School Management

School Management

S. Gupta
J.C. Aggarwal

SHIPRA

(2018, 2013, 2010, 2008, First Published in 2007)

Rs. 1500, US$ 50

ISBN: 978-93-86262-73-8

2024 Impression, PoD

School Management

Published by:
SHIPRA PUBLICATIONS
LG 18-19, Pankaj Central Market,
I.P. Ext., Patparganj, Delhi 110092
11 47322068; 22235152/ 6152; 9650028065
info@shiprapublication.com
www.shiprapublication.com

Preface

The book highlights the significance of the observations made by the Kothari Commission (1964-66) that "the destiny of India is now being shaped in her classrooms". It covers a wide range of issues and theories relating to the organization, management and supervision of educational institutions. It lays emphasis on the need for giving a new dimension to problems like the roles of the head of an educational institution, the teachers and supervisors and inspectors. So that the students develop ideals and values needed in an enlightened citizen of a democratic state.

This publication is divided into four sections as given below:

Section I deals with the concept, process and approaches to school management.

Section II covers the role of the head of the institution in the management of the school and that of teachers in the classroom management.

Section III relates to educational administration and organization of co-curricular activities.

Section IV discuss the various issues involved in the construction of school time-table, maintenance of school records.

It also details the role of the supervisors and inspectors in ensuring better management and organization of schools.

The book is designed as a textbook for students but should also serve as a handy volume for in-service programme for teachers and heads.

The authors are greatly thankful to all the writers and publishers whose works they were made use of in preparing this book.

S. Gupta
J.C. Aggarwal

Contents

SECTION III

SECTION IV

SECTION I

1

School Management: Concept, Characteristics and Scope

1.1 MEANING OF THE CONCEPT OF SCHOOL MANAGEMENT

School management is the dynamic side of educational enterprise. Educational philosophy sets the objectives of education, educational psychology explains the principles and school management is the operational side of the principles for the realisation of the objectives.

'*A Cyclopaedia of Education*' (1913) by Paul Monre states the meaning of school management in these words: "School management, as a body of educational doctrines comprises a number of principles and precepts relating primarily to the techniques of class-room procedure, and derived largely from the practice of successful teachers. The writers in the field have interpreted these principles and precepts in various ways usually by reference of larger and more fundamental principles of psychology, sociology and ethics." This concept of school management hardly fits in the modern times when far-reaching changes have taken place in various disciplines especially with the explosion of information and communication technology (ICT). Management as a distinct discipline has emerged. Accordingly, the concepts of educational management and school management are increasingly being used.

In the present context, school management may be defined as an art and science in coordinating human and material resources of the school in such a way as to attain the objectives to optimal level of satisfaction of those served and with a high degree of morale and sense of attainment on the part of those rendering the service.

School management is to forecast, to plan, to organise, to command, to coordinate, to motivate and complement school.

1.2 CHARACTERISTICS OF SCHOOL MANAGEMENT

Following are the chief characteristics of school management:

1. School Management as an Organised Structure to fulfil Certain Objectives—School management implies the practical and pragmatic measures which the school takes to ensure that the system of work which it uses will be of the greatest possible assistance in fulfilling its objectives and of the greatest possible value to the students in their all-round development.

Management may be functionally defined as an organised body or system or structure or arrangement or framework which is used for ensuring unity of effort, efficiency, goodwill, harmonious relations and appropriate use of resources.

2. School Management as an Embodiment of Ideas—School management is the embodiment of an ideal and of a spirit. It must enable different limbs of the school organism to function harmoniously in happy coordination, blending themselves into a composite personality like a collage of different colours and shapes which attracts persons of all shades and provides a soothing environments.

3. School Management as a Lens—School management may be compared to a lens that brings everything about the school system as well as educational system into focus—faculty (staff), students and the community. If it is a poor lens, the image is fussy and obscure and no one in the school system or the community gets a clear picture of what the educational system or the school system is trying to do. If it is a good lens, the school system becomes a clear-cut and vivid projection of the ideals, ideas and values that have been envisaged to bring into being in the school system.

4. School Management is the Coordination of Various Elements of the School—This is illustrated in the following figure:

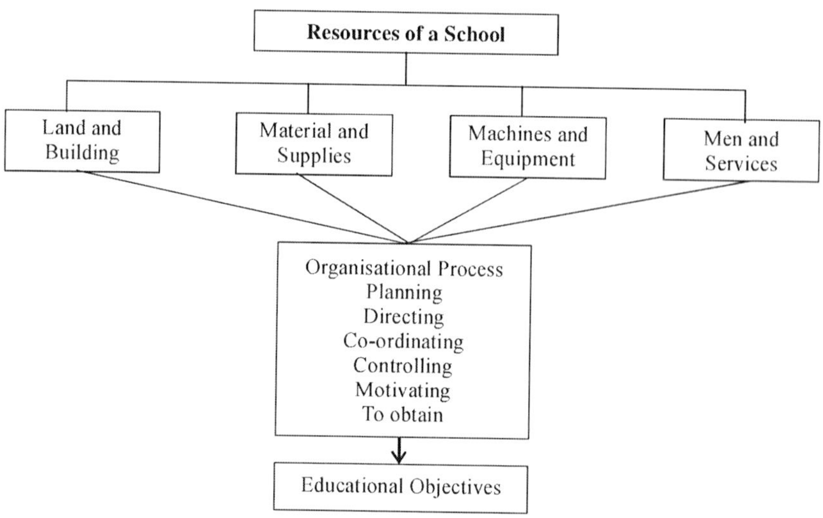

Fig. 1.1: School Management as Coordination of Various Elements of the School

5. School Management is Dynamic—School management changes with the concept of changing times. Its objectives undergo changes in the philosophy of the education as reflected in the constitution of a country. Its processes are influenced by philosophy as well as changes in information and community technology (ICT).

1.3 ORIGIN AND MEANING OF SCHOOL MANAGEMENT

Until the beginning of the 20th century, the term 'management' was not in common use in educational literature, although it had figured as far as back

1872 when the title of a publication by Harding was *Practical Handbook of School Management by Teachers*.

The development of school management as a field of study began in United States in early part of the 20th century. Development in the United Kingdom came as late as the 1960s.

An article entitled *Some General Principles of Management Applied to the Problems of School Systems* was published in 1913 by Franklin Bobbit of the University of Chicago.

In India, the concept of school management hardly existed before 1980. This is borne out of the fact that *Encyclopaedic Dictionary and Directory of Education* (with special reference to India), Volume II (1990), A. Biswas and J.C. Aggarwal, while listing the books relating to school organisation, mentions only one book *School Management* by R.C. Sharma (1983). The concept of school management became popular only in the last decade of the 20th century.

1.4 OBJECTIVES OF SCHOOL MANAGEMENT

The objectives of school management must be in accordance with the objectives of the school for the fulfilment of which it is set up. In a simple language, the objectives of the school are to educate the students in such a way as they become aesthetically rich, culturally refined, emotionally stable, mentally alert, morally sound, physically strong, socially efficient, spiritually enlightened and vocationally oriented. Naturally, therefore, the school management must be geared to these objectives.

Broadly speaking, the objectives of school management may be considered from two points of view which are complementary and supplementary and certainly not competitive.

A. Objective of School Management from the Point of View of the Society

The objectives of school management from the point of view of the society are:

1. Consolidating the spiritual strength of the society.
2. Maintaining the historical continuity of the society.
3. Securing the past achievements of the society.
4. Guaranteeing the future progress of the society.

B. Objectives of School Management in Relation to the Development of the Students

A school should be organised to:

(i) train the faculties of the students,
(ii) widen their outlook,
(iii) cultivate their minds,
(iv) form and strength their character,
(v) develop and cultivate their aesthetic faculty,
(vi) build up their bodies and enable them to acquire health and strength,
(vii) teach them their duties to themselves, the community and the State,
(viii) enable them to be emotionally well-balanced,
(ix) prepare them to be spiritually well-balanced,
(x) enable them to and adjust themselves with the Society.

Objective of School Management is not merely to prepare the students for Examination.

The objectives and functions of the present day school management may be summed up in the words of P.C. Wren as "Organise the school to benefit the scholar, to train his faculties, to widen his outlook, to cultivate his mind, to form and strengthen his character, to develop his aesthetic faculty, to build up his body, and give him health and strength to teach his duty to himself, the community and the State. Organise the school for this and not to prepare him for the Matriculation Examination".

1.5 MAIN FUNCTION OF SCHOOL MANAGEMENT

The main function of school management is to make the optimum use of the human and material elements of the school system for the optimum fulfilment of the objectives of the school as stated above.

The human elements include:

(i) Students, (ii) Staff, (iii) Parents, (iv) Community, (v) Board of Education, (vi) Department of Education, (vii) Managing Committee of the School and the Governing Body, (viii) In-service and pre-service training institutes like DIETs etc.

Material elements include:

(i) Finances, (ii) School plant, (iii) Instructional supplies and equipment.

1.6 SCOPE OF SCHOOL MANAGEMENT: 5 MS

School management includes five elements which may be expressed as 5 Ms, i.e., Men, Money, Materials, Machines and Methods.

Elements	*Inputs*	*Process*	*Outputs*
1. Men	Cooperation of students, teachers, parents, community managing committee, Department of Education	1. Planning 2. Organising 3. Staffing 4. Directing 5. Coordinating 6. Reporting 7. Budgeting 8. Monitoring	(i) Aesthetic Development of students (ii) Cultural Development of Students (iii) Ethical Development of Students (iv) Intellectual Development of Students (v) Moral Development of Students (vi) Physical Development of Students (vii) Recreational Development of Students (viii) Social Development of Students (ix) Spiritual Development of Students (x) Vocational Development of Students
2. Money	Use of school funds		
3. Material	Use of furniture, stationery, raw material etc.		
4. Machines	School workshops, Laboratory Apparatus etc.		
5. Methods	Appropriate – Teaching Learning – Class-room Management – Evaluation – Supervision		

Scope of school management is very vast. As a matter of fact, anything and everything having to do something with the education of the child through the agency of the school comes under the purview of school management.

Following may be listed as necessary components of school management. These are the outcomes of the management of 5 Ms (Men, Money, Materials, Machines and Methods) as listed above:

1. Providing and organising the human material—teaching staff, non-teaching staff and the students.
2. Providing and organising the material equipment such as school building, furniture, farms, laboratories, library etc.
3. Preparing the curriculum for different classes.
4. Preparing the time-table.
5. Management of co-curricular activities.
6. Maintaining discipline.
7. Organisation of student government.
8. Organisation of health and physical education.
9. Organisation of educational and vocational services.
10. Organisation of mid-day meals.
11. Organisation of various ancillary services like drinking facilities.
12. Organisation of labour and social service weeks.
13. Organisation of home-work time-table.
14. Organisation of evaluation of machinery.
15. Maintenance of school records.
16. Financing and budgeting.
17. Making purchases of different kinds.
18. Following department rules and regulations.
19. Organising admissions.
20. Organising transport for students.
21. Establishing liaison with other organisations and institutions including parents.

1.7 SCHOOL MANAGEMENT PROCESS

Planning	*Organising*	*Motivating*	*Controlling*	*Monitoring*
Forecasting and fixing goals Collecting and comparing data Selecting best alternative and decision-making Formulating policies, procedures and programmes	Doing division of work Assigning tasks Delegating authority and responsibility Fixing accountability	Providing effective leadership Communicating effectively Providing incentives Humanising organizational process	Laying down standards Evaluating performance Finding out reasons for deviation Taking corrective measures	Checking Progress from time to time

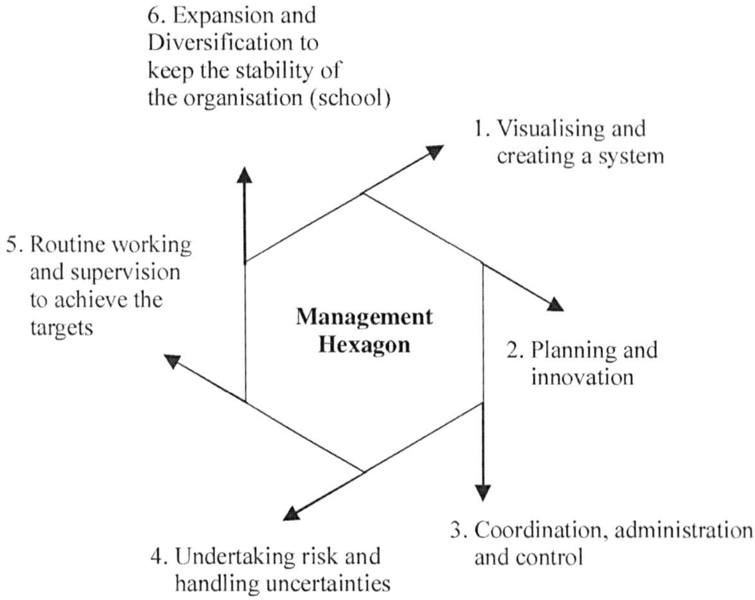

Fig. 1.2: School Managerial Hexagon

1.8 FACTORS INFLUENCING EFFICIENT SCHOOL MANAGEMENT

Important factors are:

1. Principles of democratic management.
2. Scientific collection of the data.
3. Systematic and optimum use of the school machinery.
4. Judicious use of school finance.
5. Target fixing.
6. Monitoring.
7. Periodic checking or evaluation.
8. Flexibility.

1. Principle of Democratic Management—An efficient management must be based on the following principles:

(i) Principle of harmonious human relations.
(ii) Principle of sharing responsibility.
(iii) Principle of equality.
(iv) Principle of freedom.
(v) Principle of cooperation.
(vi) Principle of justice.
(vii) Principle of recognising individual worth.
(viii) Principle of leadership.
(ix) Principle of coordination.

2. Systematic and Scientific Collection of the Data—This implies that the school records must be maintained in a proper manner. They must be kept up-to-date, complete in all respects and quite accurate. Any lapse in this direction is likely to upset the whole planning of management. The manager, that is, the head of the school must devote adequate attention to this aspect of school management.

3. Optimum Use of the School Machinery—What is school machinery? By school machinery we mean the building, the teachers and the students. The work of the school should be distributed among members of the staff in such a way that the right teacher teaches the right class. This implies that work should be distributed among members of the staff according to their qualifications and experience. A good time-table will enable the head to make the best use of the school staff and school building.

Attempt should be made to associate the students with the management of different school activities. A limited form of self-government is very helpful in enlisting their cooperation.

4. Judicious Use of School Finance—The school money is a trust in the hands of the school authorities. Most of the troubles in schools may be attributed to the wrong use of the funds, especially the Boy's Fund which gives a handle to the students to create mischief and cause indiscipline. It is, therefore, very necessary that the Boy's Fund must be spent for the welfare of the students.

5. Target Fixing: Institutional Planning—Term-wise programme should be chalked out. The entire syllabus to be covered during the academic year should be divided into four terms. Programme of all activities must be carefully planned so as to make the best use of school and community resources.

6. Monitoring—Monitoring implies establishing a suitable mechanism for the identification of milestones of achievement, collecting and analysing data and establish information flows among different levels.

7. Periodic Checking—Terminal and monthly tests should be conducted to judge the progress of the students as well as of teachers.

8. Flexibility—It must be stressed that management is a means and not an end. It must not dominate the end. The end is the many-sided development of the personality of the child. The curriculum, the methods of teaching, the evaluation the time-table and in fact every aspect of school management is devoted to this end. Therefore, it is but proper that the management should be kcpt flexible.

1.9 FLEXIBILITY AND NOT RIGIDITY IN SCHOOL MANAGEMENT: MANAGEMENT GOOD SERVANT BUT A BAD MASTER

In view of rapid changes, new developments and new situations encountered with while implementing educational programmes, it is essential that we should have an open mind. Planning as visualised may not remain a realistic one with a change in situation. One plan for a particular school system or a class system or teacher may not be suitable for the other. After all school organisation is a means and not an end. The means should not be allowed to dominate school organisation which is for the pupils and its effectiveness and efficiency must be measured to the extent to which it contributes to teaching and learning. No doubt, there must be planning but there should be no absolute rigidity in it.

H.G. Stead has rightly said that management should be 'fluid.' In the words of Mort Paul, "Adaptability, stability and flexibility are really facets of the same thing. A school must have these three characteristics if it is to achieve its purpose and at the same time give due regard to all persons immediately or remotely concerned. It must hold fast to the good, change what requires change and be fertile in considering individual differences and in all personalities involved." A fluid system believes in evolution rather than revolution.

Freedom should be given to the teachers to use their own methods of teaching. Similarly, students should not be forced to obey a multiplicity of rules and regulations. Self-discipline cannot be achieved through rod and punishment. It can only be realised through love and sympathy.

Similarly, monthly tests should not be treated all in all. They are a means to the end as enumerated above. All the aspects of school management and management itself are the servants of the students, the teachers and the head and as such it must not be given the place of a master. It should be dynamic and not static and should change according to the circumstances.

1.10 CHANGING CONCEPT OF SCHOOL MANAGEMENT: FACTORS AFFECTING SCHOOL MANAGEMENT

In view of the new challenges, the roles of the present day school have been radically changed and accordingly the concept of school management. Change is the order of the day and the school management must reflect a positive note in this regard. The old principles and practices of school management are now fading into insignificance in the dazzling light of the new ones.

Organisation of the Traditional School (Organisation was the earlier term)

H.G. Wells has said, "If you want to feel the generation rushing to waste like rapids—you should put your heart and mind into a private school." This remark was meant for some of the private schools of England of the past and is certainly not applicable to the present day schools of that country but is absolutely true for the large majority of our schools whether public or private.

A traditional school was considered to be a place where knowledge was manufactured and this used to be bookish, mechanical and stereotyped. Education being uniform; no importance was attached to the individual needs of children. Rote memory and memorisation played the dominant role. Children were regarded just like dumb driven cattle. Examination dominated the entire system of education. Rod was the chief weapon to educate the educand. 'The fear atmosphere' prevailed in the school. The teacher was called a policeman and drill sergeant. Co-curricular activities were almost unknown. No attempts were made to enlist the cooperation of the parents. Technology of teaching-learning was very simple.

Management of the Present-Day Schools

1. Ideals and Values of Democratic India—The functions of the present-day schools have undergone a great transformation in India since the advent of Independence. Our country is wedded to the ideals of democracy. Democracy imposes many responsibilities on the citizens of a country. It is based upon love, cooperation, tolerance, open-mindedness, truthfulness and fellow-feelings. If democracy is to survive, education must develop certain qualities needed for its survival. It must enable an individual to take part effectively and freely in the affairs of the group to which he belongs. Education is essentially a social affair. According to Dr. Radhakrishnan, all education is social. Education is the transmission of technical skill and cultural traditions from one generation to another. Education is literacy plus discipline—a kind of an appreciation of the values of society of which we happen to be members. Education is not worth the name, if it does not help an individual to live harmoniously and cooperatively in the society.

2. Ideals of Socialism and Secularism—Besides democracy, we have accepted socialism and secularism as our ideals. Our educational institutions, therefore, must serve these ends and produce individuals imbued with the ideals and attitudes of secularism and socialism.

3. New Concept of Education—Education in terms of traditional 3 Rs has been replaced by the present 7 Rs, i.e., Reading, Writing, Arithmetic, Recreation, Rights, Responsibility and Relationship.

4. Guidance and Counselling—Individual differences of children must be taken into account and diversified courses provided. School curriculum is considered more in terms of activities and not subjects. Besides subjects such as English, Mathematics, Hindi etc., it is increasingly being realised that a variety of co-curricular activities must be considered as important as other school subjects. A well organised system of guidance and counselling is also needed.

5. Activity Methods—New activity methods such as Dalton Plan, the Project Method, the Heuristic Method, the Montessori Method, etc., have brought about far-reaching changes in our methods of instruction.

6. Impact of New Technology—New technology has affected the old system of school management. Information Technology (IT) has placed new processes and equipments at the disposal of school organiser which must be made use of profitably.

7. Impact of the New Pattern of Education, i.e., 10+2—Far reaching changes have taken place in the entire philosophy and practices of school management. School curriculum and methods of teaching-learning have undergone important changes with the introduction of the new pattern of school education in 1975. All this had implications for principles and practices of school management.

8. Introduction of Vocational Courses and Socially Useful Productive Work—These two elements have greatly influenced the philosophy and practices of school management.

9. Multifarious Co-curricular Activities—A present day school is expected to provide for a number of co-curricular activities which need an altogether a new concept of school management.

10. Increase in the School-Going Population—People are becoming increasingly education conscious. Today we find a large number of students attending the school. They differ in tastes, needs, aptitudes and in various other ways. Family and social background of the students also vary. This has made the problem of educational management very complex.

11. Multifarious Functions of the School—The school of today is not only concerned with the intellectual development of the child but is also to train him in the 'art of living together' which in itself is a complicated affair.

12. Role of the School in Fostering Values of Emotional Integration and National Unity—There is a growing recognition of new demands upon management and the necessity of an imaginative response in transforming the principal's job.

Schools are expected to help in achieving national unity and as such the importance of its impact on educational management can hardly be ignored.

1.11 AUTOCRATIC AND DEMOCRATIC SCHOOL MANAGEMENT

Why Democratic School Management: We are wedded to a democratic philosophy and a democratic way of life and as such it must be reflected in all our institutions and organisations including educational. If this point is lost sight of, the very purpose of school management goes into oblivion. As observed by the Secondary Education Commission, "The educational system must make its contribution to the development of habits, attitudes and qualities of character which will enable its citizens to bear worthily the responsibilities of democratic citizenship". The school is an important social agency which provides numerous opportunities to the students to imbibe democratic values and train them in the 'art of living together'.

	Democratic School Management	*Autocratic School Management*
1.	An environment of mutual trust exists.	An environment of mutual distrust exists.
2.	Cooperative planning is done by the entire staff.	Planning is done by the management.
3.	'We' feelings prevail in the school environment.	'I' feelings are predominant. Ego of one individual prevails.
4.	The committees are chosen to do the work.	The head or management chooses committees and dominates them.
5.	Managers discuss problems with teachers and accepts suggestions.	Management tells teachers what to do.
6.	The organisers and the Head respect teacher's personality and plans cooperatively with him.	The Management/the Head sometimes embarrasses teachers before children.
7.	The Head gives co-workers credit for success.	Management/Principal takes credit for all success.
8.	The Head encourages faculty to make use of human resources in the community.	Management/Principal gives no recognition to parents and leaders.
9.	Managers, administrators and principals are educational leaders as well as administrative persons.	Managers, administrators and heads are concerned only with the details of management and administration.

(*Contd.*)

(Contd.)

	Democratic School Management	*Autocratic School Management*
10.	The managers, administrators and principals make possible an active in-service programme for teachers.	The managers, administrators and principals take the attitude of 'get it yourself'.
11.	Teachers plan with the supervisors in special fields for work to be done.	Special supervisors outline course for teachers to follow in teaching special subjects.
12.	The management allows teachers to make flexible programmes which best suit the interests and needs of children.	Management requires a set type of common programme.
13.	Faculty meetings are cooperatively planned by the entire staff.	Faculty meetings are planned only by principal.
14.	The teachers can adopt an exploratory attitude.	The teachers give directions in a firm manner.
15.	Teachers are encouraged to use cumulative records.	Cumulative records are only for the use of principal.
16.	Teachers participate in selection of text-books.	Text-books are selected by the management.
17.	Audio-visual materials are made easily available to the teachers.	Audio-visual programme is operated on a rigid time schedule, prepared by the management.
18.	The staff and children are allowed to plan social gatherings after school time.	Such occasions are very rare.
19.	Students are teacher-guided.	Students are teacher-dominated.
20.	The students are guided by the teachers in the choice of many activities.	The teacher plans activities without conferring with the pupils.
21.	The budget is prepared cooperatively, with teacher's participation.	The budget is prepared by the managerial and administrative staff.
22.	The teachers are sympathetic.	The teachers spring awe and fear.
23.	Students committees also assume responsibility for selecting equipment and supplies needed.	Teacher or the principal assumes responsibility for selecting and purchasing equipment.
24.	The teachers try to understand the child.	The teachers work according to set procedure.
25.	The daily programme is flexible and can be changed as the group decides.	Daily programme is rigid.
26.	Students are encouraged to correct their mistakes.	The teacher directs pupil activities.
27.	Students are encouraged by the teacher to make suggestions concerning their work.	The teacher ignores suggestions of the pupils.

(Contd.)

(*Contd.*)

	Democratic School Management	Autocratic School Management
28.	The students share with the teacher the responsibility of appraising their work.	The students are not conferred with in appraising their growth.
29.	The pupils share with teachers establishing standards of achievement.	The teachers set-up standards of achievement without conferring with the pupils.
30.	The students assist in planning the academic work, make suggestions and proposals.	The students answer questions asked by the teacher.

1.12 CHIEF CHARACTERISTICS OF A WELL MANAGED SCHOOL

The pen-picture of a well manage school has been outlined by S. Bala Krishna Joshi in the words, "A school is not a mere brick and mortar structure housing a miscellany of pupils and teachers; a school is not a market place where a heterogeneous crowd gathers with diverse objects; a school is not a rigorous reformatory where juvenile suspects are kept under vigilant watch. A school is a spiritual organism with distinctive personality of its own; a school is a vibrant community centre, radiating life and energy all-round; a school is a wonderful edifice, resting on the foundation of goodwill—goodwill of the public, goodwill of the parents, goodwill of the pupils. In a word, a well-conducted school is a happy home, a sacred shrine, a social centre, a state in miniature and bewitching Brindavan, all beautifully blended into a synthetic structure."

According to the Secondary Education Commission (1952-53), "The secondary school must make itself responsible for equipping its students adequately with civic as well as vocational efficiency—and the qualities of character that go with it—so that they may be able to play their part worthily and competently in the improvement of national life. They should no longer emerge as helpless, shiftless individuals who do not know what to do themselves". The school is one of the most important formal agencies of education. It plays a major role in moulding the ideas, habits and attitudes of the children with a view to producing well-balanced personalities, culturally sound, emotionally stable, mentally alert, morally upright, physically strong, socially efficient, vocationally self-sufficient and internationally liberal. Informal agencies of education such as the church and the home fail to satisfy the increasing educational requirements of a complex society and thus are losing their hold on the people. The school is a social institution set up by the society to serve its ends. It is a place where men of tomorrow are trained and disciplined in certain forms of activities.

It is not without reason that the Education Commission 1964-66 wrote, "The destiny of India is now being shaped in her class-rooms. This, we believe, is no mere rhetoric". In a world based on science and technology, it is education that determines the level of prosperity, welfare, and security of the people. On the quality and number of persons coming out of schools and colleges will depend our success in the great adventure of national reconstruction whose objectives are to raise substantially the standard of living of our people and to create a new social order based on the human values of the dignity of the individual, freedom, equality and justice.

The most important and urgent reform needed in education is to transform it, to endeavour to relate it to the life, needs and aspirations of the people and thereby make it a powerful instrument of social, economic and cultural transformation necessary for realisation of the national goals. For this purpose, education should be so developed as to increase productivity, achieve social and national integration, strengthen democracy, accelerate the process of modernisation and cultivate social, moral and spiritual values."

The above mentioned objectives can be realised if the school is managed in such a way as to make provision for the following:

1. Provision of a stimulating environment.
2. Transformation into activity school.
3. Provision for experimentation.
4. Training students in the art of living together.
5. Opportunities for developing self-discipline.
6. Making library as the hub of school activities.
7. Providing work experience and socially useful productive work.
8. Use of progressive methods of evaluation of students' performance.
9. Organising self-government in some select areas of school work.
10. Making school a centre of community service.

1.13 PRINCIPLES OF EFFECTIVE AND INSPIRATIONAL SCHOOL MANAGEMENT

1. Principle of development of harmonious relationships among all those connected with the school.
2. Principle of forward planning.
3. Principle of realistic target fixing.
4. Principle of periodical evaluation of the planning and implementation of the programmes and activities.
5. Principle of cooperation.
6. Principle of coordination.
7. Principle of democratic philosophy.
8. Principle of equality.
9. Principle of reasonable freedom.
10. Principle of flexibility.
11. Principle of justice.
12. Principle of dynamic leadership.
13. Principle of introspection.
14. Principle of optimum output.
15. Principle of optimism.
16. Principle of recognition of individual differences and worth.
17. Principle of sharing responsibility.
18. Principle of budgeting.
19. Principle of accountability.

1.14 ADMINISTRATION, MANAGEMENT AND ORGANISATION

Earlier literature on education usually used the word school organisation but in recent literature words 'management' and 'administration' are increasingly being used in place of school organisation.

In the B.Ed. curriculum of most of the Universities, the word organisation has been replaced by administration and management. In essence, all these three words connote the same meaning.

The *Webster's New Collegiate Dictionary* gives the following meaning of these terms:

Administer	*Manage*	*Organise*
1. To manage or supervise 2. To perform the office of the administrator.	1. To handle or direct with a degree of skill. 2. To direct or carry on business of affairs.	1. To cause to develop an organic structure. 2. To arrange or form into a coherent unity or functioning whole. 3. To set-up an administrative structure. 4. To arrange elements into a whole of interdependent parts.

Administration:

1. The act or process of administering.
2. Performance of executive duties.
3. The execution of public affairs as distinguished from policy-making.
4. (a) A body of persons who administer,
(b) A group constituting the political executive in a presidential government,
(c) A government agency or board.
5. The terms of office of an administrative officer or body.

Management:

1. The act or art of managing; conducting or supervising of something (as a business).
2. Judicious use of means to accomplish an end.
3. Capacity for managing: executive skill.
4. The effective body of those who manage.

Organisation:

1. (a) The act or process of organising or of being organised,
(b) The condition or manner of being organised.
2. (a) Association or society,
(b) An administrative and functional structure (as a business or political party: the personnel of such a structure).

2

Management Approaches and Decision-Making

2.1 APPROACHES TO MANAGEMENT

The following chart illustrates the management approaches advocated by management experts.

Approaches to Management

- (1) Manpower Approach or Human Resource Development Approach
- (2) Cost benefit Approach or Rate of Return Approach
- (3) Social Demand Approach
- (4) Social Justice Approach

2.2 MANPOWER APPROACH

Manpower is a primary resource without which other resources namely, money, material etc., cannot be put to use. Even a fully automatic unit or say even unmanned satellite requires manpower to execute it and plan further improvement activities. In order to achieve any goal, manpower requirement needs to be assessed, located, trained and harnessed.

Most of the economists prefer this approach. It starts with the proposition that providing manpower is the most dynamic function of an educational system. It is argued that it is more prudent to estimate future manpower requirements systematically than to guess them. Forecasts of manpower needs (however defective) can be accurate enough to be useful guides.

Ideally educational development at the higher level should be broadly related to the pattern of jobs and the estimates of demand in the economy for educated manpower. This is important both for the individual and the society. The individual is enabled to take decisions about future careers with the assurance that his training will be put to proper use and he would be productively employed. The gain to society flows from the fact that a timely view of educated manpower required to achieve the varied tasks of economic development makes it possible to provide adequately, yet not excessively, for the scale and pattern of educational development which will best serve the purpose.

The Kothari Commission (1964-66) has stressed the need to pay due attention to the relationship between enrolment and manpower requirements;

"If India is to achieve its targets of economic growth, it must have an adequate supply of educated specialists for each category of job to be performed. Conversely, if there is an excess of trained people in any category, it implies an imprudent use of scarce resources and also creates difficult problems of unemployment of the educated. Even from the point of view of the individual some matching of educational patterns and job opportunities is vital. Nothing is more frustrating than to be under-qualified or over-qualified for a job or to be unemployed because there is no call for one's qualifications. We believe, therefore that estimates of future manpower needs, form a useful basis for regulating enrolment patterns above the primary level."

Relating Manpower Estimates to Output of Educational Institutions at Two Levels

The Commission points out that the following measures will have to be taken to relate the output of the educational system to manpower needs:

1. *National Level.* Planning at the national level should be done by the Centre in consultation with the States and should cover all sectors crucial for national development. These should include engineering, agricultural and medical education, and the preparation of teachers for higher education.

2. *State Level.* The planning of remaining sectors should be done at the state level by State Governments. The planning of facilities in secondary and higher education (excluding the sectors for which planning would be done at the Central level) should be done at the State level.

Vocational education, both of school and college standard, will have to be expanded in all areas on a priority basis in keeping with manpower needs.

For enrolment in general education, however, which is under-developed in some areas and over-developed in others, a policy of equalisation will have to be adopted.

Limitations of the Manpower Approach

1. The employment classification and manpower ratios used in most manpower studies in developing countries, as well as the assumed educational qualification corresponding to each category of jobs, are usually borrowed from industrialised economies and do not fit in the realities of less developed ones.

2. It is extremely difficult to make reliable forecasts of manpower requirements to be of significant value to educational planning.

3. It gives the educational planners only limited guidance.

There is no doubt that there are uncertainties inherent in the task. Long-term forecast of the growth of the economy has to be made and in order to provide guidance for educational planning it must be not only sufficiently detailed but also fairly authoritative. As new facts emerge and better methods of analysis are involved, fresh estimates will need to be made.

4. Manpower approach needs an interdisciplinary approach to educational planning. This requires an elaborate process and pooling of resources of various disciplines.

2.3 COST BENEFIT APPROACH OR RATE OF RETURN APPROACH

Maureen Woodhall explains this approach in these words: "A systematic comparison of the magnitude of the costs and benefits of some form of investment (in case of education it is investment in human capital) has to be made. All forms of investment involve a sacrifice of present consumption in order to secure future benefits in the form of higher level of output or income. Cost-benefit analysis provides a means of appraising these future benefits in the light of the costs that must be incurred in the present."

Education as an investment implies two things: (1) As a result of education, the productive capacity of an individual increases. He is in a position to add to the total sum of production. There is difference between the productive capacity of an educated person/skilled person and an illiterate/unskilled one. The difference between the two is called 'productivity' and this element is assigned to education/training.

(2) The level of earnings of educated persons must be higher than those of the uneducated/illiterate. In such a situation, it is said that return to education is 'possible'.

Alfred Marshall refers to 'education as a national investment' in his *Principles of Economics*. Marshall writes: "There are few practical problems in which the economist has a more direct interest than those relating to the principles on which the expenses of the education of the children should be divided between the state and the parents. But we must now consider the conditions that determine the power and the will of the parents to bear their share of the expense, whatever it may."

John Vaizey has observed: "Education has become a major source of skills and trained talent. Higher the level of education an individual has, the higher his earning powers will be."

Rate of return could be higher only when right type of skills are developed. This means appropriate educational reforms.

Limitations of this Approach

This approach when implied to education suffers from two handicaps—availability and estimation of adequate cost data and the calculation of future benefits. This approach at its present experimental stage of development tells us more about the past than it does about the future.

In the end it may be said that none of these approaches provides an adequate basis by itself for educational planning. A synthesis of all these is needed.

Mark Blaugh and J. A. Lauwerys point out in the *Yearbook of Education*: "Each is only an index, a guide—certainly not an exclusive guide—to the formulation of educational policy. In one sense they are not even indices of the same thing, but rather different views of the nature of education."

2.4 SOCIAL DEMAND APPROACH

Several educators and political leaders favour the social demand approach to planning. This approach implies that the educational planners must give due attention to the aggregate popular demand for education while drawing up educational plans.

It is argued by the protagonists of this approach that education is the most important instrument of social change.

In a country like India which remained under foreign rule for more than two centuries, education remained neglected. After independence there grew persistent demand for education from almost all sections of population. According to social demand approach to planning in education, all those who wish to study or receive education must be provided educational facilities. This approach implies that educational facilities should be extended in proportion to the degree of demand for education. This in other words, may mean 'an open door' policy to education.

In a welfare and democratic state like India, maximum educational facilities must be provided to all those who put forward demand for education.

Limitations of Social Demand Approach

This approach has been criticised on the under-mentioned three grounds:

1. It does not take into consideration the larger national problem of resource allocation.
2. It ignores the character and pattern of manpower needed by a country.
3. It tends to overestimate popular demand and underestimate costs. This may result in their spreading of resources over too many students thereby reducing quality and effectiveness.

2.5 SOCIAL JUSTICE APPROACH

A democratic, secular and socialist state without social justice has no meaning. A welfare state without education is a contradiction in terms. The right to education is a fundamental right. It is needed for the optimum development of all individuals or citizens of a democratic state.

Appropriate type of education is considered a 'potent leveller' of all disparities.

Social justice approach demands that all should be provide equality of opportunity in education.

The Preamble to the Constitution of India '*inter alia*' emphasises—Justice: social, economic and political.

Keeping in view the role of education in national development and social justice, the Constitution makers made specific provisions for education in the Constitution.

Realising the importance of elementary education, Article 45 provided for free and compulsory education to all children of age of six to fourteen years. In 2002, this Article was amended and Article 21A, Right to Education, was added.

With a view to meet the demands and requirements of social justice, Indian Constitution has provided special safeguards and special reservations in services, educational institutions and in the Panchayati Raj Institutions (PRIs) for the uplift of the weaker sections like the SCs, STs and OBCs. Special provisions are also made not only for admission to minority groups but also in the functioning of minority institutions. Several concessions like free tuition, free uniforms and stipends, etc. are given to the children belonging to these classes. Hostel facilities are also provided where needed. Assessment for special coaching and compensatory classes are also made.

Summing Up

It is not advisable to put faith in any single approach. For effective planning, a harmonious and balanced approach is needed.

2.6 DECISION-MAKING

Decision-making includes the following elements:

1. Significance of decision-making.
2. Types of decisions.
3. Types of administrative behaviour decisions.
4. Decision-making process.
5. Factors and problems in decision-making.
6. Competencies and skills needed in decision-making.

2.7 SIGNIFICANCE OF DECISION-MAKING

Decision-making is considered as the "heart of administration and management." The strong the decision-making ability of the leader and the organisation, the 'strong heart' or the healthy state of affairs of the functioning of organisation. Decision-making is the most critical dimension of educational administration and management. The institution, the organisation and the individuals rise and fall in proportion accordance to the impact of a decision.

Decision-making in educational administration is a very challenging, critical, delicate and difficult task. It needs a lot of administrative skill and foresight.

2.8 TYPES OF DECISIONS

There are innumerable classifications of types of decisions. However, these can be classified broadly into three categories, depending upon the concern or focus. These are:

1. Institutional decisions.
2. Strategy decisions.
3. Administrator's behaviour decisions.

Institutional Decisions. Institutional decisions are mostly decisions related to policy-making or scheduling concerning activities and programmes. These include: (i) Allocation decisions, (ii) Expenditure decisions, (iii) Planning decisions, (iv) Facilities decisions, and (v) Miscellaneous decisions.

The growth and development of an institution largely depends upon these type of decisions.

Strategy Decisions. These decisions follow institutional decisions, i.e., decisions regarding implementation of institutional decisions. Strategy decisions call for identifying appropriate tactics to take the institution to further heights. These relate to (i) 'whom' to involve, 'why' to involve, 'when' to involve, 'how' to involve, 'where' to involve. Priorities and training considerations of the personnel may also be considered.

Administrative Behaviour Decisions. The behaviour of the administrator plays a determining role in all situations. No administrator can afford to behave in an arbitrary and in a random manner. To meet new situations effectively, meaningful, relevant and specific behaviours are needed. It is, therefore, very important that the administrator should himself know thoroughly. It is very rightly said: "Man know thyself." "Physician heal thyself before healing others." Likewise the administrator should know not only about the behaviour of others but also about his own behaviour—his assets and liabilities.

2.9 TYPES OF ADMINISTRATIVE BEHAVIOUR DECISIONS

Types of Administrative Behaviour Decisions

(1) *Status Quo* Decisions

(2) Deferred Decision

(3) New Course Decisions

(4) Response Decisions

'Status Quo' *Decisions. Status quo* decisions emerge when the administrator does not want to change the situation. It is 'no intervention policy.' Decisions for the 'sake of change only' should not be taken. *Status quo* may be allowed to remain in case the administrator feels that after taking a new decision, it is not possible for him to implement it.

Deferred Decisions. Sometimes situations arise when the administrator has to observe and watch the situation for sometime before taking a decision. In unavoidable circumstances, decisions may be deferred.

New Course Decisions. Sometimes, situations are such as warrant radical changes. While taking such decisions, sufficient thought should be given to study the situation in all its dimensions. Views of all concerned may be ascertained as to have a wider field of choice. New course decisions need a deep analysis of the situation.

Response Decisions. Response decisions are those decisions which are taken in response to situations. Such decisions are taken, by and large, at the spur of the moment.

Classification of Decisions as Given by Stuffe Beam

(1) Planning Decisions to Determine Goals

(2) Implementing Decisions

(3) Structuring Decisions Relating to Actual Means to Achieve Decisions

(4) Recycling Decisions

2.10 DECISION-MAKING PROCESS

Important characteristics of the decision-making process are as under:

1. Cyclic nature.
2. Four-stage process of decision-making.
3. Four-settings of decision-making.
4. Decision models.

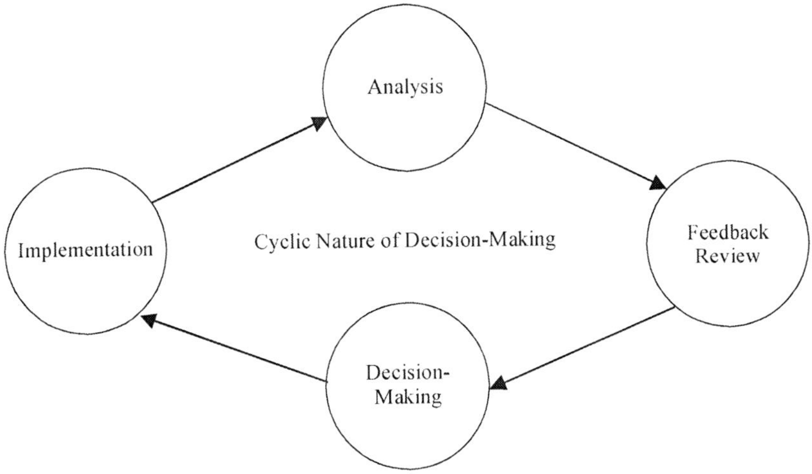

Fig. 2.1: Cyclic Nature of Decision-Making Process

2.11 FOUR-STAGE PROCESS OF DECISION-MAKING

The stages are:

(a) Becoming aware of the need for a decision.
(b) Designing the situation.
(c) Selecting an alternative.
(d) Implementing the decision or taking action on the decision.

Four Settings of Decision-Making. A setting implies the total set of environmental conditions which influence analysis and choice. Following are the four settings:

(i) *Metamorphic Decision Setting.* This type of setting exists when the situation or environment is such that a complete change is needed through the decision.
(ii) *Haemostatic Decision Setting.* This type of setting involves a low degree of change and a higher degree of information grasp.
(iii) *Incremental Decision Setting.* Incremental decision setting implies a situation that results in a shift to a new balance by the process of series of small changes. In this setting, reliance is placed on expert judgement, special studies, committees and discussions rather than on information collected routinely.
(iv) *Neomobilistic Decision Setting.* Neomobilistic decision setting refers to a decision that is taken in a situation which needs new solutions for solving a significant problem and when considerable change is envisaged after the implementation of a decision. In such a situation very little information is available.

Decision Models. Three decision models have been identified. These models correspond to three settings of decision-making excluding the metamorphic decision setting. These are:

(a) Synoptic model corresponding to haemostatic setting.
(b) Disjointed model suitable for incremental stage.
(c) Planned change model appropriate for neomobilistic decision setting.

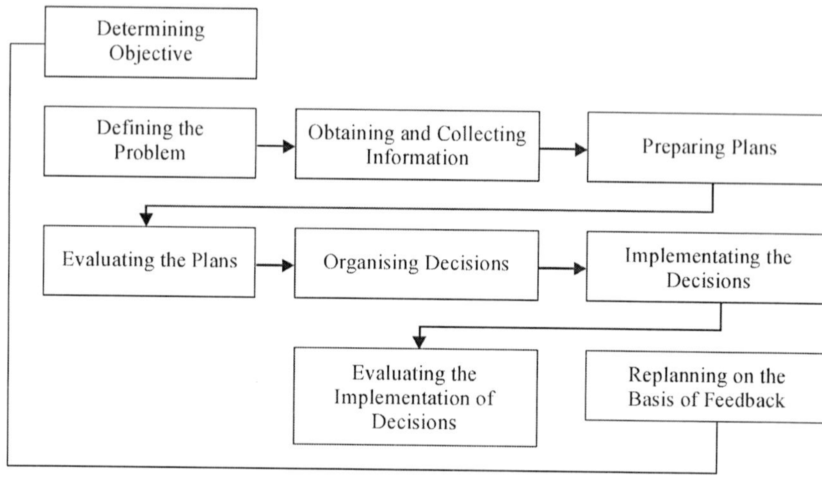

Fig. 2.2: Process of Decision-Making or Problem Solving

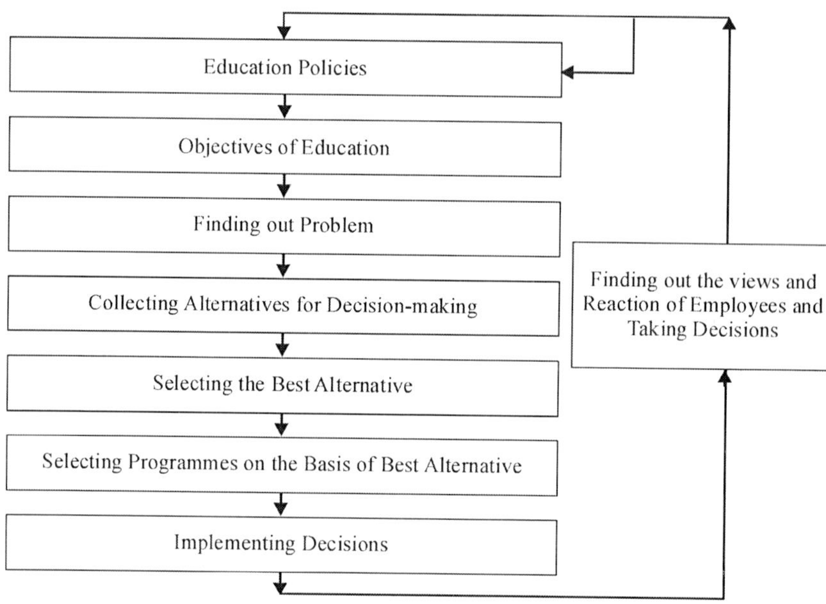

Fig. 2.3: Proposed Outline for Decision-Making

2.12 FACTORS AND PROBLEMS IN DECISION-MAKING

Following factors and problems influence the decision-making proces:

1. Problem of availability of adequate information.
2. Problem of deadline of taking a decision.
3. Problem of involvement of appropriate group in the process of decision-making.
4. Problem of conflicts and pressures of interested individuals or groups.
5. Problem of commitment.

6. Problem of administrative behaviour.
7. Problem of resources.
8. Problem of secrecy.

2.13 COMPETENCIES AND SKILLS NEEDED IN DECISION-MAKING

Decision-making, as already stated, is a very challenging task. It depends upon a host of competencies and skills possessed by the educational administrator and manager.

Following are the basic/essential competencies and skills needed for arriving at sound decisions. In this regard, it may be stated that all these elements are closely related to each other. There is no single competency or skill which is adequate to find a working solution. Only a balanced blend of these qualities is helpful in making correct decisions.

Administrative Competencies and Skills Needed in Decision-Making

1. *Planning*
   (a) Setting objectives.
   (b) Assessing resources.
   (c) Formulating broad policies and programmes.
   (d) Fixing targets.
   (e) Planning procedures.
   (f) Monitoring and reviewing.
   (g) Revising plans when needed.
2. *Organising*
   (a) Determining assignments.
   (b) Dividing assignments.
   (c) Assigning authority.
   (d) Establishing a chain command and coordination and channels.
   (e) Determining span of control.
   (f) Setting out guiding principles
3. *Establishing and Maintaining Controls*
   (a) Preparing guidelines.
   (b) Preparing orders.
   (c) Fixing responsibilities.
4. *Communicating Skills*
   (a) Expressing oneself clearly and precisely; both orally and in writing.
   (b) Conferencing.
   (c) Instructing employees/co-workers.
   (d) Securing participation of employees/co-workers.
5. *Forecasting*
   (a) Interpreting Data.
   (b) Evaluating Information and Resources.
6. *Decision-Making*
7. *Reviewing and Evaluating*

3

Physical Infrastructure of the School

3.1 EFFECTIVE PHYSICAL INFRASTRUCTURE OF THE SCHOOL

Adequate, attractive, well-equipped and properly maintained school physical infrastructure serves as a great motivating force in the teaching-learning process. It is very important that the school infrastructure becomes the learning laboratories, directly as well as indirectly.

Winston Churchill, a former Prime Minister of England, has expressed the significance of the school plant as "We shape our buildings and ultimately they shape us."

A school is a life-giving and vital environment. Therefore, a concerted attempt on the part of all concerned with the school should be put to bring about aesthetic improvement in the drab, dull and ugly environment which most of our educational institutions provide. There must be artistic appeal, beauty and grace in the buildings, furniture, the equipment, the grounds and the general layout of our schools.

A school cannot be put up everywhere and anywhere. The importance of school environment is apparent when we realise that the students spend a good deal of their time in the school premises. A healthy, beautiful and refreshing environment soothes the eyes and pleases the soul. In such an environment the intellectual forces of teachers and students function at their best. It has been very aptly observed by Yeager William: "Nothing in the whole educational programme is more conducive to cooperative attitude among the pupils and a love of school than an attractive and wholesome environment."

In this regard K. G. Saiyidain has observed: "Ideally a school building should be planned spaciously, functionally and with pleasing architectural features. It should stand out in the village or the city as something of which the local community can be proud. In fact in some educational by advanced and wealthy countries, schools are housed in beautiful buildings, which are not only stimulating centres of education for children but also vital centres of community life."

3.2 MEANING OF PHYSICAL INFRASTRUCTURE OF THE SCHOOL

Broadly speaking, physical infrastructure of the school includes all physical and material resources of the school other than human resources.

It includes the following elements:

1. Building and its Fittings.
2. Equipments like furniture and stationary, etc.

3. Playgrounds and their Equipment.
4. Hostel Building and Equipment.
5. Agricultural Land and Its Implements etc.
6. Gardens and Its Products, if any.
7. School Farm and its Products.
8. School Workshop and its Equipment.
9. School Library, Books and Equipment.
10. Instructional Aids like Television, Computers etc.

Building: It includes:

(i) Principal's Office
(ii) School Office
(iii) Staff Room
(iv) Reading Room
(v) Library Room
(vi) Assembly Hall
(vii) Auditorium
(viii) Museum Room
(ix) Workshop room
(x) Laboratories
(xi) Sanitary blocks.
(xii) Class-rooms

3.3 AVAILABILITY, ADEQUACY AND UTILISATION OF INFRASTRUCTURE

For the successful running of the school, the necessity of availability, adequacy and proper utilisation of infrastructure hardly needs to be emphasised. There are certain norms fixed by the Department of Education of each State and every management is expected to make available the infrastructure according to norms. Norms for school site and construction of building are fixed. Likewise appliances and equipments needed for laboratories, libraries, farm and workshop etc. are fixed.

Sometimes space for school site is not easily available in metropolitan towns. Schools, therefore, are being run in shifts.

Utilisation of the infrastructure of the school primarily depends upon the quality of leadership of the head of the school. This efforts should be to make the optimum use of available infrastructure. Some broad principles of the utilisation of school infrastructure are given here.

3.4 PRINCIPLES OF MANAGING PHYSICAL INFRASTRUCTURE

1. Principles of determining the needs of various physical resources.
2. Principles of acquiring material resources.
3. Principle of availability.
4. Principle of adequacy.
5. Principles of utilising material resources.
6. Principles of maintaining and keeping material resources in order.
7. Principle of keeping records of material resources.
8. Principle of determining accountability criteria in handling material resources.

9. Principle of developing indigenous material aids.
10. Principle of mobilising community resources.

General Principles of Planning and Designing School Building

(i) Principle of adequacy.
(ii) Principle of safety.
(iii) Principle of durability.
(iv) Principle of economy.
(v) Principle of accessibility.
(vi) Principle of mobility.
(vii) Principle of flexibility.
(viii) Principle of coordination.
(ix) Principle of simplicity.
(x) Principle of comprehensiveness.
(xi) Principle of utility.

All the above mentioned points are discussed separately.

Principles of Acquiring and Using Equipment

(a) Principle of standardised equipment.
(b) Principle of durability.
(c) Principle of serviceability.
(d) Principle of economy.
(e) Principle of adaptability.
(f) Principle of simplicity.
(g) Principle of aesthetic sense.
(h) Principle of maintenance and timely repairs.
(i) Principle of keeping inventories.
(j) Principle of keeping records.
(k) Principle of observing financial and technical rules.

3.5 GENERAL PRINCIPLES OF DESIGNING SCHOOL BUILDING

1. Principle of Adequacy of Space—The school plant must provide for all the necessary facilities for curricular and co-curricular activities.

2. Principle of Safety—The building must be planned in strict conformity with safety and hygienic considerations. Full attention must be given to site, soil, ventilation, light and other allied problems. The school plant must be able to protect the health of the students and teachers.

3. Principle of Durability—As far as possible, the building must be *pucca* rather *kachcha*.

4. Principle of Economy—The school plant should be economical in original cost, upkeep and operation. Economy can be affected by the adoption of a standard class-room unit.

5. Principle of Accessibility—The school should be built at a place which is easily accessible to the students and free from road dangers.

6. Principle of Mobility—The question of easy movement, particularly in large schools of more than one storey is important.

7. Principle of Flexibility—There should be no rigidity in the design and use of the plant. Scope must be left for modification in accordance with the needs.

8. Principle of Coordination—There must be full coordination among the various parts and their location at particular place must have a purpose. For instance a workshop will be away from the class-room and staff room very near to principal's room.

9. Principle of Simplicity—The design of the building should be simple but artistic.

10. Principle of Comprehensiveness—A comprehensive vision is necessary in which function, form and space are so harmonised that the soil from which the synthesis grows, will be enriched by such a pattern.

11. Principle of Utility—It must give the maximum utility to the students as regards accommodation, protection from weather, maximum light and ventilation, free movement and comfortable stay in rooms for longer hours.

3.6 SCIENTIFIC PLANNING OF SCHOOLS

In the opinion of School Buildings Committee (1971), general considerations that should determine the planning of schools of all types are set out below:

1. Due regard should be given to aesthetic standard, e.g., form, design and colour, in school buildings, in order that objectives of lessons in good taste may remain at all times before the eyes of the pupils.

2. The question of easy movement, particularly in large schools of more than one storey is important. Corridors should be wide enough and staircases should be so placed as to avoid congestion when classes change and above all in the event of fire.

3. Similar considerations should apply to the location of cloak rooms, changing rooms, bicycle sheds, etc. where provided.

4. Latrines, urinals and lavatories should be, from the point of convenience, as accessible as possible from all parts of the schools, subject always to their being so placed as to create neither a nuisance nor an eyesore.

5. The possibility of extension being required at some future date should always be borne in mind.

6. Verandahs can be made a most useful adjunct to almost every school in India.

7. Kindergarten rooms and rooms for young children should always be on the ground floor.

8. Where ample sites are available, single storey buildings have certain advantages. They facilitate elastic grouping of rooms as well as the use of light form of construction.

9. The orientation of all class-room and verandahs and of many practical rooms needs careful consideration. Local climatic conditions will largely determine this and sites should be chosen with this factor in mind.

10. Provided that the arrangement is convenient and design harmonious, the particular shape of the plan is of little Importance. The quadrangular plan popular in Western countries has definite disadvantages; the most obvious being that it renders impossible the best orientation of many rooms.

11. Economy can be effected and planning facilitated by the adoption of a standard class-room unit which can be multiplied if necessary where larger

rooms are required. It would be an advantage if sound proof adjustable partitions could be provided and where partition walls are provided they should be left free from carrying loads, so that they can be moved if, at some future date, it should be necessary to rearrange the rooms.

12. The plan must provide for a plentiful supply of pure drinking water.

3.7 SELECTION OF SCHOOL SITE OR PLACE

In the selection of school site, important considerations which must be taken into account are given below. It must be stressed that the selection of the site which is the first requisite of a good environment needs careful consideration.

1. Surroundings—The site should be located in healthy surroundings. It should be near a road so as to be accessible by bus or other means of transport, yet back from the road. It should be located in a quiet and pleasant environment.

2. Level—The level of the area should be little raised so that water logging does not take place. There should be no danger of floods or breach of any canal.

3. Direction—The site selected should permit the construction of the rooms in such a way that no corner remains without sunlight.

4. Shape—The shape of the site preferably should be rectangular.

5. Service Conditions—Various public services like drainage, water-pipe arrangement and lighting arrangement should be easily accessible.

6. Scope for Future Expansion—The site for a school should be so selected as to allow normal expansion towards one direction at least.

Situations to be avoided in the Selection of Site/Space for the School

1. Noisy and busy roads.
2. Public places like bus stand, railway station, grain market, etc.
3. Places like cremation grounds and burial grounds.
4. Marshy lands.
5. Uneven and undeveloped lands.
6. Stagnant pools, cattle ponds and other unhealthy surroundings.
7. Places of public entertainment like the cinema houses.

3.8 AREA REQUIREMENTS: SPACE FOR THE SCHOOL

It is not possible to prescribe any definite limit. The area required for a school site depends upon many factors.

1. Strength of the School—As every child is to be provided with 15 square feet of floor space, the area of the site will depend upon the number of students in a particular school.

2. Type of School—For residential schools, a big area is required. They will require provision for hostel and staff quarters also. A modern public school which provides a swimming pool etc needs much large area.

3. Subjects Taught—Schools which provide for the teaching of agriculture must have agricultural farm. Naturally, such schools will stand in need of a far greater area than an ordinary school. Likewise vocational subjects would need workshops and various types of equipment. Therefore, their needs would be quite different.

4. Co-curricular activities—Generally speaking greater area is required for the public schools as they organise a large number of co-curricular activities than the ordinary schools. They provide activities like swimming etc.

5. Other Considerations—In big cities where land is not easily available, there may be several storeys of school building. In such cases, the area required would be small. Moreover there is an acute shortage of place for playgrounds. A cluster of schools is provided a common playground. Likewise different yardsticks will apply to schools in hilly areas. In the rural areas, there may not be any problem of getting enough land for school buildings, playgrounds, farms and workshops.

Quarters for the School Staff—The Secondary Education Commission has greatly stressed the necessity of providing quarters for the school staff as possible. The Commission writes: "We feel that the presence of the headmaster and at least some of the staff in or near a school, particularly if there are hostels attached or where the schools are residential, will be of the greatest benefit to the school going population."

Minimum Size of a Class-room—Minimum size of a class-room depends upon the number of students to be accommodated. On the basis of the 10 sq. ft. each for 40 pupils in a Primary School and 12 sq. ft. each for 35 in a Middle, High and Higher Secondary school the minimum area of a school room will vary between 400-420 sq. feet.

Dimensions of a Room—The standard class-room unit of approximately 400 sq. ft. should be 20′-20′. The length and breadth may be varied by 2′ on either side.

Lighting—Short-sightedness is very common among children of school-going age. This imposes additional responsibilities upon the school authorities for providing proper means of lighting. Important considerations are: (a) Light should be well-diffused. (b) It should not fall directly on the eyes of the students. (c) Light should come from the left. (d) Where left light is not possible, right light may be allowed. (e) Direct front light is not allowable in any case. (f) The colour of the walls should be such as it does not tax the eyes of the pupils.

Windows—The windows serve two purposes: (a) Admission of light, (b) Admission of air. The window area should not be less than one-fifth of the floor area. Every part of the school should be well lighted. The window sills should be placed at not more than four feet and not less than three feet and a half above the floor of rooms in which the pupils are seated at desks.

Ventilation—There are two methods of ventilation, natural and artificial. Natural ventilation depends upon natural forces while artificial ventilation is brought by the use of fans etc.

Following points should attended to:

(i) Ventilation is of use only when there is cross ventilation. Doors and windows provided only on one side of the room will not severe the desired purpose.

(ii) The window should be fixed at three to four feet above the floor level. They should be sufficiently wide and high to allow adequate air to come into the room.

(iii) The windows should be wire-gauzed so that it is possible to keep them opened in the event of dust also. The wire-gauzed provides protection against excessive cold, head, dust, rain and insects.

(iv) There should be supplementary arrangements for ventilation such as the ventilators which serve as outlets for foul air and the floor ventilators which allow plenty for fresh air from outside.

(v) When there is the possibility of smoke and gas inside the room, an outlet should be provided in the form of a chimney.

Flooring—The floors should be such that can wear and tear and can be cleaned easily. Cemented floor is the best floor. It is durable and can be swept and washed conveniently. Brick floors should be the last alternative. In hilly areas, asphalt tiles or linoleum blocks and wooden sleepers can be used.

Sanitation Facilities: Toilets and Lavatories

It is universally agreed that the provision of proper and adequate sanitary facilities is essential. But it is only here that there is a wide gap between the standard recommended by different authorities and the actual conditions. An ideal toilet room should consist of flush latrines, urinals, wash basin etc. However, this is not possible. The lavatory block should be located at a place easily accessible from all the wings of the school buildings.

In several urban areas and rural areas, there is no water supply arrangement. The dry latrines will be the only alternative. These latrines require cleaning every two to three hours. Phenyl and other disinfectants must be used regularly.

Following are the desirable provisions:

(i) Latrines of W.C.: One for every 100 students or part thereof.

(ii) Urinals: 1 for every 25 students or part thereof.

(iii) Water tap with troughs: 1 for every 50 students or part thereof. For girls separate arrangements should be made.

3.9 TYPES OF BUILDING DESIGN OF A SCHOOL

Important types of design are:

I Type	:	This is the simplest form of school building. It consists of a number of class-room in a single row. This can be a temporary arrangement and allows scope for further expansion.
L Type	:	This is an improvement of I type. In this pattern I type will have an expansion on one side.
T Type	:	This consists of I type with extension on one side both ways.
U Type	:	This has two I's joined on one side.
E Type	:	In this design I type will have three extensions on the same side of the main block.
H Type	:	This consists of two I's joined in the centre with the block of rooms.

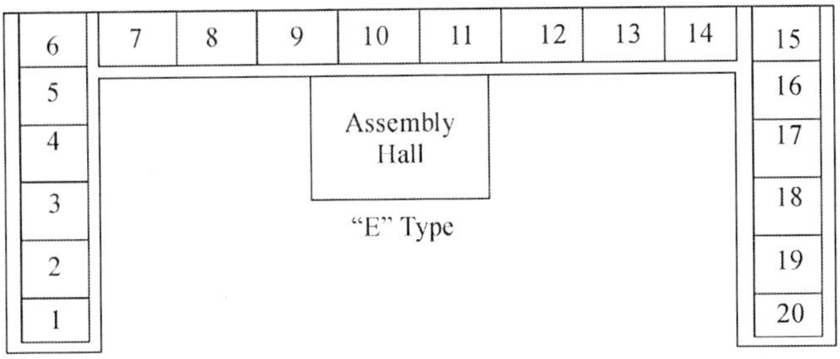

Fig. 3.1: E Type School Building

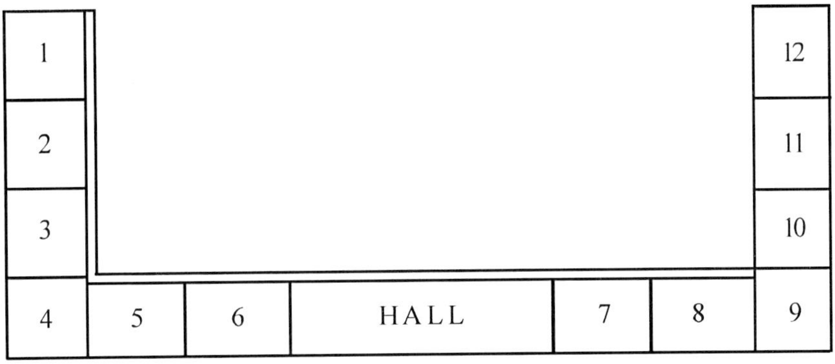

Fig. 3.2: U Type School Building

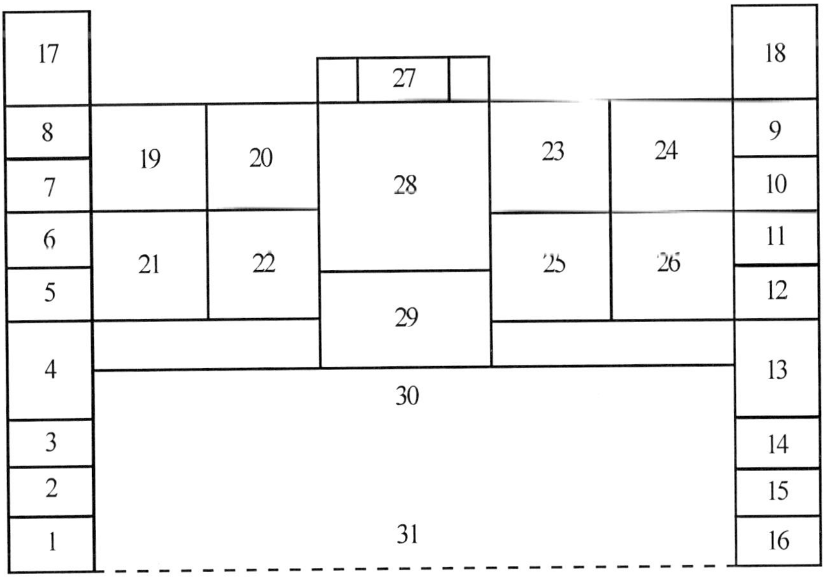

Fig. 3.3: H Type School Building

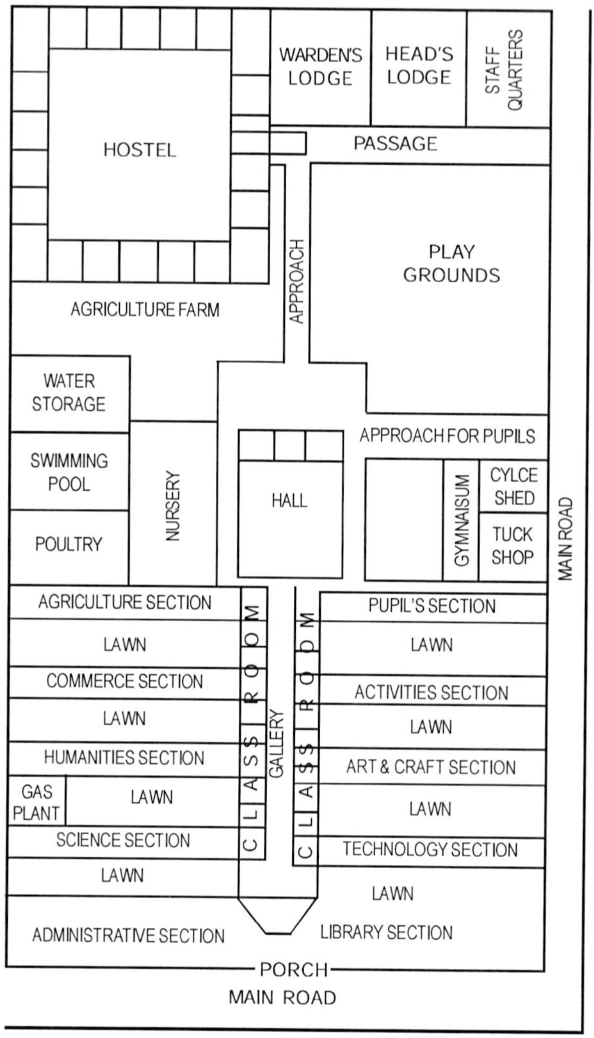

Fig. 3.4: Master Plan for a Progressive School

Note: Several public schools make provision for swimming pools, gymnasium etc. They provide a number of activities normally not provided in government schools. Thus they have their own plans for school buildings.

3.10 CLASS-ROOM EQUIPMENT/INFRASTRUCTURE

The class-room equipment is usually divided into three categories, i.e., essential, less essential and desirable.

Essential equipment—It includes:

(i) Desks and chairs for the pupils or matting if they are required to sit on the floor.

(ii) Black-board, preferable a wall black-board.
(iii) A chair and a table for the teacher.
(iv) A map stand or a chart stand.
(v) Dustbin

Less essential equipment—This includes:
(i) A bulletin board.
(ii) Foot pad, door mat, wash basin etc.
(iii) Decorative items such as flower pots, table cloth etc.

Desirable—
(i) Curtains
(ii) Matting under the desks.
(iii) A dais or a raised platform for the teacher.
(iv) An almirah or cup-board carved into the walls for chalk duster, illustrative aids etc.
(v) An attendance board.
(vi) A notice board.
(vii) Wooden rallings round the walls of the room with hooks and nails for display of charts, pictures and portraits.

School Building and Health of the School

Following points should be taken note of:
(i) Healthy surroundings of the school.
(ii) Airy and well-ventilated rooms.
(iii) Suitable colour of the walls.
(iv) Cleanliness of the school building.
(v) Good seating arrangements.
(vi) Suitable chairs and desks.
(vii) Right type of black-boards and use of right type of chalk.
(viii) Fresh drinking water.
(ix) Sanitation of latrines and urinals.
(x) Spacious playgrounds.

Aesthetic Aspect and School Building

Our present system is dominated by a material outlook and provides very little scope for the growth of aesthetic sense in our students. Aesthetic education has a great value in life. Man does not live by bread alone. He has to satisfy his senses also. Aesthetic education enables us to appreciate the wonderful face of nature. Delightful scenes whether in nature, painting, photography, music or poetry have cheering and soothing influence on the body, as well as the mind. Aesthetic values sometimes provide relief to the students from the dull and dreary life of the school. Aesthetic imagination if properly developed can become one of the greatest assets of man. Appreciation of 'truth', 'beauty' and 'goodness' is the watchword of aesthetic education.

Following factors can be very conveniently employed for the introduction of aesthetic elements in our schools:
1. Healthy school surroundings.
2. Building well-designed and tastefully decorated.

3. Occasional excursions to places of natural scenery, e.g., valleys, lakes, river sides, open fields, etc.
4. Introduction of activities such as gardening, photography, etc.
5. Well-furnished reading rooms.
6. Teaching of poetry and other subjects like nature study, arts and drawing.
7. Musical competitions.
8. Organisation of various programmes like dramatics.
9. Arranging competitions in art and craft work.
10. Giving due appreciation to the activities of children.
11. Planning and execution of various projects like pageant on the life of Buddha.
12. Emphasis on personal cleanliness.
12. Orderly arrangement of desks.

School Furniture

Desks

Desks have a great bearing on the health and especially of the postures of the students. As a child spends a good deal of his time at desk, it is but obvious that right postures can be maintained only when good seats are provided. A child who is comfortable is likely to pay more attention and concentrate on his work than one who is not. The seat and the desk should be made to fit the child—not the child to the seat and the desk. J. Mace Andress states: "If a child is properly seated he should be able to rest his feet comfortably on the floor without pressing upon the nerves and blood vessels under the knee; the seat should be so shaped as to encourage the sitter to it with the pelvis well back in the chair, the distance of the chair from the desk, its height and slants should be such that bending forward will not be encouraged".

Dressler states: "If the back of school bench or chair be just a little lower than the shoulder blades of the pupils when sitting properly, the best results, other things being equal, may be obtained".

P.C. Wren has described the importance of good furniture for the students in these words: "Furniture plays an extremely important part in the physical, moral and mental welfare of scholars. If the desks be of the wrong kind, or if benches be used instead of desks, curvature of the spine, contract of chest, roundness of the shoulders and a confirmed stoop may result as a physical injury; bad discipline, irritation, discontent and discomfort may result as moral injury and inability to sustain attention and concentration owing to lack of bodily ease may result as mental injury".

Following points should be borne in mind while providing furniture to the students:

(i) There should be, as far as possible, a single desk with a slight slope towards the seat.
(ii) The seat should be supported by a back.

(iii) The maximum length of the desks should be twelve feet.
(iv) Inkpots should be fitted in the desks.
(v) The desks should not be arranged more than six rows deep.
(vi) 18″ of space should be provided to each pupil.
(vii) There should be sufficient space between the rows of desks as well as between desks and walls so as to have free movements.

Black-Board

The black-board plays a significant role in making the teaching efficient and effective. It is a necessary equipment of a class-room and a handy apparatus at the hands of a teacher.

Types of Black-Board

Following are the various types of black-boards:

(i) Fixed black-board.
(ii) Easel or removable.
(iii) The sliding black-board.

Use of Black-Board

Black-board should be placed at a place from where the writing on the black-board could be seen very easily. It should never be placed between windows. Its back should not be towards the light as in this position its surface would be in the dark and it will tax the eyes of the students in trying to read what is written on the black-board. It should be either black or green in colour and should not be glossy, otherwise it will adversely affect the eyesight of the pupils. Its height from the floor should vary from 26 to 39 inches according to the height of the students. It should be four feet wide. Easel black-board is better as its both sides can be used and it can be raised or lowered. It is also easily removable. Damp duster should be used to clean it so to avoid the inhalation of chalk dust which leads to consumption.

Seven factors to be kept in view in the use of black-board are:

(i) Location
(ii) Distance
(iii) Colour
(iv) Surface
(v) Dimension
(vi) Chalk and duster
(vii) Washing and varnishing

State of School Buildings in India (1993 and 2002)

The following tables illustrates the state of school buildings in India in 1993 and 2002. From this it is concluded that there has been an appreciable change in the situation. However, some schools including secondary and senior schools were without building. It is strange that 327 secondary schools and 27 senior secondary schools were running in the open space.

Table 3.1: Type of School Buildings in India (2002-2003)

Sl. No.	*Type of School Building*	*Primary School*	*Upper Primary School*	*Secondary School*	*Higher Secondary School*
1.	*Pucca*	527404	201751	76529	40198
2.	Partly *Pucca*	79302	32573	10896	3348
3.	*Kuchha*	27898	7215	2903	359
4.	Tent	1001	171	106	19
5.	Open space	15776	3564	327	27
	Total	651381	245274	90761	43951

Table 3.2: Percentage of Type of School Building in India (1993 and 2002)

Sl. No.	*Percentage of Type of School Building*	*1993*	*2002*
1.	Percentage of Primary Schools		
	(i) Without building	4.20	2.58
	(ii) With *kuchha* building	12.07	4.52
	(iii) With *pucca*/partly *pucca* building	83.73	92.85
2.	Percentage of Upper Primary Schools		
	(i) Without building	1.92	1.80
	(ii) With *kuchha* building	8.78	3.35
	(iii) With *pucca*/partly *pucca* building	89.30	94.85
3.	Percentage of Secondary Schools		
	(i) Without building	0.51	0.61
	(ii) With *kuchha* building	8.35	4.00
	(iii) With *pucca*/partly *pucca* building	91.14	95.39
4.	Percentage of Higher Secondary Schools		
	(i) Without building	0.29	0.13
	(ii) With *kuchha* building	2.38	1.23
	(iii) With *pucca*/partly *pucca* building	97.33	98.64

Note: Without building includes schools functioning in tents and open space.
Source: "*Seventh All India Educational Survey, Provisional Statistics as on 30.9.2002*". NCERT.

3.11 MANAGEMENT OF SPACE

Management of space involves two problems as given below:

1. Problems relating to acquiring space for school site.
2. Making the best use of the available space. This has the following problems:
   (i) Type of school building – single storey or more.
   (ii) Allocation of space to different activities and programmes.
   (iii) Framing of suitable time-table.
   (iv) Running of schools into shifts.

3.12 PROBLEMS OF SCHOOL BUILDINGS AND RECOMMENDATIONS OF COMMISSIONS AND COMMITTEES

I. Recommendations of the Panel on Higher Secondary School Buildings (1960)

The panel appointed by the National Buildings Organisation of the Ministry of Works, Housing and Supply, Government of India, made the following recommendations:

Minimum Area for School site: Students 960

The minimum area for school site shall be:

(a) 3 acres, if community parks and open spaces are available for use by the school as playing fields.

(b) 5 acres where community parks or open spaces are not available for use as playing fields.

Norms as under

1. Enrolment in the school. Ordinarily schools shall be planned for enrolment of 960 students.

2. Enrolment in the section. Maximum number of students per class/section shall be 40.

3. Area per student. An area of 12 sq. ft. per student shall be provided in a class/section.

4. Laboratories. Laboratories shall be planned for even number of students subject to a minimum of 20. The area of laboratory shall be worked out at 20 sq. ft. per student seat provided. Store 80 to 120 sq. ft. may also be provided.

5. Library. A library of 600 sq. ft. shall be adequate to meet the present educational needs. In certain cases the area may be increased to 690 sq. ft.

6. Assembly hall. Ordinarily assembly hall shall be planned in all school designs for future construction only.

Assembly hall shall be planned for 50 per cent of the total enrols at the rate of 7 sq. ft. per seating capacity. The areas of the hall so arrived at shall be inclusive of internal passage gangways but shall be exclusive of the area of stage.

7. Scale of accommodation. The following scale of accommodation is recommended for administrative units:

(1) Principal's office	200 sq. ft.
(2) Staff common room	For 75 per cent members of the total teaching staff at the rate of 20 sq. ft. per staff member subject to a minimum of 200 sq. ft.

(3) General office, record and 200 sq. ft. files room.

(4) Guidance room 200 sq. ft. which may also be used as visitors' room.

(5) First-aid or doctor's room 150 sq. ft. with attached lavatory.

8. Built-in storey. Adequate built-in storage space in the shape of cup-board, open shelves, etc. shall be provided in a class-room.

9. General space. General storage space hall be in the neighbourhood of 5 percent of the teaching area.

10. Cafeteria. Cafeteria and students' common room, etc., need not be provided except under special circumstances.

11. Sanitary fittings. The following scale of sanitary fillings is recommended:

Latrines or W.C.	1 for every 100 students or part thereof.
Urinals	1 for every 25 students or part thereof.

(In case of girls schools urinals shall be provided in separate enclosures with foot squatting).

Water taps with troughs	1 for every 50 students or part thereof.

12. Area under circulation. The area under circulation shall not exceed:

(a) 20 per cent of the total area in case of single storey structures or double storey structures with doubly loaded corridors.

(b) 33½ per cent of total billing area in case of double storey structures.

Area for light shall be 15 to 20 per cent of the floor area.

Area for ventilation shall be 28 sq. inches per student.

13. Residential accommodation. Residential accommodation in school compound for the following members of staff is recommended.

Urban areas	Principal, a member of staff, chowkidar and a sweeper or peon.
Rural areas	Principal and 50 per cent of the staff.

II. Recommendations of the Education Commission (1964-66)

Problems of School Buildings (Including Problem of Space)

The Commission considered the following problems:

1. Problem of space.
2. Reduction of the building costs.
3. Expeditious construction.
4. Supervision and standardisation of school building
5. Problem of necessary funds.

1. Problem of space for school buildings. The problem of school buildings needs to be discussed separately for urban and rural areas. In the former case, land values are high; and very often enough land is not available at all. Sophisticated structures are, therefore, necessary, even in order to keep in tune with the immediate environment. In the rural areas on the other hand, land is cheap and readily available; and sophisticated structures often look grotesque in a village atmosphere.

We recommend that everything should be done to encourage local initiative and local contribution in cash, kind or labour for the erection of schools. A special device that can be of great use is that government should supply only the framework—which can be pre-fabricated—and the local people should be expected to raise the plinth and fill up the walls. (*See* also pages 42 to 45).

2. Reduction in costs of construction: Building in Urban Areas. In urban areas, the following steps should be taken for achieving economy in the construction of educational buildings:

(i) Judicious selection of specifications and local materials. The existing practice of playing safe by adopting conventional specifications is not conducive to economical construction. Economy can be achieved through the selection of locally available materials, use of cheaper materials, omission altogether of certain finishes and acceptance of a lower standard of construction. In all these steps, the governing factors would, however, be the availability of materials, climatic conditions, safety of buildings and recurring costs on maintenance.

(ii) Techniques of construction. With careful planning and designing, even the so-called 'temporary' structures can be made to serve a better purpose than many of the rented buildings in which schools are often housed. Such structures should be built, wherever climatic and other conditions permit. If pucca buildings are absolutely necessary, an increasing reliance is needed on the improved techniques of construction such as the use of framed structures, cavity walls, pre-fabricated components, RCC frames for doors and windows and components evolved by the Central Building Research Institute and other research organisations.

3. Expeditious construction. In order to expedite the construction of school buildings, the following steps are recommended:

(i) Rural areas. In rural areas, there are no local contractors available. Contractors from urban areas generally charge higher rates when they are required to work in villages. The departmental machinery is also not adequate to reach most of the outlying villages. For the construction of village school buildings, therefore, we recommend that the agency of the local communities or village panchayats should be utilised to the fullest extent possible.

(ii) Urban areas. In urban areas, we recommend that the local agencies like municipalities and corporations should be utilised fully for construction of school buildings. They have the necessary technical staff and can also contribute towards the cost of such buildings. If the responsibility for providing buildings for local schools is placed on municipalities and if a suitable system of grant-in-aid is devised, the progress in this sector would be accelerated.

4. Supervision and standardisation of school buildings. For construction of government school buildings, to assist the voluntary organisations for the purpose, to supervise the general programme of construction of school buildings in a State, and to continually introduce improved economic techniques, we recommend the adoption of the following additional measures:

(i) Formation of educational building development groups. Each State should have an Educational Building Development Group within the Public Works Department but working in close association with the Education Department and consisting of an architect, an educationist, an administrator, a civil engineer and a cost accountant, all working on a full-time basis (with power to co-opt representatives of special technical skills). The main function of the group would be to improve the planning and construction of government school buildings but its advice should be available for private schools also. There should also be a Building Development Group working at the Centre for effectively coordinating the working of State-level Groups.

The other functions of the Groups will be

(a) to study building requirements in the light of new teaching techniques, (b) to develop in cooperation with manufacturers new building techniques and specifications, (c) to evolve functional and economic type plans for various types of educational buildings, (d) to arrive at a correct assessment of costs of materials and labour required, (e) to conduct field trials, (f) to evaluate the plans, specifications and building techniques already in use, and (g) to study methods of maximising the use of indigenous materials. The Group at the Centre could profitably bring out a journal highlighting the latest techniques of construction, and researches at home and abroad on conventional buildings.

The State Government should ensure that the recommendations of these Development Groups are followed.

When the Groups in the different States are well-established, the possibility of making them function within a rigid framework of 'maximum cost per place and minimum standards' as is being successfully done in the United Kingdom, should be explored.

(ii) To avoid delays in the construction of government buildings a separate unit of PWD should be set up for execution of educational buildings programmes.

(iii) Formation of educational building consortia. After the Educational Building Development Groups have standardised the plans and the technique of construction, the possibility should be examined of establishing Education Building Consortia (on the lines of similar associations, popularly known as CLASP in the UK) to exploit fully the advantages of industrialised buildings.

(iv) Standardisation. Layouts, dimensions, specifications and methods of construction for any particular region should be standardised by the Educational Buildings Development Group mentioned above so that mass production of the different components on a factory scale can be undertaken resulting in economy as well as speed of construction. Considerable work in the field of standardisation has been done by organisations like the Indian Standards Institute which could serve as a basis for further studies.

(v) Buildings for private schools. The economy measures worked out by the Educational Building Development Group in each State for reducing the cost of educational buildings should be made known to the managements of private educational institutions in the State, and the grant-in-aid given to a private management for a building should be subject to the upper cost limits worked out.

5. Funds for school buildings. We recommend that the allocations for construction of school buildings in the Central and State budgets should be increased. This is one area where the local community can make a significant contribution. Schemes of grant-in-aid should, therefore, be devised under which assistance from the State will be available to local communities on a basis of equalisation, for the construction of school buildings. Wherever possible, loan programmes for the construction of buildings should be encouraged. Grant-in-aid and loans should also be available to private schools on a fairly liberal basis for building construction.

III. Recommendations of the Committee on School Buildings (1976)

The Committee appointed by the Central Advisory Board of Education, Government of India, Education Ministry, made the following recommendations:

It is considered desirable to set up a Central Financing Corporation for educational buildings. An outlay of Rs.14 crores spread over a period of 7 years at the rate of Rs.2 crores per year would allow a revolving fund to be set up to be administered by the proposed Corporation.

In order to mobilise local resources for school buildings following steps are recommended:

(a) Funds may be collected through lotteries.
(b) Local people may be asked to donate one or two rooms at the time of birthday, marriages, etc.
(c) Religious institutions may be encouraged to donate buildings as part of their programme.
(d) Other avenues like staging plays, organising exhibitions should be explored for raising funds for school buildings.
(e) Contributions in kind such as cement, food for paying for labour, etc. may be collected.

3.13 SCHOOL BUILDING AND PLAYGROUNDS AS PER H.P. EDUCATION CODE

The Himachal Education Code prescribes the following requirements:

General

In this modern age, a school building is required to be designed properly keeping in view the needs of the institution. The building should be constructed on a proper and suitable site that is large and provides for the present and future needs of the institution. An ideal school building should have a healthy locality and a respectable neighbourhood having proper ventilation, lighting and sanitary arrangements. Since the resources available for construction of buildings are meagre, it is not government alone to construct a large number of new buildings. Donations/cooperation of the Public, Panchayat and other such arrangements will accordingly be necessary to augment the necessary sources in this regard.

Size and Construction

A school building shall be constructed according to the specifications approved by the Education Department from time to time. Normally, a primary school building shall have a minimum of the dimension of 8 × 6 meters and a varandah in front of the room.

A middle school building will consist of three rooms of 8 × 6 meters, with varandah and one office room.

High school building shall consist of a Headmaster's room, an office room for clerks, a staff room for all classes in accordance with the requirements of the institution, a science laboratory, an a room, a library and reading room, NCC room, a store room and a big assembly hall.

For a senior secondary school, in addition to the accommodation for high school their will be separate rooms for physics, chemistry, biology, computer-*cum*-information technology and sports. Rooms will be of such dimensions as approved by the Education Department from time to time.

Separate toilets for boys, girls and staff will also be provided as per requirement.

No school is to be made functional/taken over/upgraded unless the people of the area provide accommodation for the purpose.

Repairs

The school building will be maintained by the concerned agencies such as Panchayats, Education Department and P.W.D. or any Government agency out of regular maintenance budget provided by the department through building fund. Essential minor repairs will be carried out by building fund committee, to be constituted by the Head of Institution out of building fund available at their disposal to ensure the maintenance of the school building.

Playgrounds

Every school is expected to have a playground in order to promote sports activities and inculcate spirit of sportsmanship among the youth.

An institution/school will only be able to take up physical activities, co-curricular activities and recreational items when it has the facility of a playground attached with it. A play ground is also for the all-round development of a child.

Table 3.3: Type of School Buildings in Himachal Pradesh (2002)

Sl. No.	*Type of Building*	*Primary*	*Upper Primary*	*Secondary*	*Higher Secondary*
1.	*Pucca*	7897	1252	934	626
2.	Partly *pucca*	1876	261	296	152
3.	*Kuccha*	983	207	83	29
4.	Tent	0	3	1	0
5.	Open space	112	179	6	0
6.	Total	10866	1902	1320	807
7.	School without building, tents and open space	112	182	7	0

Utilisation of Space and Infrastructure of the School: Double Shift System in Schools

Beginning of the Double Shift

The system was first adopted in Delhi to provide a quick solution to a big problem—the problem of providing immediate schooling facilities to tens of thousands of displaced students from West Pakistan. It was, then, perhaps the only solution of the problem in 1948. But its continued to meet the problem of expansion of educational facilities. The double shift system is gradually coming up in all the towns.

Limitations and Drawbacks of Double Shift School System

The following are some of the defects of the system which inevitably lead to a lowering of standards. They apply to both types of double shift schools—those with a single administration and those with a double administration. They may be classified under two heads (i) educational and psychological defects, and (ii) administration and other general drawbacks.

I. Educational Drawbacks

1. The school hours under this system are unnatural and are not conducive to effective learning. Both the students and the teachers of the second shift are relatively not fresh when they come to school at about mid-day, especially in summer. The first shift people find themselves greatly handicapped in winter when they have to come to school by half past seven or so in the morning.

2. The hours of work are shorter in double shift schools than in single shift schools, whereas the curriculum and the syllabi to be covered are the same for both. This has an adverse effect on the achievements of the students which do not compare well with that of students in single shift schools.

3. By making the children work under abnormal and difficult conditions we are helping the formation of poor habits of study and wrong attitudes towards work both among students and teachers. It tends to develop an indifferent attitude to, school work.

4. The teachers have either the morning or the afternoon entirely free. This provides a temptation for them to undertake outside work consequently, those who have to work in the second shift are too tired to work zealously. Besides, they come to regard school work as secondary and this attitude affects the quality of their effort and output.

5. Co-curricular activities which should find an important place in the school programme are, for all intents and purposes, stifled for lack of time.

6. The ill effects of the system are accentuated in the case of those schools which are housed in tents.

II. Administrative Drawbacks

1. There is generally very little time—at the most, half an hour—between the two shifts. This makes it very difficult to have the school cleaned before the second shift commences. The cleaning and sweeping work often goes on while the school is working. Thus the school does not get properly started.

2. The upkeep and repair of the school furniture and other property constitute a disturbing problem. Generally, it is the responsibility of one of the shifts; but while the wear and tear is double, the contingency provision is the same as for a single shift school, as only the school owning the property can legitimately claim any expenditure under this head. The same is the case with the charges for water and electricity which have to be borne entirely by one of the two shifts.

3. The number of children in the various classes in two schools is often different with the result that the seating arrangements require adjustment everyday before each shift begins. This often takes away sometime from the already too short hours of work besides creating a great deal of noise and doing damage to the furniture.

4. There is also difficulty with regard to the class IV servants. More often than not they do not cooperate and throw the blame on one-another for not doing things like sweeping the floor or cleaning the window panes. Sometimes their quarrels lead to misunderstandings between the heads which result in unfortunate consequences.

5. The setting apart of special rooms for subjects like science, domestic science and drawing, etc., and of offices for heads of schools and staff rooms for teachers poses quite a big problem in school buildings which have not been specially constructed with two shifts in view.

6. It is extremely difficult, if not impossible, to organise cultural educational programmes after school hours so that school life remains poor in these respects. This is specially so where one of the shifts is for girls and the other for boys.

Suggestions

Conscious as we are of the fact that it will not be possible to discard the system overnight, we have formulated some suggestions which might be conveniently adopted to minimise or to overcome some of the difficulties listed above. But in no way do they constitute a permanent solution which consists only in the discontinuation of the system.

(i) Though the hours of work may remain more or less as they are, it should be possible for the teachers of the second shift to come about an hour before the school begins and utilise the time in correction of assignments, etc., for which there is hardly any time during the actual school hours. Similarly, the teachers of the first shift may stay back for the purpose. But this cannot be done unless there is a clear departmental regulation fixing the hours of work.

(ii) Both the teachers and the students of the second shift should be asked to plan their work in their free hours in such a way that they have a long period of rest before they come to school. Of course, there can be no binding force to get them to do this; it must be impressed upon them that they need to come to school physically and mentally fresh.

Similarly, first shift students and teachers may be well-advised to have an adequate period of rest before they take up their out-of-school assignments.

(iii) To meet the difficulties of double shift schools of having to cover the syllabus in a shorter period than in single shift schools, it would be advisable:

(a) To plan the syllabus very carefully and thoughtfully avoiding overlapping and repetition.

(b) To plan home assignments very carefully to make up the deficiencies in the work in school.

(c) To adopt a double period time-table, wherever possible. At least those subjects which are allotted more than one period daily should be given consecutive periods.

(d) To make proper lighting arrangements in double shift schools to enable the school hours to be stretched to the utmost extent possible and desirable under the circumstances.

(iv) Teachers should be required to prepare detailed lesson plans to economise on the time available. These should be regularly checked by the Head.

(v) The co-curricular programme should be planned co-operatively by the two Heads. The activities should be so interwoven into the curricular programme that they do not really need time outside of the school hours. Where a school has playgrounds nearby, the second shift children should be allowed to utilise them when the first shift is on, and *vice versa*. Of course, the games programme will have to be planned cooperatively by the two Heads. In the case of those schools which have no playgrounds of their own, an effort should be made to take the children to nearby public park and give them as much time as possible per week for games and physical education. With thoughtful planning, it should be possible to make some provision in this respect which is better than none.

(vi) If the school is housed in tents, quick growing trees and bushes should be planned to provide protection against the sun and dust-storms.

(vii) There should be close cooperation and communication of ideas not only between the heads of the two shifts but also among the staff of the two shifts. The aim should be to bring about a feeling of oneness and unity among the heads, teachers and students of both shifts. To ensure cooperation between the two heads it is advisable that they meet daily. It should be so arranged that either the second shift head comes an hour earlier or the first shift head stays on for some more time. But to get the best results from this arrangement, it would be necessary to keep records of such meetings and of the decisions taken therein for future reference. These should be open to inspection by the departmental authorities.

(viii) The Heads should, in turn, be held individually responsible, though by mutual arrangement, for the cleanliness of the school building for a period varying from one week to a fortnight. The sweepers of both the shifts should work together for a fixed period before each shift and should be held jointly responsible for the proper cleanliness of school. It would be better if both the sweepers and chowkidars are provided residential accommodation in the premises of the school. The students should be made responsible for picking up pieces of paper, etc., in and around their own class-rooms. They should be trained not to throw scraps of paper in the rooms, but to use the dustbins supplied for the purpose. The expenditure on the maintenance of buildings should be divided and a case made out for additional allotment under this head. If the heads cooperate there should be no difficulty in this regard.

(ix) The number of students in the classes in the two shifts occupying a particular room should, as far as possible, be equalised. The number in the classes in the two shifts should be an important factor in deciding the allotment of rooms; or the items of furniture supplied to a particular room should be based on the number in the larger section occupying that room. To avoid damage to furniture and to ensure its better care as also to fix the responsibility for breakage, a diary system should be evolved. Each head should make a note of the breakage taking place in his or her shift and pass it on to the other through the chowkidar of the latter.

4

School Library, Laboratories, Playground and Hostel

4.1 IMPORTANCE OF THE SCHOOL LIBRARY—HUB AND CENTRE OF INTELLECTUAL AND LITERARY LIFE

In the words of the Secondary Education Commission (1952-53): "The library will be the hub and the centre of the intellectual and literary life of the recognised school and play the same part *vis-à-vis* all the other subjects as the laboratory plays for science subjects or the workshop for technical subjects."

The Commission further observed: "Individual work, the pursuit of group projects, many academic hobbies and co-curricular activities postulate the existence of a good, efficiently managed library."

K.G. Saiyadain, a well-known thinker and educationist has stated the importance of library as "No school or university without a library, adequate for its needs and size should be recognised as a worthy centre of education."

The dynamic role and the educational possibilities of the school library have long been realised in all progressive countries. In countries like the United States and Great Britain, the school libraries are usually well-equipped and are used very profitably in the education of children.

4.2 ORGANISATION OF A GOOD LIBRARY: ROLE OF THE LIBRARIAN

The organisation of a good library may be discussed under the following heads:

1. The librarian
2. Books
3. Cataloguing
4. Library rules
5. Library room and equipment

I. The Librarian

The Secondary Education Commission observed that if the library is to be the hub of the academic and intellectual life of the school, if it is not only to meet but also to guide the reading interests of the students, if it is to work as a centre of free and supervised study as well as group work on projects undertaken by them—if it is to do all these things, the librarian will surely have to be wide–awake and remain active.

Arnold Benett states that if libraries spend less on books and more on educated staff, far better results would be obtained. A librarian should possess the following qualifications:

(i) General education.
(ii) Professional, i.e., indexing and cataloguing.
(iii) Pedagogical, i.e., adept in child psychology, familiar with the present trends in the educational field, sympathetic nature, etc.

A librarian is expected to perform the following functions:

1. Preparing and displaying library rules and regulations.
2. Preparing catalogues.
3. Classifying books.
4. Numbering books.
5. Stocking books properly.
6. Training students in the art of looking up reference and other material.
7. Instructing students to keep books neat and tidy.
8. Taking annual stock of books.
9. Making plans for the purchase of books of different types.
10. Attaining skills in the use of modern technological aids like computers, etc.
11. Making an environment of perfect silence conducive to self-study.
12. Displaying cuttings and foldings on the new books and journals, etc. on the library notice board.

II. Books

According to Secondary Education Commission, the guiding principle in selection should not be the teachers' own idea of what books the students must read but their natural and psychological interests. The contents of a library may be classified as:

1. Books for Younger Children—Well illustrated and attractive books giving information on fairy tales and fables, etc.

2. Books for Older Children—

(i) Books depicting stories of travels, explorations, adventures. discoveries and inventions.
(ii) Biographies of great men and women.
(iii) Suitable works of fiction, fun and hobbies.
(iv) Parallel text-book.
(v) Books on different subjects.

3. Reference Books—

(i) Source books.
(ii) Dictionaries.
(iii) Encyclopaedias.

4. Books for Teachers—A faculty committee including representatives of each department should be appointed with the librarian as the convenor. The committee should determine policies for the development of the library, draw up rules, governing its use, and use funds in such a way that each department of the school work is provided for equitably.

5. Books for Adults—To serve as a centre of community service, the school library should contain books for adults also.

III. Cataloguing

Views of Tagore are worth noting when he writes, "The usual thing is for a library to say: Here is my catalogue, come and select for yourself. But in the usual catalogue there is no Introduction, no invitation, no spirit of welcome. That library alone can be called hospitable, which shows an eagerness to invite readers to the feast at its disposal. It is such hospitality that makes a library big, not its size. That the readers make the library is not the whole truth, the library likewise makes the readers."

IV. Library Rules

Among other rules, the following must be included:

(i) Library periods may be allotted.

(ii) For the changing and distribution of books, a certain time may be fixed.

(iii) Each student may be asked to keep a diary wherein name of the books read with date and comments be entered.

V. Library Room and Equipment

Regarding this, S.R. Ranganathan observes, "It should be equipped with plenty of attractive, well-built, well-printed, well-illustrated, with comfortable furniture, open shelves, charming pictures, flowers, hangings and bright and cheerful outlook, with a librarian who loves children as well as books."

Reading, lending, borrowing and returning should be the watch words of a library room. Spitting, smoking, noise making, sleeping, and quarrelling should be prohibited.

4.3 CENTRAL OR CLASS LIBRARY

Both of these have got a definite place in the school. By class-room library we mean library in the room of each class. It contains well-selected books suited to the needs of the class. Class library is not competitive to central library. It should supplement the work of the central library. "The class library is an important and essential adjunct to the central school library," writes the Secondary Education Commission. It has great educational potentialities.

Class-room library is easier to administer. It does not require an elaborate method of recording. Its organisation can very easily be entrusted in the hands of the students thus giving them an opportunity to manage their own affairs.

Class-room library affords opportunities to the teachers to see how much reading each pupil is doing and can thus encourage the keen students and stimulate the slowgoers. The teachers can also test whether the pupils are reading carefully and intelligently. As a class teacher spends much of his time with the students, he is in a better position to suggest suitable books to the students according to their tastes and aptitudes.

4.4 SUBJECT LIBRARIES

The Secondary Education Commission recommends that besides the class library in every high school, there should be subject-libraries under the charge of subject teachers. In addition to text-books, there should be advanced works, reference books, books on related subjects and allied fields. Such collections will help the teachers in enriching their teaching greatly. The students also will get a wide view of the subject in all its bearings.

4.5 ENCOURAGING STUDENTS TO MAKE THE BEST USE OF SCHOOL LIBRARY

Usually it is observed that the students do not take adequate interest in the use of school library. Only a very negligible number of students make the profitable use of library material. Concerted efforts are needed to develop interest in this regard. Following measures may be adopted towards the end:

1. The library should be made the most attractive place in the school so that it may attract the students in large numbers.
2. The cooperation of the students should be sought in decorating the library in order to give them the feeling that the library belongs to them.
3. The librarian should behave very sympathetically with the students.
4. Books suiting different tastes and interests should be provided in large numbers.
5. The teachers should give occasional talks to pupils on the importance of extra-reading.
6. The librarian should give thorough instructions to the students in not only how to find out books and other material in the library but also how to make the best use of the material which the library contains.
7. Library periods should be provided for each class in the time-table.
8. As far as possible the open shelf system should be introduced so that the students may have free access to books.
9. Students should be asked to maintain a diary in which they should enter date-wise the names of all the books they have read. They may also be asked to write brief quotations or extracts from the books that may appeal to them. They may also write short reviews and appreciation of these books.
10. Marks may be allotted for extra-reading and entered in the monthly progress report.
11. Book competitions should be arranged from time to time and questions on titles, authors and subject-matter may be set.
12. The school library should be kept open during the vacation and long holidays.
13. The beautiful picture-cuttings from newspapers and illustrations from current events and topics should be displayed on the library Bulletin Boards.
14. The furniture should be as per the needs of the students.
15. A catalogue of library books should be available in the library for ready reference.
16. Library day may be organised once a year to popularise the school library.

We may sum up the discussion with a quotation from Tagore: "In order to bring a library into the fullest use, it is necessary that its contents should be clearly and specifically brought to notice, otherwise it is difficult for the ordinary man to find his way about them, and the library is left as a city of vast accommodation that lacks sufficient means of communication. Those who frequently visit libraries on some special means of communication. Those who frequently visit libraries on some special quest of their own may manage to make a track for themselves by dint of the urgency of their particular pursuit. But the library itself should recognise its share of responsibility in the matter. Because it has the books, it is incumbent on the library to get them read, for then alone it is justified. It is not enough that it passively permits visitors; its invitation should be active. For, as the Sanskrit proverb tells us *tannashtam yannadiyate*, that which is not given is wasted."

Role of the Teachers in Encouraging Students to Use Library

Teachers and librarians must make attempts to break down the old barriers that completely separate library and class-room. They must join together so that students make the optimum use of school library.

The teachers should acquaint themselves with the contents and interesting aspects of books and other reading material within the school library and inform students accordingly.

In the day-to-day class-room teaching, they should make pointed references to important books and other reading materials available in the school library.

They should guide the students to the type of books they should read.

The teachers may give assignments and project work which the students may complete independently by self-study.

They may maintain records of books read by the students.

They may give extra credit to the students when they read supplementary books.

4.6 SCHOOL LABORATORY

Meaning and Significance of School Laboratory

A school laboratory is a big room in which practical work relating to science is done. It is considered as the 'hub' of science activities. It is a field of experiments. Students learn here by doing.

In a secondary and senior secondary school, separate laboratories for history, chemistry and physics are provided. Teaching of these subjects cannot be imagined without a laboratory.

Main Objectives or Purposes or Need for a Laboratory

1. To develop scientific temper among students.
2. To develop the power of observation of the students.
3. To provide real knowledge of scientific phenomenon.
4. To provide conducive environment for learning.
5. To provide opportunities to verify scientific laws.
6. To provide opportunity to students for training in the use of scientific method.
7. To help students in developing values of cooperation and working

together.
8. To help students in developing initiative and self-confidence.
9. To provide opportunities to observe, think, analyse and synthesise facts.
10. To draw conclusions on the basis of cause and effect relationships.

Equipment for Different Types of Laboratories

General Science Laboratory:

(i) Working tables (ordinary) with drawers.
(ii) Demonstration table (8′ × 4′) provided with gas and water points.
(iii) A minimum of two sinks in the corners of the laboratory.
(iv) A black-board.
(v) Stools (in two sizes)
(vi) Almirahs (steel or wooden)

Biology Laboratory:

Biology laboratory should be equipped with the following:
(i) Tables (6′ × 2′ × 2.5') with water fittings and drawers.
(ii) Two sinks at the corners of the laboratory.
(iii) Almirahs.
(iv) Stools (in two sizes).
(v) Wall board or black-board.
(vi) Small table racks.
(vii) Wall shelves.
(viii) A froggery, where necessary.

Special attention be paid to lighting arrangement in biology laboratory. It should have glass panes on the northern side and pendent lights over the tables.

Chemistry Laboratory:

The equipment for chemistry laboratory is as under:
(i) Almirahs (wooden and steel).
(ii) Wall board or black-board.
(iii) Demonstration table (8′ × 4′) with cupboards, water and gas points.
(iv) Working tables with cup-boards, shelves, water and gas points.
(v) Balance room should be attached to the laboratory.
(vi) Sinks on each working table or at least two large sinks at the corners of the laboratory.
(vii) A fume cup-board.
(viii) A wooden box half filled with sand for use as waste material box.
(ix) Acid proof drainage system.
(x) Shelves for reagent bottle on each working table and wall shelves for storage of reagent bottles.

Physics Laboratory:

Physics laboratory should have the following equipment:
(i) Working tables (ordinary) with teak wood top.
(ii) At least one table having gas point fitted to it. This may be used for

experiments on heat.

(iii) Projected platforms for balances.
(iv) Almirahs.
(v) Demonstration table having drawers, water and gas points.
(vi) Wall board or black-board.
(vii) Two large sinks at the corners of the laboratory.
(viii) Stools (in two sizes).
(ix) Physics laboratory should have an attached dark room.

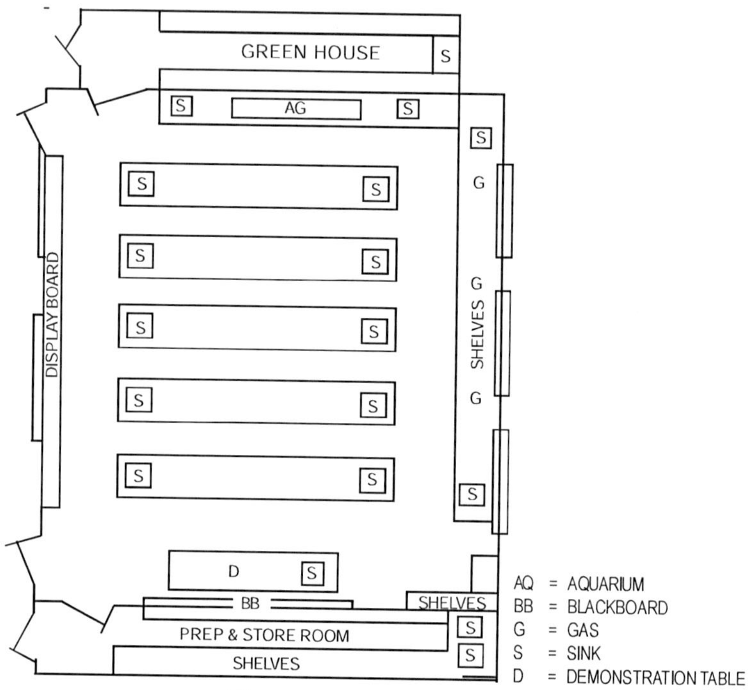

Fig. 4.1: Biology Laboratory

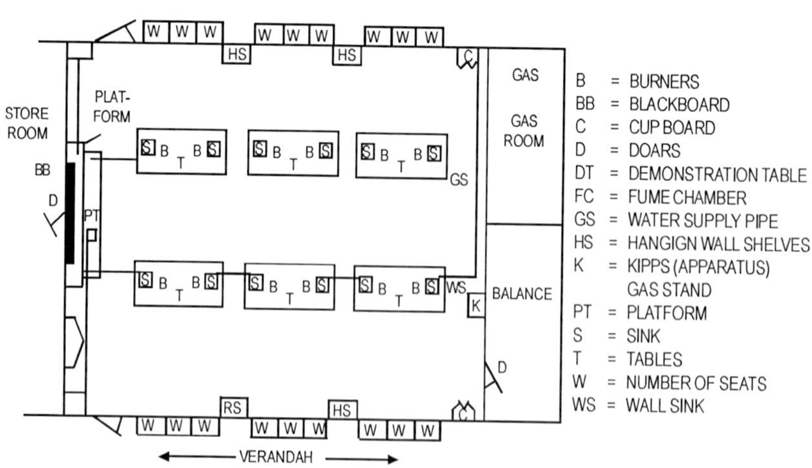

Fig. 4.2: Chemistry Laboratory

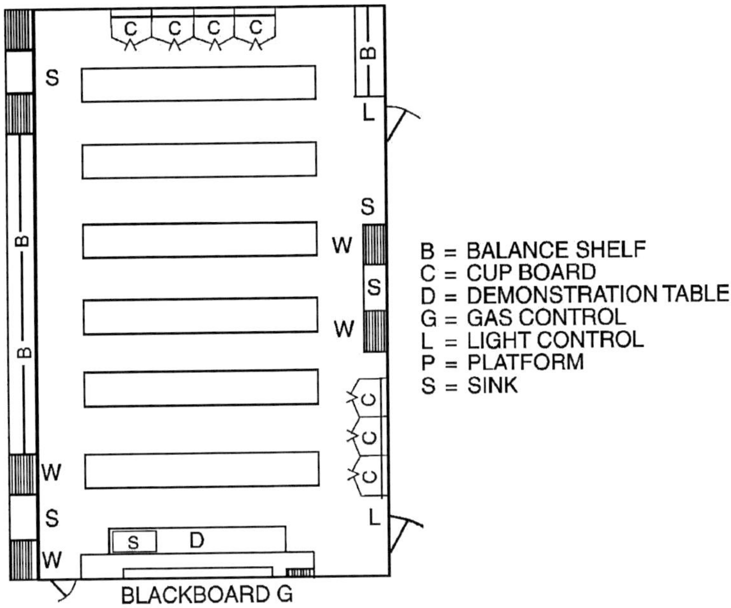

Fig. 4.3: Physics Laboratory

4.7 THE PLAYGROUND AS THE UNCOVERED SCHOOL

The playground is said to be the cradle of democracy. Various co-curricular activities and especially the games and sports contribute a lot for the development of all the major qualities needed to be an ideal citizen. It is called the 'uncovered' school as it is a place where character and personality develop.

The playground serves the following purposes:

1. Games Teach Cooperation—Team work is the pivot round which the wheel of games revolves. If the members of the team do not work for the team but for their individual distinctions, the team is sure to go to the walls. Games and sports bring home this fact to the students that loyalty and cooperation are the important contributory factors for the honour of the team. These serve to eliminate selfishness and teach the students to subordinate their own interests for the sake of a broader aim of winning the game. This lesson is very important and every citizen is expected to follow it.

2. Preparaing for Life Situations—The players have to play sometimes against heavy odds. Courage, patience, steadfastness and perseverance are needed to play well and effectively. The players get accustomed to face very critical situations and this stands in good stead when they enter life. We cannot think of an ideal citizen without possessing these qualities.

3. Providing Opportunities for Leadership—Games and sports provide opportunities for leadership of a very high order. The captain of the team has to put right players at their right places and has to bring harmony among the different members of the team. Only a man of self-confidence, imagination and enterprise can lead others.

4. Development of Various Senses—The games and sports call for a variety of movements—physical and mental. "School games involve a wide range of activity. Most of the senses are called into action. Comparison and judgment are needed," says William Gowers. The mind has to be kept alert to meet the changing situation to the ball. Body and mind work in harmony.

5. Physical Development—Games and sports promote good health, which is perhaps more important than wealth. Good health is also a sign of a good citizen.

6. Emphasis on Struggle—They teach the lesson that struggle is more important than success. Baron de Conbertin states, "The important thing in sports is not to win but to take part. The important thing in life is not triumph but struggle. The essential thing is not to have conquered but to have fought well. To spread these precepts is to build up a stronger and more scrupulous and more generous humanity."

7. Satisfaction of Various Urges of Children—Games satisfy one of the important urges of the children. Play is a biological and social necessity for the children. It is the most fundamental thing about a child—play for the child is one of the most serious facts of life; it is a form of work for the young and the basis for all education.

8. Development of *Esprit de Corps*—Tournaments develop in the minds of the students love for the school. 'We' feeling comes to the forefront. Tournaments if properly conducted help in developing the idea of corporate life in the minds of students. The players play for their respective schools and the other students of the respective schools cheer up. It is thrilling to witness the students clapping and encouraging the players of their sides. The love for the institution is clearly manifested in the minds of the students.

Important Elements of the Playground

(1) Spacious space for different games

(2) Boundary wall

(3) Free from thorns

(4) Shady trees

(5) Regular up keep

Area of Playground

An Ad Hoc Enquiry Committee on games and sports appointed by the Government of India (1958) recommended the following area for playground:

Type of Institute	*Recommended Area*
1. College (with a student population of 1,000 to 1,500 students)	10 Acres
2. A High School of Senior Secondary School (with a student population of 500 to 1000 students)	5-6 Acres
3. A Middle School (with a student population of 200 to 500 students)	3-5 Acres
4. A Primary School	1 Acre

Where separate playgrounds cannot be made available for each educational institution, a common pool for a group of institutions should be created.

National Policy on Education (1986, 1992)

Sports and physical education are an integral part of the learning process. A nation-wise infrastructure for physical education, sports and games will be built into the educational edifice.

The infrastructure will consist of play-fields equipments, coaches and teachers of physical education as part of school improvement programme.

Available open space in urban areas will be reserved for playgrounds if necessary by legislation.

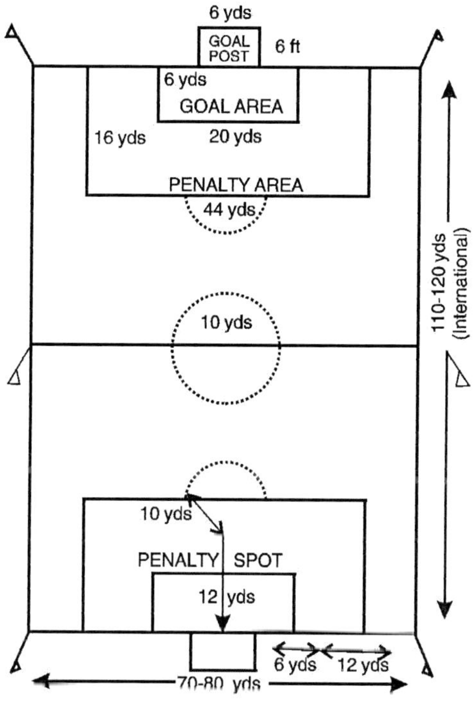

Fig. 4.4: Football Ground

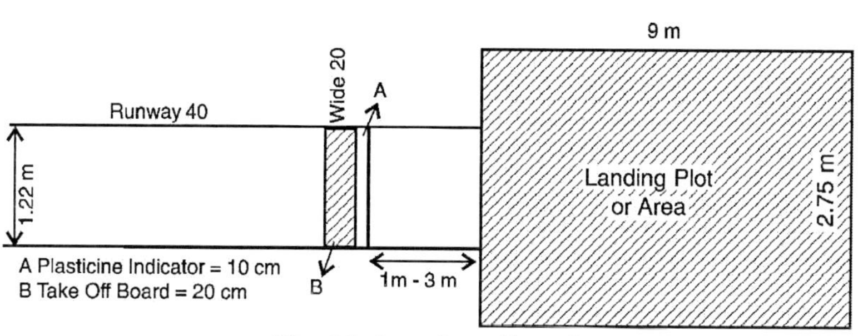

Fig. 4.5: Long Jump Ground

4.8 SCHOOL HOSTEL

Significance and Need for a School Hostel

It is universally accepted that a good hostel can serve as an enlarged ideal family for developing a spirit of corporate living, self-reliance and self-discipline in the student. An ordinary school sets limits to the possibilities of developing the 'art of living' amicably and graciously.

A well-supervised hostel is very conducive to the training of ideals and values of citizens.

A well-organised hostel can serve as a great cementing factor in uniting students coming from different regions with their distinct languages, customs, and manners, etc. Values of appreciation of varying cultures is developed. Ideals of emotional integration and national unity are strengthened.

Hostel becomes a necessity in the event of frequent transfer of parents of students.

Sometimes parents send children to protect them from unhappy and unhealthy home environment.

Role of the Hostel Superintendent

The proper management and organisation of a hostel depends to a great extent on the personality and character of the hostel superintendent. He is the person who can provide an appropriate environment for the desired development and training of the students.

Sympathetic and enlightened supervision of the various communities of the hostel life by the superintendent with the help of students' committees will go a long way in making the lives of the hostellers, riches, fuller, nobles and conducive to the ideas of citizenship.

If the superintendent is careless, negligent and devoid of psychological knowledge, the boarders are likely to go astray. Broadly speaking the hostel superintendent must be a parent substitute. All the essentials of home life must be made available to the students so that they may not think that they are living at a place which is quite separate from them. To develop this kind of attitude, introduction of self-government in hostels is very helpful.

Too much of liberty to students regarding stay outside the hostel is very harmful. No student should be allowed to spend the night away from the hostel except with the prior permission of the hostel superintendent.

A proper check on the visit of the friends of the hostlers should be kept. Undesirable elements should be disallowed to visit the hostel.

To minimise the chances of extravagant expenditure, the hostel superintendent should act as a banker. He should teach them the virtues of thrift and economy.

Proper time-table for studies and games, provision for co-curricular activities, formation of students committees for the management of different activities, etc. are very essential for organising hostel life.

Important Duties of the Hostel Superintendent

Following are some of the important duties of the hostel superintendent:

1. To look after the morals of the students.

2. To look after the studies of the students.
3. To look after the diet of the students.
4. To look after the health of the students.
5. To look after the cleanliness of the hostel.
6. To look after the recreational activities.
7. To look after the spending habits of the students.
8. To look after the corporate life of the students.

Important Qualities of the Hostel Superintendent

The hostel superintendent is expected to possess the following qualities:

(i) He should be a man of vision.
(ii) He should be democratic in his outlook.
(iii) His treatment with the students should be parental.
(iv) He should be academically and professionally well-qualified to guide students in their intellectual pursuits.
(v) He should command respect and obedience through his qualities of head and heart.
(vi) He should understand the adolescence psychology.

Self-Government in the Hostel

Principle of sharing responsibility with the students should be the key-note of the functioning of hostel.

Following committees may be constituted to carry on various activities of hostel life.

(a) Mess Committee—The function of this committee will be to prepare a suitable menu, to make necessary purchases in connection with the meals and to supervise the preparation of meals. It will be its concern to see that wholesome diet is supplied to the boarders.

(b) Sanitation Committee—Its function will be to look after the general cleanliness of the hostel, urinals, lavatories, etc.

(c) Literary Committee—It will be entrusted with the task of supervising the study habits of the students. Perhaps this is the most difficult task.

(d) Cultural Committee—It will be entrusted with the work of organising daily prayers and arranging talks on moral and spiritual matters. Social and religious functions may also be planned by this committee.

(e) Dramatic Committee—This will organise dramatics to make the hostel life richer from the recreational point of view.

(f) Games Committee—This Committee will be entrusted with organising games regularly.

(g) Discipline Committee—This Committee will frame general rules and code of conduct to be observed in the hostel.

These committees are intended to provide opportunities to students to develop the ideas of cooperation, mutual help, fellow-feeling and love for rules and regulations. The students will feel that they are residing in their own homes and it is their responsibility to enhance the reputation of this home, i.e., hostel. By obeying the laws framed by different committees, they will develop an attitude of respect to laws whether framed by the superintendent or school authorities. Dignity of labour will also be developed in them. They learn how to adopt the policy of 'give and take'.

A Word of Caution

Lack of appropriate supervision by the hostel superintendent may lead to the following undesirable elements:

1. Indulgence in gossips.
2. Undesirable habits.
3. Mutual bickering and jealousies.
4. Extravagant expenditure.

To avoid ugly situations and indisciplinary tendencies, it is very essential to prepare a time-table for studies, provision for co-curricular activities and formation of students committees to look after various activities.

SECTION II

5

School Head: Qualities and Duties

5.1 SUPREME POSITION: AS THE HEAD, SO IS THE SCHOOL

W.M. Ryburn compares the position of the Headmaster in a school to the captain of a ship.

According to Jaswant Singh, "The Headmaster or the Principal of a school is the hub of the education process."

P.C. Wren has described the role and position in the following words:

"Schools are good or bad, in a healthy or unhealthy mental, moral and physical condition, flourishing or perishing as the headmaster is capable, energetic and of high ideals or the reverse. "Schools rise to fame or sink to obscurity as greater or lesser headmasters have charge of them."

In the words of the Central Advisory Board of Education: "No scheme of educational reconstruction will produce the desired result unless it is administered with vision and efficiency". The school is aptly called the lengthened shadow of the Head because the environment of the school reflects the personality of the Head.

Will French and others stress the role of a principal in these words: "If a teacher fails, the principal fails, if the teacher succeeds, the principal succeeds. To sum up what the principal's job is, we may call him a referee—the captain of the ship—the boss of the firm—a juvenile judge before whose tribunal come not only the culprits but the adults who frequently contribute to the pupils' shortcoming. He is a promoter who must project the future of his institution and convert the public to this plan. He is a social physician to every parent who has a wayward son who needs attention. He is a friend in need to pupils and to all the homes in which misfortune comes. His power, his activities, even the good he does, cannot be measured by a measured yardstick."

General Grant is said to have remarked that there are no poor regiments but poor colonels.

Sultan Mohi-ud-din rightly states that no school can succeed if the teachers in it work only as individuals and not as a group. But just as every group needs a leader, so also a school must have a leader who would stimulate and direct its work. Such a leader is the Headmaster. And so is the case with the school. He is the hub of the education process. The success of the school system depends on his ability and skill as a sound and effective educational leader. The success or the failure of the school depends upon its Headmaster.

"The character of the school reflects and proclaims the character of the headmaster."

"He is the seal and school is the wax."

"What the main spring is to the watch, the flywheel to the machine or the engine to the steamship, the Headmaster is to the school."

In the words of S. Balakrishna Joshi: "By virtue of his office, he has to be a nexus between the government and the school authorities, the management and the staff, the masters and the pupils, and the parents and teachers—character rather than capacity, tact rather than authority, sympathy rather than severity are his forte."

The Secondary Education Commission (1952-53) has stated the role of the Head of the School as:

"In him proper working of the school depends."

"The reputation of the school and the position that it holds in the society depends in a large measure on the influence that he exercises over his colleagues, his pupils and the general public".

"He acts as a liaison between it (the school) and the department and the general local community."

"He holds an important place in the life of the community, where he can exercise a very healthy influence."

"By his contact with the parents and the general public he can help to forge that link between the school and the larger community which we have repeatedly stressed."

According to S.N. Mukherji, "The Headmaster is a link between internal and external administration of the school."

"The Headmaster is a keystone of the arch of school administration."

It is stated, "He is an organiser, leader, governor, business director, coordinator, superintendent, example: teacher, guide, philosopher and friend."

5.2 MULTIPLE ROLES, RESPONSIBILITIES AND RELATIONSHIPS OF THE HEAD OF THE SCHOOL

In the past, the duties of the Head were confined mostly to routine work at school and beyond that he had practically no responsibilities. The new ideal of secondary education entails heavy responsibilities. Now he is required not only to deal with correspondence, office work, scholar's registers and cash-books but also to discharge his duties to the society. He has to coordinate the efforts of teachers, students and the community at large.

The functions of Headmaster are very complex. He has to supervise each and every activity in the school. He has to play a very delicate and critical role. He has always to work with four varied interest and groups: pupils, people, teachers and the authorities. He has often to come across and strike a balance in the practical fields among quarrelling and fighting students, complaining parents and exacting departments. He is expected at various times and various interests to play different roles. He must, by nature of his position, be:

1. A *teacher* of teachers.
2. A *supervisor* not only of teachers but of service personnel.
3. A *disciplinarian*, just but effective.
4. A *psychologist*, at least to the extent of being able to detect

maladjustments, especially of teachers, which definitely hinder effective instruction and achievement of desired goals.

5. A *financier* in organising the school budget.
6. A *lawyer* at least to the extent of knowing his obligations, rights and legal abilities as well as of those of all school personnel.
7. A *sociologist* to the extent of at least being able to understand the relation of school with a social forces.
8. A *technical* expert is educational measurement and evaluation.
9. An *expert in group dynamics* to the extent of working effectively with staff, pupils, public and the authorities.

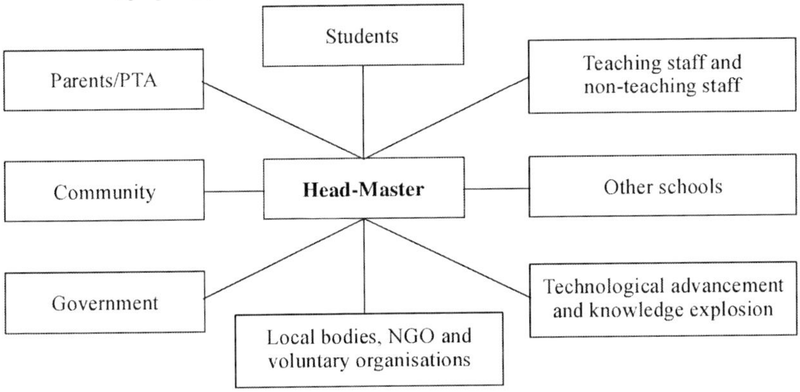

Fig. 5.1: Multiple Roles and Responsibilities and Relationships of the Head of the School

5.3 IMPORTANT MANAGEMENT ROLES

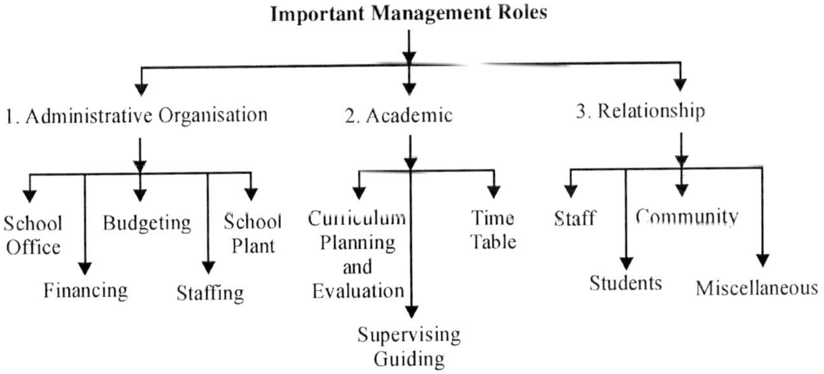

Note: Roles, responsibilities and relationships overlap.

The head is responsible for the smooth running of the school. He is responsible for carrying out the policies and programmes of the Department of Education. He is the coordinator of educational work. He sets the tone of the school. He acts as a 'liaison' between the Education Department and the management or the general of head and heart he possesses.

Hundreds and thousands of eyes watch him, judge him, measure him and are eager to follow his noble example.

He has to be sweet and soft as well as stiff and stern.

Goldsmith said: "Oil, vinegar, sugar and saltness in him to agree!"

Unless he has a seeing eye, an understanding heart and an all adjusting mental poise, he is bound to falter and tumble.

The Headmaster is in the strategic centre of a web of instructional inter-relationships—teacher-pupil, teacher-teacher, teacher-supervisor, teacher-parent and teacher-superintendent.

The Headmaster is the solar orb round whom all the planets (teachers) revolve.

5.4 WHAT IS THE HEAD LIKE?

1. The Head is the hub of the education process.
2. The Head is the leader of the school.
3. The Head is the seal and the school the wax.
4. The Head is like the main spring of the watch.
5. The Head is like the flywheel to the machine.
6. The Head is like the engine of the steamship.
7. The Head is a liaison.
8. The Head is the strategic centre.
9. The Head is the solar orb.
10. The Head is the link.
11. The Head is the key-stone.

5.5 QUALITIES OF THE HEAD AS PER HIMACHAL PRADESH EDUCATION CODE

The Himachal Pradesh Education Code (2001) does not prescribe any special qualities for the head of the school. This implies that the qualities of head of the school which find mention in educational literature and research work in the field are also applicable to the heads of school working in schools. However, the Code explains the term 'Quality of Education' by quoting Mannheim. According to him education means "Fostering the free development of the person through the unhampered unfolding of his or her innate qualities". The Educate Code further states, "Quality Education should consist of training the intelligence, widening the mind and enlarging its interest and teaching the technique on which modern civilisation is based. Education demands discipline of reasoning and discipline of emotions. This discipline should help us to rise in society and focus our creative instincts. While living in society it is essential that man should try to adjust himself within the social code. Socially maladjusted people create problems for the society in general. Though everybody knows the XYZ of everything, nobody knows the ABC of anything. Education should produce better human beings rather than artisans and technicians".

In view of his supreme position, the head enjoins in the school, he is expected to possess certain qualities to discharge his functions effectively and efficiently and to justify his position. These qualities are given here.

1. Considers the Administrative Machinery as an Instrument of Social Service—"An educational administrator is more than an official punctilious about administrative routine; he is a leader guiding and directing a sacred undertaking. The official apparatus that is at his disposal, the education department that is under his control, is more than a bureaucratic machine. It is an instrument of social service." —*Chitra Naik*

2. Cooperative Attitude—"The leader of the school can be successful only when he secures willing cooperation from his co-workers; when he makes those co-workers feel that the problems of the school are theirs and not his own." —*Mohi-ud-din*

"Dignity does not consist in aloofness and in maintaining an air of superiority; it rather consists in being helpful and doing the right thing.

—*Mohi-ud-din*

3. Democratic Attitude—"A democratic administrator should look upon the personnel as socially equal to himself; he should not take decisions by himself, but with his colleagues; he should make them feel responsible and share in administration; he should have a code of set rules of administration which he and his colleagues should follow rigidly, making no discrimination in their application; and lastly, he should want no special privilege." —*R.R. Kamria*

4. Educational Statesman—In the words of E.P. Cubberly: "He must learn to lead by reason, by his larger knowledge and courageous enthusiasm rather than to drive by reason of his superior power.... He must reach up out of the routine of school supervision and execute duties into the higher level of educational statesmanship."

5. Expert in Human Psychology—An ideal head always remembers that all people cannot be equally intelligent and hard working. A trouble shooter needs to be handled firmly in the very beginning. Praise and appreciation sometimes help even if a person does not deserve it. Sometimes sympathetic hearing is all that is needed to blow off the steam of emotions. Sometimes valuable suggestions help in easing the tension.

6. Faith in Human Nature—"It is essential, therefore, that he be a man of faith, faith in his vocation, faith in his pupils, faith in human nature, and faith in his staff." —*W.M. Ryburn*

"He must have unlimited faith in himself and his creator."—*Jaswant Singh*

7. Recognition to Good Work Done—Ryburn writes, "Nothing will more encourage a man or woman, a boy or girl, to greater effort, than an encouraging recognition of good work done, of sincere effort made, or good qualities shown. If those in-charge of institutions, and those carrying on the administrative work of department wish to enable those working with them to do their best, they should always realise the value of ungrudging recognition of all that merits such recognition."

8. Judicious Decision-Making—(i) Decides cases promptly. (ii) Gives judgements only after weighing and considering relevant evidence. (iii) Perceives true nature of cases. (iv) Decides cases on the basis of principles rather than expediency. (v) Makes decisions without bias and prejudice.

9. Headmaster not by Appointment but by Superior Ability—"It must not be known by his staff and scholars that he is their headmaster by appointment but felt that he is their master by superior ability, energy and character."

—*P.C. Wren*

"He is the organiser, leader, governor, business director, coordinator, superintendent, teacher, guide, philosopher and friend."

10. Health—"A person with indifferent health and poor stamina will not be able to discharge the multifarious and heavy responsibilities of his office."

—*Jaswant Singh*

11. Life one of Immolation—In the words of S. Balakrishna Joshi: "The progress of the school community is his thought by day and dream by night, and his aching passion is to wear himself out in the service of the shrine in which he feels spiritually wedded. It is his conviction that while the life of a teacher is one of consecration that of the headmaster should be one of immolation."

12. Leader by Courage and Reason and not by Power—"He must learn to lead by reason, by his larger knowledge and courageous enthusiasm rather than to drive by reason of his superior power.... He must reach up out of the routine of school supervision and execute duties into the higher level of educational statesman.

—*E.P. Cubberly*

"The successful administrator gets people to work with him, not primarily because he has power over them and can order them but because he is the kind of leader for whom they want to do their best."

—*Pagors and Myers*

13. Man of Integrity—He fights all temptations to pad his purse with money to which he is not entitled. To quote S. Balakrishna Joshi: "He does not try to exploit school influence for private gains because he realises that if he does it, he signs his moral death-warrant. The result is that no amount of pressure can wean him from the path of duty and justice. Authority, cannot coerce him, nor can temptation reduce him into any course of conduct not conducive to the highest interests of the school."

14. Optimistic Outlook— He has unlimited faith in himself. He does not accept defeat. He always think of success all the time. Ryburn stresses, "It is essential, therefore, that he be not only a man of high character but also that he be a man of faith; faith in his vocation, faith in his pupils, faith in human nature, and faith in his staff."

15. Patience— "Patience is a virtue that will pay very generous dividends to assists, not to control the educative process."

—*Reaves*

"Go slow the first day, the first week, the first month, and even the first year, make changes slowly and always with the cooperation of the faculty."

—*William T. Melchor*

16. Philosophy of Education—"A good Headmaster needs to have a sound philosophy of education."

—*Jaswant Singh*

17. Planning Capacity—"If a principal is not careful, he will find himself spending much of the time in answering telephone, running errands for teachers, signing excuses, making repairs to the buildings, handling money, raising campaigns, and performing other minor duties and then budget his time accordingly."

—*Margaret Grag*

18. Professional Devotion—"He should derive the same satisfaction from working for institution as the artist or the sculptor derives when working late hours over his handiwork, fully attentive to the smallest details, never tiring."

—*Jaswant Singh*

19. Progressive Outlook—"It is reasonable to expect that a headmaster should be progressive in his outlook." —*Mohi-ud-din*

20. Rising Equal to any Occasion—"He rises equal to any occasion, and by his resourcefulness and readiness to render service, solves knotty problems. To him it is not beneath his dignity to strike the gong in time if the peon is engaged otherwise, or to lead a band of devoted volunteers to flush the latrine if scavenger is absent. Again he is prepared to 'referee' a match if the umpire has not turned up or step into a class and teach any subject if a teacher is called suddenly. Thus his willingness and ability to do any piece of work pertaining to the school, wrest for him the confidence and regard of all concerned.

21. Scientific Attitude—An ideal head is particularly careful in making judgement about persons for whom he cherishes a positive like or dislike. He observes correctly without letting personal feeling, prejudices, and wishes to influence him, draws valid conclusions from given facts and makes sound generalisations as the facts warrant. He does not see things through coloured spectacles. He is able to detach his personal likes and dislikes from the performance of others. He is conscious of the fact that monopoly of truth is not held by anyone.

22. Sense of Humour—Dr. Jaswant Singh writes about this quality: "It will enable him to get over an impasse with the help of a smile, a light hearted chuckle, or a jocular remark which will ease the tense atmosphere. The sense of humour will help break resistance, overcome opposition by injecting a spirit of comraderie into the situation. Many a difficult situation can be resolved by a witty remark."

23. Sensitive to the Needs of the Community—"In whatever community the principal finds himself, he should study the characteristic social conditions and needs of his pupils and endeavour in appropriate ways to secure increased cooperation between the school and the community in meeting these needs."

—*W. Johnson Frank*

24. Sensitive to the Needs of the Students—A good Headmaster should be profoundly sensitive to the physical, mental, moral, intellectual and spiritual needs of his pupils and should know how to minister to them."

—*V.S. Jha*

25. Sensitive to the Needs of Teachers—"The principal should not interrupt classes, unless invited to do so." —*Jacobson and Others*

"If the principal stays to the end of the class period, he should observe good manners by expressing in a sentence or two his pleasure on visiting the class." —*Jacobson and Others*

26. Sensitive to the Needs of the Parents—"He should always treat parents with scrupulous courtesy." —*W.M. Ryburn*

27. Source of Inspiration—The members of staff should look to him for guidance, help and inspiration. "Under any authoritarian regime, where basis of relationship is fear of one sort or another, it is often possible to get certain routine done efficiently. But under such conditions, it is impossible to bring into rapport the best elements in the personality of the teacher—thus education loses its formative influence."

"He gives up the time-old tradition of checking his teachers, frightening his teachers, weakening his teachers and examining them; but manipulates things so as to train his teachers, inspire his teachers, encourage his teachers and trust them."

—*D.I. Lall*

28. Thinking Capacity—"Experience is an indispensable qualification for a head master. This is certainly true. But experience alone without the capacity to think out and plan out new progressive programmes is inadequate."

—*Mohi-ud-din*

29. Vision and Imagination—

(a) Makes decisions which later events show to be sound and reliable.

(b) Searches new practices and techniques.

(c) Seizes opportunities to develop new patterns of action.

30. Not an Awful Man—"In a school worth its name the Head will neither sit in his room like a large spider waiting for a chance to pounce on his prey nor he is like an awe inspiring God on the Olympian Heights who visits the earth once in a way to thunder disapproval or to subjugate the people by his presence."

—*A.M.D. Razario*

Personality of the Headmaster

To justify his place as the inspiring leader and guide, the Headmaster must have a strong personality. R.A. Lamb remarks, "To make the perfect head of the school, there is needed in addition to all these, a quality which is undefinable—and which resides in the personality of the individual. It is not possible to analyse this quality any more than it is possible by dissecting a man's brain to find wherein resides the soul or the spirit of life. But that it exists is beyond question."

5.6 DUTIES OF THE HEAD OF SCHOOL AS PER HIMACHAL PRADESH EDUCATION CODE

Chapter II entitled "Internal Administration" mentions the following duties of the head of the school

1. General Control of the School. It is the duty of the Head to exercise general control of the school and connected wings (like hostels, stores, farm, shop) in his charge.

2. Maintenance of Discipline. To maintain discipline among staff and pupils.

3. Instruction Work. To organise, guide, stimulate and supervise the instruction.

4. Text-books. To prescribe approved text-books.

5. Teaching work. To take a regular part in the teaching work especially in classes and subjects in which his personal guidance is desirable as prescribed from time to time.

6. Physical Education. To arrange for the games, physical education and other extra moral activities of the pupils.

7. Maintenance of Registers. To see that all registers are regularly and accurately maintained.

8. Maintenance of Accounts. To keep precise accounts of all money entrusted to him and to see that they are properly disposed of in accordance with the rules laid down in that regard.

9. Welfare of Pupils. Generally to promote the physical, intellectual and moral welfare of the pupils under his charge.

10. Annual Confidential Reports. The annual confidential reports of all the ministerial staff should be initiated by him by 15th of April every year (even in those cases where the ACR forms have not been received from the concerned official after having recorded his resume of work/self appraisal). The ACRs in such cases be initiated *suo-motu* and submitted to the reviewing officer by 22nd April. In the case of teaching staff the reports be initiated by 15th of September every year and submitted to the reviewing officer by 22nd September positively irrespective of the fact whether self appraisal/resume of work has been recorded by the teacher concerned or not. Such ACRs may also be initiated *suo-motu* by due date and be submitted to the reviewing officer for further action.

11. Submission of Vacancy Position. The monthly vacancy position and quarterly establishment returns should be submitted to the Directorate and District Education Office, by 7th of the following month.

12. Submission of Retirement Cases. The list of staff due to retire during the following year ending 31st December should be prepared and submitted to the Directorate in the month of January every year.

13. Expenditure Statement. The expenditure statement for the previous year and the budget requirement for the following financial year should be submitted to the District Education Office in the month of April.

14. Submission of Data. The institutional and numerical data as on 30th September will be submitted to District Education Officer concerned by last week of October every year. The scholarship forms of students complete in all respect are submitted to the Directorate and to District Education Officer wherever applicable by October end every year.

15. Court Cases. The matters relating to Courts/Tribunal/Vidhan Sabha and disciplinary matters should be attended on priority and in a time-bound manner.

16. Due permission to be taken to start any new subject/stream of study (Commerce, Science etc.). No stream is to be started if number of students studying in that particular stream (Commerce, Science etc.) is less than 20. Similarly, no subject is to be started, if number of students opting for the study of a particular subject is less than 10. Teaching of Punjabi as an optional subject for 9th and 10th classes be started, if number of students opting is 20 or more than 20 in each class. However, in case of sub-cadre/ hard area, the criteria of enrolment for starting new stream/subject shall be 50per cent that of mentioned herein.

17. Relieving of Teachers. The employee under transfer/promotion should be relieved within the stipulated time limit and not allowed to continue beyond such time limit under any circumstances unless extension has been granted by the competent authority for specific period and the LPCs are issued. The salaries of such staff for the following month be drawn only from their new place of posting. It will also be ensured that no staff surplus/maladjusted to the sanctioned strength is retained in the institution except in cases where specific directions from the Government/Director of Education has been received.

18. Maintenance of Teachers' Diaries. All the teachers should maintain teacher diaries mentioning therein yearly teaching details divided in four quarters subject-wise, class-wise and get it signed from the head in the first two weeks of academic session. Teaching task accomplished in the previous month will be got signed by the concerned teacher from the head in the first week of the next month.

19. Preparation of School Calendar. A calendar of school, mentioning all the activities, viz., beginning of the academic session, vacations, collection of dues, dates and timings of various co-curricular activities including sports, celebration of important days should be prepared and maintained.

20. Holding Annual Function. The school must hold its annual function once in a year between September to February every year.

21. Organisation of Co-curricular Activities. Every head of institution will ensure that all the teachers are given administrative as well as other co-curricular assignments by giving at least one administrative and one co-curricular assignment to every teacher.

22. Corporal Punishment Authority. Corporal punishment in any form, for any reason, is totally banned. However, the head of institution may impose special fine not exceeding Rs.5/- in any one case, for breach of school discipline or misconduct which shall be understood to include un-punctuality, irregular attendance, use of bad language and slovenly habits as well as breach of school rules and such delinquencies so as to set a bad example. Written report of misconduct shall be sent to parents or guardian of the student.

23. Expulsion, Rustication and Suspension only for Classes IX upwards. The penalty of expulsion or rustication of a student for serious misconduct may be imposed with the approval of the concerned District Education Officer. The period of rustication or expulsion shall not exceed one academic year. The head of the institution may suspend a student temporarily for misconduct for immediate deterrent effect and this punishment will be terminated if the student gives in writing a promise of good conduct in future along with an assurance of the student's good conduct by the parent or guardian failing which, the head may recommend expulsion of the student for one year to the concerned District Education Officer.

24. Private Tuition. The teachers in Government Schools shall not undertake any private tuition. Strict vigilance shall be maintained and those who force the students to attend/enrol for private tuition shall be penalised. It is general duty of head of institution that special coaching classes for weak students may be arranged before or after school hours. Nothing is to be charged from the students on account of such special coaching. All the teachers are expected to prepare the students in such a manner so that the students attain confidence and are able to develop proficiency and pass in different subjects.

25. Minimum Teaching Work-Load in Schools. (a) Principal and headmasters will teach 6 and 8 periods per week respectively.

(b) School lecturer will teach minimum of 30 periods per week.

(c) Each TGT and C&V Teacher will teach minimum 36 periods per week.

Head of the institution can assign any extra teaching, administrative or co-curricular work to any of the teachers.

26. Subject-wise distribution of 54 periods per week. The Head should ensure the following:

A. Classes 6th to 8th

Compulsory subjects:

English 8, Maths 8, Hindi 6, Science 6, Social Studies 6, Sanskrit 6.

Optional Subjects:

Drawing/Home Sc./Music 6,

Non-examination subjects.

Library 1, Moral Education 1,

Physical Education 4, Co-curricular Activities 2.

Total = 54 periods

B. Classes 9th to 10th.

Compulsory subjects:

English 8, Maths 8, Hindi 6, Science 6,

Social Studies 6.

Optional Subjects-I:

Drawing/Home Sc./Music/Economics/Agriculture/IT Education 6.

Optional Subjects-II Indian Modern Languages:

Sanskrit/Urdu/Punjabi/Tamil/Telgu 6.

Non-examination subjects:

Library 1, Moral Education 1,

Physical Education 4, Co-curricular Activities 2.

Total = 54 periods

27. House Examination. The head must ensure that there are two house examinations in an academic year for all classes. The first house examination for under matric classes will be conducted in last week of May and last week of August in winter closing and summer closing schools respectively. The second house examination will be conducted in last week of August and first week of December in winter closing and summer closing schools respectively. For plus two classes these two house examinations are to be conducted in last week of August and in first week of December, both in winter and summer closing schools. The progress report including mark sheet of the house examination of the student and detail of attendance, conduct, and turnout will be sent to the parents after each house examination.

28. Students number in class. The head may keep in view that the number of pupils in a class or section shall not exceed that for which accommodation is available in the class-room, nor shall it ordinarily exceed 60 for classes 6th to 10th, and 80 in case of Plus One and Plus Two classes. A new section should be formed only, if in the opinion of the head of institution, the total number in that class, justifies it on grounds of efficiency, economy and feasibility.

29. Attendance of Teachers. The attendance of the teachers shall be recorded regularly and punctually in a register kept for the purpose. Teachers will not leave the school premises during school hours without the permission of the Head. Whenever, the head of the institution leaves station on official duty or on leave, he must make an entry in the order-book and assign the officiating duty to the next senior teacher.

30. Time-table. A class time-table of six hours daily teaching and 54 periods in a week, showing the routine of study for each day of the week, shall be displayed in each class-room and a general time-table showing the work of all the teachers and classes and time-table of each teacher will be similarly displayed in the Head's room and in the staff room.

31. Students Attendance/Registration. (i) The Roll shall be called at the time when the school opens, and again at the beginning of the second meeting after recess. No blank shall be left and no pupil's attendance shall be marked after the roll has been called. When a pupil leaves the school due to sickness, or any other cause before he has completed 2 hours of secular instruction, his attendance for that school meeting shall be cancelled.

(ii) Correct admission number should be entered in each class attendance register to avoid complications while issuing School Leaving Certificates. This must be got checked once in a year by the Head of the Institution and every month by the checker of the register.

32. Correct Age Entry. The head of the institution is required to make every endeavour to ensure that the age of a pupil is recorded with scrupulous accuracy on his first admission to a school and to make it clear to the parent or the guardian that the date of birth when once recorded will not be subsequently changed.

Sometimes, it may so happen that at the time of change of department/ seeking readmission/transfer of school the entries are wrongly made in the admission withdrawal register. If these are merely clerical errors, corrections should be made by the Head of the Institution instead of going into the whole of the procedure laid down for the change in the date of birth.

33. Conduct Register. The conduct register shall be in the charge of the head of the institution. Remarks need only be entered in this register when a pupil is commended for special merit or reported for misbehaviour, besides achievements of a student in different subjects. If no entry is made against the name of a pupil it would be presumed that his conduct has been satisfactory. The periodical progress report sent to the parents should include remarks on the conduct, physical standard and regularity in attendance of the pupil concerned.

34. Attending Half-Yearly Review Meetings for the Head of the Institutions. It will be the duty of every head of institution of Senior Secondary and High School to attend every meeting of the heads of the institutions which will be held half yearly and will be convened by the DEO of the district concerned.

First Half-Yearly Meeting

This meeting is to be convened in the 3rd week of April every year. The points for interaction in this meeting are to be as follows:

(i) Submission of expenditure statement of the previous year ending 31st March.
(ii) Projected Budget of the next year.
(iii) ACRs of ministerial and other cadres except for teachers.
(iv) Establishment return and vacancy position on prescribed proforma.
(v) Action taken report in inspections carried out in the previous year.
(vi) Inquiry, disciplinary and legal cases, if any.
(vii) Submission of UCs of the sanctions out of any scheme during the previous financial year.
(viii) Clear-cut vacancies and vacancies to be caused due to retirement in the next year of each cadre.
(ix) Status of audit reports/audit paras in schools/DEO offices and their disposal.
(x) Any other item referred to from Directorate, District and Zonal offices.

Second Half-Yearly Meeting.

This meeting is to be convened in the last week of October every year. The points for interaction in this meeting are to be as follows:

(i) Submission of institutional data on prescribed proformas.
(ii) ACRs of teachers.
(iii) Expenditure statement of April, May, June, July, August and September months.
(iv) Establishment return and vacancy position on prescribed proforma.
(v) Submission of scholarship forms.
(vi) Any other item from district, zonal offices or directorate.

5.7 ROLE OF THE HEAD IN PLANNING, MONITORING, SUPERVISION AND EVALUATION

Role of the Head of the School in Planning

Smooth and efficient running of the school depends upon skill in planning. Planning is the pre-requisite of any administration. Before the opening of the new session, Headmaster is expected to plan out all the activities that are likely to take place during the course of the year. An activity calendar may be prepared and it may be got printed or cyclostyled and distributed to the teachers and the students. For preparing this. The head would do well to discuss it with his colleagues, parents and students, where desirable. Planning will bring order and system in the school programme; of course, there would always be a scope for changes according to new situations. Regarding non-planning Jacobson writes, "In extreme cases there are teachers without students, classes without teachers, sections with enrolment twice the capacity of the room. The teachers are handicapped because of the shortage of supplies, lack of books and equipments and improperly classified students. In many schools it is the custom to close school at noon of the first day to allow the principal and teachers to organise the work so that it may begin properly on the second day. Such a waste of time is inexcusable"

Meaning of Planning

The concept and essentials of planning may be illustrating by pinpointing the significance of each letter forming 'planning.' By and large, significance is applicable to planning at all levels including school planning by the Head.

P stands for— (a) Purpose, (b) Policy, (c) Priorities, (d) Pupil's participation, (e) Parents' participation, (f) Perspective plan.

L stands for— (a) Liaison among different authorities, (b) Division of responsibility, (c) Long-term and short-term objectives.

A stands for— (a) Administrative structure, (b) Advisory bodies, (c) Appraisal of the Plan from time to time, (d) Attitude formation.

N stands for—(a) National goals, (b) National integration, (c) Numbers (Data).

N stands for— (a) New needs, (b) New developments.

I stands for— (a) Inputs, (b) Indigenous resources, (c) Investment, (d) Internal resources, (e) Involvement of teachers and others, (f) Institutional plan.

N stands for— (a) Nomenclature, (b) New priorities.

G stands for— (a) Government rules and regulations.

Long-Term Planning and Short-Term Planning

Long-term educational planning involves many specialists and institutions in the education sector and other sectors and indeed the community itself. The process has to be continuous, and point in time. Five year plans are useful not only in reviewing progress of the recent past but also in setting broad goals and macro-strategies for the ensuring planning period.

Short-term planning for implementation should be decentralised so as to place appropriate aspects of planning responsibility as close as possible to those who are responsible for implementation at all levels. Long-term planning involves the integrated efforts of educators, sociologists, economists, psychologists and political scientists. J.P. Naik has observed, that practically all the previous plans did not look beyond five years. There is a great need to have a perspective plan of educational development with in the framework of our economic plan. In the light of the perspective plan, short-term plans of economic and educational development should be prepared and implemented.

5.8 ROLE OF THE HEAD IN MONITORING

Meaning of Monitoring

The *Oxford Dictionary* explains monitoring as "To watch and chart something over a period of time in order to see how it develops, so that you can make necessary changes."

"*Webster's New Collegiate Dictionary*" gives the meaning of monitoring as "To watch, observe or check especially for a specific purpose: to keep track of, regulate or control the operation of a process."

From above, it becomes obvious that the term monitoring embraces in its meaning a wide scope of activities.

Applying these meanings to monitoring by the Head, it implies watching and charting the progress of school programmes over a period of time by him in order to see how it develops so that he can make necessary changes.

Thus the monitoring role of the head of the school has the focus to maintain and control the school functioning in accordance with the set plans.

In monitoring, the Head of the school shares responsibility with his colleagues. He assigns some duties to them.

Merits of Monitoring

The monitoring has the following merits:

1. It brings continuity in carrying out work.
2. It makes administrative functioning efficient and smooth.
3. It is based on the democratic educational management principles.
4. It brings system in functioning.
5. It is based on the principle of sharing responsibility.
6. It is based on the principle of delegation of authority.
7. It provides for improvement by bringing new ideas into operation.
8. It is conducive to discipline.
9. It is based on the principle of accountability in educational arrangement.

Limitations of Monitoring

1. It is likely to introduce rigidity in the plan.
2. It relies more on rules and regulations.
3. It may ignore the element of human relations.
4. It is more concerned with quantitative targets.
5. It entails more of paper work.

5.9 ROLE OF THE HEAD IN SUPERVISION

We have earlier discussed the various dimensions of supervision and laid stress on the basic fact that there is no area of school work which needs no supervision by the Head of the school.

Supervision does not mean 'fault finding.' It means guiding and motivating the staff to put in their best for the all-round development of the students.

In brief, supervision by the Head includes the following elements:

1. Supervision of school office.
2. Supervision of instructional work.
3. Supervision of curriculum transaction.
4. Supervision of school plant (including building etc.)
5. Supervision of school supplies.
6. Supervision of school workshop, farm, etc.
7. Supervision of physical and health programme.

8. Supervision of guidance and counselling.
9. Supervision of co-curricular programme.
10. Supervision of moral development of the students.
11. Supervision of school finances.
12. Supervision of vocational programme.
13. Supervision of overall physical and social environment of the school.
14. Supervision of professional development of the staff.
15. Supervision of school community relations.

Guidelines/Criteria for Supervision

Before supervising, the supervisor will bear in mind the following points:

1. The supervisor should prepare in advance a schedule of his activities.
2. The supervisor should keep his schedule flexible.
3. The supervisor should afford opportunity to teachers to participate actively in planning the programme of supervision.
4. The supervisor should provide assistance in interpreting the community background of his pupils.
5. The supervisor should provide assistance in modernising methods and techniques of instruction.
6. The supervisor should provide assistance in interpreting the results of the evaluation programme.
7. The supervisor should guide the teachers in the construction and evaluation of the daily lesson plans.
8. The supervisor should assist in using enrichment material.
9. The supervisor should guide in using the audio-visual aids.
10. The supervisor should guide the teachers in the maintenance of school records.
11. The supervisor should provide opportunities to participate in the activities of professional organisations and study groups.
12. The supervisor should provide an opportunity to participate in the selection of professional literature for the professional library.
13. The supervisor should provide an opportunity to teachers to participate in the selection of new verbal and non-verbal instructional materials.
14. The supervisor should make efforts in the development of cooperative relationships with other departments or levels of instruction.
15. The supervisor should assist the teachers in the procurement of necessary instructional materials.
16. The supervisor should on occasions put himself in the position of others.
17. The supervisor should welcome constructive suggestions.
18. The supervisor should make efforts to understand his staff thoroughly.
19. The supervisor should live up to his promise.
20. The supervisor should help each individual teacher to feel conscious of his worth.
21. The supervisor should help teachers to work cooperatively.
22. The supervisor should encourage new ideas.
23. The supervisor should infuse desire to improve.

24. The supervisor should assist in promoting adaptability and other personality traits.
25. The supervisor should make efforts towards promoting better understandings.
26. The supervisor should encourage self-effort and self-improvement on the part of teachers.
27. The supervisor should utilise individual differences of intelligence, talent, initiative and energy of the staff and students.
28. The supervisor should assist in improving teacher morale.
29. The supervisor should offer effective leadership.

5.10 ROLE OF THE HEAD IN MONITORING AND SUPERVISION

Broadly speaking there is no difference in the objectives of monitoring and supervising. Both aim at achieving maximum output and making the optimum use of input.

Monitoring lays more emphasis on the attainment of quantitative targets. It depends upon, by and large, on observing rules rigidly. It relies heavily on paper work.

Supervision takes note of quantitative as well as qualitative aspects. It relies heavily on human elements. It provides guidance to workers.

Decision taking and decision implementing are inherent in supervision. Monitoring keeps track on the fulfillment of decisions or targets. In this sense, monitoring is a part of supervising or supervision.

The Head of the school is both a monitor as well as a supervisor.

5.11 ROLE OF THE HEAD IN EVALUATION

Meaning of Evaluation

Evaluation involves skills in defining goals and establishing standards by which to judge the amount of change; collecting evidence of change; applying the criteria of making judgments about the worth of the change; and revising plans in terms of judgement.

Purposes of evaluation. Following are the purposes of evaluation:

1. *Diagnostic.* This means that evaluation in supervision should lead to the discovery of the strengths and weakness of the educational institutions and the causes that have contributed to these.

2. *Improvement of School System.* Diagnosis enables the concerned authorities to chalk out an improvement programme and then re-appraise and re-improve it. Thus continuous evaluation and continuous improvement go together.

3. *Providing Motivation.* Evaluation motivates the school personnel to achieve all the more better results.

Principles of Evaluation

Following are the important principles of evaluation in this respect:

1. Principle of functional utility.
2. Principle of cooperation.
3. Principle of comprehensiveness.
4. Principle of continuity.

5. Principle of critical appreciation.
6. Principle of forward looking.

Types of Evaluation

Following are the major types of evaluation:

1. Informal or uncontrolled evaluation.
2. Formal or controlled evaluation.
3. Self-evaluation.

Effectiveness of the Supervisory Programme

Effectiveness of the supervisory programme is revealed by measuring the various elements of the teaching-learning situations which are as under:

I. Evaluation relating to pupils.
II. Evaluation relating to teachers.
III. Evaluation relating to curriculum.
IV. Evaluation relating to psycho-physical environment.
V. Evaluation of the work of the supervisor.

I. Evaluation Relating to Pupils. It is very difficult to prepare an exhaustive list of elements relating to pupils which can or should be evaluated. Suggestive list is given below:

(a) Emotional qualities or development.
(b) Intellectual qualities or development.
(c) Moral qualities or development.
(d) Physical qualities or development.
(e) Social qualities or development.
(f) Vocational qualities or development.

II. Evaluation Relating to Teachers. Teachers' efficiency may be measured in two broad areas:

A. Teachers' traits and qualities relating to the following:

(i) Teacher's physical fitness.
(ii) Teacher's personal fitness.
(iii) Teacher's cognitive abilities.
(iv) Teacher's affective qualities.
(v) Teacher's professional skills.
(vi) Teacher's general skills.

B. Evaluation of teacher's duties and functions with reference to the following:

(i) The teacher as a director of learning.
(ii) The teacher as a friend and counsellor of pupils.
(iii) The teacher as a member of the school community.
(iv) The teacher as a member of professional association.

Instruments of Evaluation Relating to Teachers

1. Checklists, questionnaires observation, interaction analysis.
2. Records, diaries, anecdotal, etc.
3. Personal data about intelligence, health, academic achievement, etc.
4. Rating scales.

5. Tests of teaching attitudes, aptitudes, personality, character, etc.
6. Interviews, etc.
7. Objective and projective techniques.

III. Evaluation Relating to Curriculum. Constant appraisal and improvement of the curriculum is an important concern of the supervisor. The following points need consideration:

1. Are curricular and co-curricular activities child-centred?
2. Does curriculum concentrate on the experiences of the human race as a whole?
3. Is curriculum based on the twin principles of reality and utility?
4. Is curriculum broad based, flexible and changing?
5. Does curriculum possess continuity, articulation and integration?
6. Does the curriculum provide for individual differences among children?
7. Does the curriculum have social significance?
8. Does the curriculum consist of purposeful activities and meaningful experience?
9. Does the curriculum provide direct instruction?
10. Does the curriculum promote democratic values?
11. Does the curriculum achieve the all-round growth of the child?

IV. Evaluation Relating to Psycho-physical Environment. There is a need to study and appraise the richness of the materials and equipments that influence the child's activities and experiences. The appraisal will be with reference to the following:

1. Instructional materials.
2. Text-books and other books.
3. School plant.
4. The community.

5.12 DELEGATION OF AUTHORITY AND ACCOUNTABILITY

Meaning and Need for Delegation of Authority

Delegation of authority implies assigning responsibility of work to another person or group of persons, working in the same institution. The need for delegation of authority arises primarily on account of six considerations.

1. Democratic working of an institution demands that the head should share responsibility with the staff.

2. The Head of an institution, say the headmaster, has to look after several activities. He performs multifarious tasks. It is, therefore, not desirable that he himself should undertake each and every activity. Of course, overall responsibility will remain with the Head. He seeks assistance from his colleagues. All persons are not equally knowledgeable in all things. Likewise all persons have different talents and aptitudes. The Head endeavours to make the best use of the talents of his colleagues. He, therefore, delegates some of his authority in certain areas to some of his colleagues.

3. Sharing of responsibility develops a feeling of 'oneness' or 'we feeling' among the staff.

4. Delegation of responsibility is an indication of mutual faith – faith of the Head in the staff and of the staff in the head.

5. Delegation of authority makes easier the work of monitoring and supervision of the head.

6. Delegation of authority introduces an element of accountability on the part of all those who work in an organisation, say the school.

Areas of Delegation of Authority

In the earlier part of this chapter we have dealt with the role, functions and responsibility of the Head of the school.

He has to deal with various groups and individuals, associated directly or indirectly with the education of the students. All this demands that he should delegate some responsibility to his co-workers.

As a matter of fact, for routine work there are as many areas of delegation as the number of activities being undertaken in the school.

Following are the illustrative areas in which delegation of authority may be given:

1. Academic work.
2. Admission work.
3. Co-curricular activities.
4. Community liaison.
5. Cultural programmes.
6. Discipline.
7. Evaluation and examination.
8. Finance.
9. Games and sports.
10. Guidance and counselling.
11. Library and reading room.
12. Prayer and assembly.
13. School beautification and cleanliness.
14. School property.
15. School sanitation.

Principles of Delegation of Authority

1. Principle of need and requirement.
2. Principle of seniority.
3. Principle of experience.
4. Principle of aptitude and interest.
5. Principle of willingness.
6. Principle of classification of work to be delegated.
7. Principle of human relations.
8. Principle of sincerity in delegation.
9. Principle of cooperation.
10. Principle of motivation.
11. Principle of coordination.
12. Principle of monitoring.

13. Principle of supervision.
14. Principle of consultation.

5.13 ACCOUNTABILITY IN SCHOOL EDUCATION: IMPORTANCE, NEED AND MEANING

It is an accepted fact that without proper accountability, no organisation or institution can grow. Accountability brings an element of responsibility on the part of all those who work in an organisation. Where there is no accountability, there is little efficiency. Absence of accountability may result in chaos and confusion; without it, an organisation would be without any direction.

The word 'accountability' is a concrete and matter-of-fact expression of what the schools owe as duties and responsibilities to their establishing/employing organisation, to the student community and the society at large, with the ultimate aim of doing good by their performance. The idea of accountability should not appear as objectionable or foreign to the institutions and teachers if they could open-mindedly look at their own everyday activities and programmes. As explained by Prof. Ramesh K. Srivastava (*University News*, Vol. 38, 2000), "Most of us as customers, go to the market, have a definite idea of our requirements, select the best item in a particular category to suit our taste and pursue, scrutinise our merchandise and then bargain to get the best in the price range. But when the bought item does not come to our expectations, or when we visit a government office, a ration shop, or a court, and on finding that the concerned person is absent or on casual leaves, we tear our hair and our blood boils. In all these cases, we have some expectations, some codes or norms within ourselves and when the things or services don't correspond to them, we are disappointed."

Unfortunately no such set codes or norms exist in the academic world. There are no fixed qualitative targets to achieve, no tangible yardsticks against which the academic excellence could be measured. Fixing of accountability is one such step in the right direction.

5.14 MEANING AND DEFINITION OF ACCOUNTABILITY

1. *According to Good's Dictionary of Education* (1973), "Educational accountability is the theory that teachers and school systems may be held responsible for actual improvement in public achievement and that such improvement is measurable through tests of teacher effectiveness, constructed by outside agencies."

2. *The International Dictionary of Education* by Terry Page and J.B. Thomas (1987) explains the term accountability as "(i) Educational technology term for the extent to which student performance is attributable to instruction rather than ageing, selective admission etc. (ii) Extent to which a state, college or university is publicly accountable for its actions and expenditure." The same authors define educational accountability as, "Assumption of responsibility for bringing about specified results in students." Again it describes teacher accountability in these words: "Theory that teachers and school systems should take responsibility for improvement in public

achievement and that teacher effectiveness by this criterion should be measured by external agencies."

3. *The International Dictionary of Management* (1980) by Hano Jo Hannse and G. Terry Page (1980) defines accountability as "Accountability for action carried out and performance achieved to others, e.g., by a manager to his superior or by the board of directors to its shareholders. Also used more loosely to describe responsibility."

4. *The Concise Dictionary of Education* (1982) gives the following meaning of accountability, "Educational accountability is a concept in which the school system and especially teachers are held responsible for the learning and academic progress of students."

5. *The Blackwell Encyclopaedic Dictionary of Organisation Behaviour* (1995) edited by Nigel Nicholson explains the term 'accountability' as "The term denotes responsibility for particular activities, results or outcomes specification of the person(s) or group(s) who hold such responsibility in an organisation."

5.15 DIMENSIONS OF ACCOUNTABILITY

Accountability may be viewed from several aspects.

- *Moral Accountability* to those affected by one's actions; pupils, parents, colleagues.
- *Contractual Accountability* to one's employer, which in the case of teachers may be the school board, the school district, regional or State Government, supervisors and superintendents.
- *Professional Accountability* to the standards one sets oneself and one's professional aims, beliefs and mission.
- *Financial Accountability* to the standards set by appropriate authorities.
- *Social Accountability* to the society/community which has set-up the school.
- *Administrative Accountability* to the administrative standards set-up by persons concerned or authorities.

5.16 METHODS USED FOR ASSESSING ACCOUNTABILITY

All the above mentioned forms of school accountability can be assessed by the following methods:

1. Self-assessment by

(i) Managers of schools.
(ii) Supervisors of schools.
(iii) School staff, i.e., the head and the teacher.

2. Assessment by

(i) Students.
(ii) Teachers.
(iii) Supervisors.
(iv) Management.
(v) Community/Parents.

(vi) Autonomous organisation or independent organisation not connected in the running of the school to be assessed.
(vii) Affiliating and Recognising Authority/Board.
(viii) Legislatures.

5.17 ISSUES INVOLVED IN ACCOUNTABILITY

Important issues involved in accountability are:

1. Who is accountable to whom in our education system?
2. How can an institution be made accountable?
3. How can teachers be made accountable?
4. When different teachers in an institution are involved in teaching and evaluation, how could a particular teacher be held accountable?

These issues raise further issues when we consider accountability in school education.

1. Are other social institutions accountable?
2. School education is conducted by a number of agencies. Are these agencies accountable?
3. How can an institution be made accountable when it has little or no control in the preparation of the curriculum, in the prescription of text-books, in admission of students, in setting question papers etc.
4. To what extent each section of personnel engaged in education, i.e., administrators, supervisors, teachers, etc., is accountable?
5. Are students accountable for their performance?
6. Are parents accountable for the performance of their children in studies?

A host of such issues arise. Situation seems to be very complex and does not permit any ready-made answer.

While discussing accountability in school education, the aspect of accountability of the Department of Education which formulates educational policies and also sometimes runs and manages its own institutions grants aids to private schools and recognises schools without grants, is hardly taken into consideration. There seems to be no mechanism to fix-up its responsibility.

Likewise, the Examination Boards/Affiliating Boards seem to enjoy so much autonomy that their work seldom comes under scrutiny.

It is generally observed that only the heads and the teachers are made accountable for poor results at the Board's examination. Others associated with school education are not held accountable. This is a serious lacuna which needs to be removed urgently if worthwhile improvements on school education are to be brought about.

5.18 BROAD PARAMETERS DETERMINING ACCOUNTABILITY OF AN INSTITUTION

Following are the nine parameters on which the accountability of an educational institution may be assessed:

Parameter I: Institutional Mission and Objectives

Criterion 1. The objectives and mission of the institution are clearly stated, periodically reviewed, and communicated systematically to all its constituencies.

Criterion 2. The objectives and mission of the institution reflect contemporary educational needs and are relevant to the region it serves.

Parameter II: Curriculum Design and Review

Criterion 1. The programmes of teaching and learning are consistent with the objectives and mission of the institution.

Criterion 2. The process of course/programme approval is designed to make the objectives, content, expected outcomes and weighting of different segments explicit.

Criterion 3. Feedback from students, employers, and external peers is used by the institution in the review and re-designing of courses/programmes.

Parameter III: Quality of Teaching and Learning

Criterion 1. The programmes of teaching and learning offer a wide range of academic disciplines to train students to fulfil personal, societal and national needs.

Criterion 2. The programmes of teaching and learning harness advances in technology to encourage student initiative in learning.

Criterion 3. The evaluation procedures in the educational programmes are rigorous and fair.

Criterion 4. The evaluation methods test the knowledge and skills that specific programmes are designed to impart.

Criterion 5. The regularity and the confidentiality of examinations are maintained and results are announced within reasonable time.

Criterion 6. The institution has open and participative mechanisms for evaluation of teaching and work satisfaction.

Criterion 7. The faculty have opportunity for continued academic progress and professional advancement.

Parameter IV: Publications, Consultancy and Extension Activities

Criterion 1. The 'institution has a vigorous and well-scrutinised publication programme and actively encourages faculty and students to publish in academic form.

Criterion 2. The faculty of the institution participate in and contribute to advances in knowledge through research and consultancy.

Criterion 3. The institution is responsive to community needs and conducts relevant extension and awareness programmes.

Parameter V: Organisation and Governance

Criterion 1. The administrative organisation of the institution is such that powers and responsibilities are clearly assigned to designated bodies and individuals.

Criterion 2. The organisation is designed to facilitate tasks related to every aspect of the institution's goals and every segment of its constituencies.

Criterion 3. The institution has a realistic academic calendar which is generally followed meticulously.

Criterion 4. The institution's offices and departments are governed on the principles of participation and transparency.

Criterion 5. Management techniques and technologies are used, to the extent possible, for efficient running of every administrative and academic task.

Criterion 6. The administrative and academic units of the institution make optimal and innovative use of available facilities.

Criterion 7. Academic and administrative planning in the institution move hand in hand.

Criterion 8. The institution has effective mechanism to monitor the functioning and progress of its academic and administrative units.

Criterion 9. All affected constituencies of the institution have access to relevant information pertaining to their professional functions and welfare.

Parameter VI: Infrastructural Facilities

Criterion 1. The institution has adequate infrastructural facilities to run the educational programmes and administrative functions efficiently.

Criterion 2. The growth and maintenance of the infrastructure keep pace with the academic growth of the institution.

Criterion 3. The infrastructure ensures a clean and efficient environment.

Parameter VII: Support Systems

Criterion 1. The institution has sufficient and well-run support systems to ensure the physical and intellectual health of all its constituencies.

Criterion 2. The allocation of facilities is based on principles of fairness and encourages creative and optimal use.

Criterion 3. There are fair and expeditious grievance redressal mechanisms at all levels of the institution's functioning.

Parameter VIII: Student Services

Criterion 1. The institution's prospectus gives clear guidance to students about admission and completion requirements for all courses, the fee structure and refund policies, and student support services.

Criterion 2. Financial aid to students is well-publicised and fairly distributed.

Criterion 3. The students of the institution have access to competent counselling and placement services.

Criterion 4. The students of institution have adequate and equitable access to learning support systems and to the records of their performance.

Parameter IX: Sources, Adequacy and Management of Financial Resources

Criterion 1. The finances of the institution are judiciously allocated and effectively utilised to make its programmes and functioning cost effective.

Criterion 2. The budgeting and auditing procedures are regular and standardised.

Criterion 3. The institution has imaginative and effective resource mobilisation and management strategies.

The parameters are self-explanatory and relate directly to the effective functioning and development of an institution.

5.19 TOOLS AND TECHNIQUES USED

1. Survey method.
2. Interview method.
3. Research on various issues relating to school education.
4. Performance of school leavers in various fields.
5. Examination results.
6. Ratings of institutions.

In assessing accountability of school education, different sections may be involved. Views of students, parents, teachers and media may also be obtained.

6

The Teacher

6.1 TEACHING AS A PROFESSION

Writing about teaching as a profession, Tomas Englund (1997) wrote in a paper that the phrase 'teaching as a profession' has no unequivocal meaning and that the conceptual meaning of profession is a void, being no more than a 'buzzword'.

Soder Rozer (1990) observes: "A profession does not exist in the same way a stone exists, and to define and look for a profession in the same way one would define and look for a stone will only lead to confusion and frustration."

Unfortunately there is a good deal of confusion and contradiction on the phrase 'teaching as a profession'. The educators do not speak with a united voice. However, none of the educators or people involved with education should disagree with the claim that the primary professional duty of teaching profession is to the student – technical as well as moral.

In the words of Johnson, author of *Professor and Power* (1972): "Professionalisation is a historically specific process which some occupations have undergone at a particular time, rather than process which contains occupations that may always be expected to undergo because of their "essential" qualities.

Arguments for the professionalisation of teaching usually focus on the privilege and prestige of previously established professions, referring most notably to medicine as "The ultimate in status, the elite position in the world of work" (Soder). The fundamental basis of educators' argument is that they possess a formal, esoteric knowledge base which can guide practitioners' actions, similar to that of doctor's medical knowledge. Indeed the 1986 Holmes Group report *Tomorrow's Teachers* typifies the centrality of knowledge to claiming similarity with other professions. "The established professions have, over time, developed a body of specialised knowledge, codified and transmitted through professional education and clinical practice".

Professionalism is characterised by Englund as focusing "on the question of what qualifications and acquired capacities, what competence, is required for the successful exercise of an occupation". Professionalism is then the quality of being professional, of allowing one's actions to be regulated by an "internal code of ethics" (McDonnel, 1998).

Peter Claim (1990) writes: "Professionalism is a state of mind. It actually has little to do with occupation, position, rank, years of service, clientele or hours worked. It also has little to do with seniority, personal ambition, remuneration, holidays, office size or mode of dress. Neither has it anything to do with years spent in a university, degrees attained, social standing, or even real or imagined codes of conduct and etiquette. It is quite simply, an ideal."

Clamp Peter (1990) characterises professionalism as being composed of four attributes — competency, integrity, reliability, and empathic humanism which he defines as evidence of "genuine caring for fellow humans". The idea of a "teaching profession" describes a special and unique set of circumstances for deep understanding complex practice, ethical conduct, and higher order learning, circumstances that define the complexity of the enterprise and explain the difficulties of prescribing both policies and curriculum in this area.

According to Darling Hammond Linda (1989), "Teachers as professionals are obliged to do whatever is best for the students, not what is easiest, most expedient, or even what the student might want."

Talbert and McLaughlin (1994) point out that "a specialised knowledge is primary among the conditions that distinguish a profession of teaching from other occupations."

The National Board of Professional Teaching Standards of the USA (1990) states: "The teacher's first responsibilities are to those being taught". The Board further states that teaching ultimately requires "skills to bring about effective student learning". Other professional characters are: competency and creativity to convey subject-matter effectively.

Myrna Copper (1988) points out: "Status and control are not the characteristics of professionalism, they are by products".

Knowledge, competence and commitment to students are truly 'prerequisites' of the teaching profession.

The process of teacher professionalisation is an exceedingly difficult task. Educators and professional organisations must speak with one voice.

6.2 CHARACTERISTICS OF THE TEACHING PROFESSION

1. Commitment to the Profession—The teacher should feel the importance of his profession. He must give his exclusive attention to the growth and development of the personalities of the children under his charge. He would be showing a dishonesty of purpose if once having entered, he is engaged in other pursuits. Without an exclusive attention to his job, he would fail in bringing forth a fine harvest of young men and women who are able to contribute their best for the welfare of mankind. If a teacher takes to his work just to make his living because nothing else is available, he will lack the essential zeal required by the teaching profession. He must be a teacher first and the teacher last. A person who wants to join this profession must feel the call for it.

In the words of the Secondary Education Commission: "They will not look upon their work as an unpalatable means of earning a scanty living but as an avenue through which they are rendering significant social service as well as finding some measure of self-fulfilment and self-expression."

2. Membership of Professional Organisation—The teachers should become members of the professional organisations, the functions of which are:

(a) To advance education ideals.
(b) To care for the welfare of children and young people.
(c) To improve teaching, supervisory and administrative procedures.
(d) To safeguard the welfare of teachers.
(e) To Improve salaries.
(f) To assure pension and tenure privileges.
(g) To secure for teachers the right to participate in educational policy-making.

3. In service education—A teacher is expected:

(a) To keep abreast of the developments in the teaching profession.
(b) To maintain membership in some professional organisations relevant to his subject or area of speciality.
(c) To manifest ethical behaviour in relations with fellow teachers and educational associates.
(d) To keep abreast of subject-matter through study of books, periodicals, papers and other sources concerning development in his field.
(e) To utilise films, filmstrips, T.V. and radio as a means of keeping abreast of new and advanced knowledge in his field.
(f) To attend conferences, workshops, seminars and meetings; to take field trips which tend to broaden knowledge.

4. Knowledge about the State Education Code—An Education Code includes rules and regulations governing various aspects of education. It is divided broadly into five categories:

1. Rules regarding recognition of school.
2. Rules regarding instructional issues, e.g., age of admission to a school, admission procedure, fees and funds, prescription of teaching material, school discipline, examination and evaluation etc.
3. Rules regarding school inspections.
4. Rules regarding service conditions and welfare of the staff.
5. School community relations.

It is very important to remember that the entire teaching-learning process is carried on in accordance with the provisions of the Education Code. Any deviation from it is likely to land the teachers into trouble.

5. Obligation of Teachers Towards His Colleagues

1. A teacher should be adept in establishing good human relationships with his colleagues.
2. He should give due regard to their personality.
3. He should not indulge in forming cliques or groups.
4. He should never criticise any of his colleagues before the students, their parents and others.
5. He should not backbite his colleagues to the head of the institution or others.

6. Professional Ethics of Teachers

Meaning. The concept of professional ethics may be described in these words of Laurie: "If a teacher has not an ideal aim he had better to take to shop keeping at once, he will there doubtless find an ideal within his capacity." The Secondary Education Commission 1952–53 has stated in this connection that "They (teachers) will not look upon their work as an unpalatable means of carrying a scanty living but as an avenue through which they are rendering significant social service as well as finding some measure of self-fulfilment and self-expression."

The professional ethics demands that a teacher does not try to exploit school influence for private gain. He realises that if he does it, he signs his moral death-warrant. The result is that no amount of pressure can wean him from the path of duty and justice. Authority cannot coerce him, nor can temptation induce him into any course of conduct, not conducive to the highest interests of the school.

He fights all temptations to fill his purse with money to which he is not entitled. He does not indulge in tuitions. He does not prescribe or recommend books on some consideration.

Need and Significance of Professional Ethics for Teachers

The teachers are called the makers of man, the makers of a nation and the real makers of history. It is, therefore, essential that teachers should have professional ethics.

Following points indicate the need and significance of professional ethics for teachers:

(i) Norms and ethics provide credibility to the teaching profession.
(ii) They help in developing a sense of commitment to the teaching profession.
(iii) They serve as beacon light to the teachers in adhering to certain important ideals and values.
(iv) They serve as warnings to teachers not to fall upon unscrupulous methods.
(v) They are constant remainders to teachers for discharging their responsibilities with a sense of purpose.
(vi) Adherence to the norms enhances the prestige of teachers.

7. General Attitude Acceptable to the Society

A teacher is a member of the society. He lives and works in the society. In view of his special responsibilities and roles, he is expected to rise above the average member of society. His general attitude in society should be of enthusiasm and optimism. He should be a man of cooperative attitude. He should be sensitive to the needs of the society. He should be guided by the ideals of democracy, secularism and socialism. He should be sufficiently appreciative of the needs and problems of the society.

8. Work Ethics. Since he ceaselessly strives to be a model to others, he regards no aspect of his work as trivial or insignificant which can conveniently be passed on to others to be done well or ill. He is too well aware of the truth of that wise statement: "Trifles make perfection and perfection is no trifle." Hence every item—be it the folding of a sheet or the writing of a circular—is done with meticulous care as if it were a religious act.

It is rightly said: "Dignity consists in being helpful and doing the right things in the right manner and at the right time." A teacher would do well to prepare his lessons daily. Bagley has rightly said: "However able and experienced the teacher he could do never without his preliminary preparation." Efforts should be made to ensure that all the work done is neat and clean, systematic and in time.

9. Ethical Code for Teachers. (A) 1. Every teacher shall remain punctual in attendance and in respect of his class work and also for any other work connected with the duties assigned to him by the head of the school.

2. Every teacher shall abide by the rules and regulations of the school and also show due respect to the constituted authority.

(B) No teacher shall:

3. knowingly or wilfully neglect his duties;

4. propagate through his teaching lessons or otherwise, communal or sectarian outlook, or incite or allow any student to indulge in communal or sectarian activity;

5. discriminate against any student on the ground of caste, creed, language, place of origin, social and cultural background or any of them;

6. indulge in, or encourage, any form of malpractice connected with examination or any other school activity;

7. make any sustained neglect in correcting class-work or homework done by students.

8. while being present in the school, absent himself (except with the previous permission of the head of the school) from the class which he is required to attend;

9. remain absent from the school without leave or without the previous permission of the head of the school; provided that where such absence without leave or without the previous permission of the head of the school is due to reasons beyond the control of the teacher, it shall not be deemed to be a breach of the Code of Conduct, if, on return on duty, the teacher has applied for and obtained, *ex post facto*, the necessary sanction for the leave.

10. accept any job of a remunerative character from any source other than the school or give private tuition to any student or other person or engage himself in any business.

11. prepare or publish any book or books, commonly known as keys, or assist, whether directly or indirectly, in their publication;

12. engage himself as a selling agent or canvasser for any publishing firm or trader;

13. ask for or accept (except with the previous sanction of the Director, in the case of an aided school, or of the managing committee, in the case of an unaided school), any contribution, or otherwise associate himself with the raising of any funds or make any other collections, whether in cash or in kind, in pursuance of any object whatsoever, except subscription from the members of any association of teachers;

14. enter into monetary transactions with any student or parent; nor shall he exploit his influence for personal ends; nor shall he conduct his personal matters in such a manner that he has to incur a debt beyond his means to repay;

15. accept or permit any member of his family or any other person acting on his behalf to accept any gift from any student, parent or any person with whom he has come into contact by virtue of his position in the school;

16. practise, or incite any student to practise casteism, communalism, or untouchability;

17. cause, or incite any other person to cause, any damage to school property;

18. behave or encourage or incite any student, teacher or other employee to behave, in a rowdy or disorderly manner in the school premises;

19. be guilty of, or encourage violence, or any conduct which involves moral turpitude;

20. be guilty of misbehaviour or cruelty towards any parent, guardian, student, teacher or employee of the school;

21. organise or attend any meeting during the school hours except when he is required, or permitted by the head of the school to do so.

10. Ethical Oath for Teachers. "I solemnly affirm that I will uphold the dignity of the teaching profession and that I will devote myself to the best of my capacity to the all-round development and well-being of any students."

11. Love for Children. It is said that if a teacher does not actually like boys and girls, he should give up teaching. He must enjoy their company in groups. A good teacher feels that some sort of energy is constantly supplied by the young. "Love the child and the child will love you; hate the child and the child will hate you." is a famous maxim. One who does not like children should not stay in teaching.

12. Specialised Knowledge. A teacher must be a master of his subject. Any weakness on his part will lower his prestige in the eyes of his student. Besides, he must love his subject. A teacher who does not love his subject fails to inspire his students and runs the risk of becoming a hypocrite.

According to the University Education Commission, "No teacher who is not master of the field, who is not in touch with the latest development in his subject and who does not bring to bear upon his duties a free and untrammelled mind will never succeed in inspiring youth with the love of truth which is the principal object of a higher education."

13. Grasp Over the Method. The Secondary Education Commission states, "Any method good or bad links up the teachers and his pupils into an organic relationship with constant mutual interaction, it reacts not only on the minds of the students but on their entire personality, their standard of work and judgment, their intellectual and emotional equipment, their attitudes and values. Good methods which are psychologically and socially sound may raise the whole quality, bad methods may debase it."

The creative teacher always keeps himself in touch with the latest methods of teaching and uses them in his class. Good methods, which are psychologically sound, facilitate learning and inculcate 'love of work'. Two farmers may possess an equal amount of land, an equally great desire for rich harvest but the one who uses the best method of farming will, other things being equal, get better results. Similarly, a teacher who adopts proper methods of teaching will show better results and make his teaching more interesting and effective. A teacher should not be wedded to any particular method and must not have a conservative outlook but use every developed and progressive method in his class as required by the intellectual attainment of particular students in the particular environment. He ought to devote some of his time in exploring new methods which may be of more help to him.

14. Daily Preparation. Perhaps there is no type of work where the results of poor planning are so devastating as in teaching. Careful and systematic arrangement of the subject-matter and the class-room activities is conducive to creative discipline. A well-prepared lesson helps to overcome the feeling of nervousness and insecurity especially so common in the first attempt at teaching.

15. Democratic Attitude. A teacher cannot afford to be an autocrat. Present day education lays much stress on the inculcation of democratic ideals in the students. A teacher who is to show the way of democracy to the students must develop in himself a democratic attitude. His role is of a friend, philosopher and guide and not of a policeman.

The Secondary Education Commission remarked: "The good teacher in our reorganised school will endeavour to win the love and confidence of his children and establish his prestige on sincerity, integrity, hard work and a sympathetic handling of their problems."

16. Respect for the Individuality of the Child. A child should not be treated just like a dumb driven cattle. His soul which is pure and very sensitive requires our most delicate care. He has his own individuality. His sense of respect should not be injured. Emerson states that "the secret of education lies in respecting the pupils." A child wants to be heard and his opinion should not be brushed aside merely because he is a child.

K.G. Saiyidain writes, "Under any authoritarian regime, where basis of relationship is fear of one sort or another, it is often possible to get certain routine done efficiently. But under such conditions, it is often not possible to bring into rapport the best elements in the personality of the teacher."

17. Knowledge of Psychology. Knowledge of psychology goes a long way in providing that basic orientation towards problems of education and child development without which there would be a considerable waste of time, energy and human resources. With a knowledge of child psychology, a teacher will be in a better position to understand and appreciate the individual differences of children, their nature, temperaments, habits and manners.

18. Intimate Knowledge of the Child. Children are not miniature adults. Their peculiar patterns of thoughts and emotions must be studied. Their names must be learnt and faces recognised. They must not be made to feel that the teacher is indifferent to them. Every source should be tapped to know about them to the fullest possible extent.

19. Fully Conscious of the Rights of the Child. A teacher must accept his duty to meet his obligations to the child in the following respects as proclaimed by the International Union of Child Welfare which is a federation of national and international organisations to promote the physical, moral and spiritual welfare of the child: (i) The child must be protected beyond and above all considerations of race, nationality or creed. (ii) The child must be given the means requisite for its normal development—materially, morally and spiritually. (iii) The child that is hungry must be fed; the child that is sick must be nursed; the child that is physically handicapped must be helped; the maladjusted child must be educated; the orphan and the waif must be sheltered and succoured. (iv) The child must be the first to receive relief in time of distress. (v) The child must enjoy the full benefits provided by social welfare and social security schemes, the child must receive a training which will enable it, at the right time to earn a livelihood and must be protected against every exploitation. (vi) The child must be brought up in the consciousness that its talents must be devoted to the service of fellowmen.

20. Emotional Stability of the Teacher. It is said in *The Education and Training of Teacher* published by UNESCO that "Various researches show clearly that the emotional stability of teachers affects that of pupils. Unhappy, frustrated, dissatisfied teachers cannot help their pupils to become happy, well-adjusted young people." The teachers should try to find out their own shortcomings and try to remove them so that the students may be saved from the adverse influence of their unbalanced personality.

K.G. Saiyidain has observed: "You cannot pour out of a vessel except that you have put into it and, if a teacher is poor and shallow from within, if there is no sparkling wire in him, he cannot quicken the mind or humanise the emotions of his children—if he is not a lighted candle himself, he will never be able to light up the flame in others."

21. Thirst for Knowledge. A teacher must refresh himself by constant reading not only about his subjects but books which touch life at every point. It would be very helpful if he would get opportunities of attending educational seminars, refresher courses and the like which enable him to get a good grip of his own thoughts and to see his own working in relation to others in the same sphere.

"A teacher can never truly teach unless he is still learning himself", remarks Rabindra Nath Tagore. A teacher should not feel shy to learn from others. There is no end to knowledge and his attitude should be like that of Newton: "I am only a child, playing in the sand by the sea-shore, picking up a pebble here and there with a vast ocean of truth lying undiscovered before me."

Although he should read books, magazines and newspapers for his own enjoyment and profit, he must keep in mind his responsibilities as a teacher. His reading must be wide enough so that he can guide his students' reading tastes.

The summer vacation usually is regarded rightly by most teachers as a period of deserved and needed rest and relaxation. However, an interested and efficient teacher is primarily a teacher for twelve months of the year. Even during his period of relaxation he makes it a point to combine pleasure with education. During summer, winter or spring vacations teachers can visit historical or literary landmarks in their immediate environment. Returning to their classes they can share their experiences with their pupils, thus enriching the content of their subject and stimulate their classes.

22. Missionary Spirit—Spirit of Service. Dr. E.A. Pires opines that the great teacher has the zeal of a missionary. There is a certain aptness in the analogy—between a missionary and a teacher, for every true missionary is first and last a teacher.

S. Balakrishna Joshi has very rightly observed: "Without a band of devoted teachers who are inspired by a holy-zeal, an institution with the paraphernalia of modern convenience will be like a beautiful corpse without spark of life, a carcass without soul." According to the same author teaching is a divinely ordained mission.

6.3 PROFESSIONAL TRAITS OF A TEACHER

Meaning of a Trait

There are some traits of personality on the basis of which we may determine professional traits of a teacher. In simple language, trait is a mode of behaviour. Following are some of the definitions of a trait.

1. "A trait is some particular behaviour such as cheerfulness or self-sacrifice which characterises the individual in a wide range of activity and is fairly consistent over a period of time." —*Woodworth*

2. "My own view is that traits are only convenient names given to types or qualities of behaviour which have elements in common. They are not psychological entities but rather categories for classification of habits."

—*May*

3. "A trait is a constant directing psychic force which determines the active and reactive behaviour of the individual." —*Baumgarten*

4. "A trait is a relation between the individual and his observers."

—*Vernon*

The word trait has several meanings:

- Generally, it refers to a *characteristic* or *property* of some *entity*.
- In *biology*, *trait* refers to a genetically inherited feature of an organism.
- In *psychology*, it refers to a component of personality as defined by *trait theory*.
- In *computer science*, trait refers to several things.

Characteristics of a Trait

1. A trait is scalable.
2. A trait is manifested in a number of activities and verbal expression.
3. A trait is not static in nature.
4. A trait is a higher order of habit.
5. A trait is readiness to respond to a variety of situations in a conscious way.
6. A trait is an organised frame of reference.
7. A trait is learnt/acquired in the interaction with the environment.

Types of Professional Traits of Teacher

I. *The Secondary Education Commission 1952-53 mentions the following traits*:

1. Initiative
2. Integrity (Moral Sense)

3. Persistence
4. Leadership
5. Self-confidence.
6. Emotional control
7. Social attitude

II. *The National Commission on Teachers I (School teachers) refers to the following*:

1. Punctuality and regularity in the performance of duties.
2. Honesty towards dealing with students.
3. Affection
4. Understanding
5. Firmness
6. Consistency

III. *Robert E. Glenn on Teacher Traits*

In *Admirable Teaching Traits* Robert E. Glenn identities 15 characteristics that principals look for in the new teachers they hire:

- Flexibility
- Organisation
- Ability to build success into the class
- Ability to communicate clearly
- Ability to create a pleasant atmosphere
- Ability to differentiate instruction
- Ability to establish successful class-room management
- Enthusiasm
- High expectations
- Content knowledge
- Good people skills (with students, staff, parents)
- Ability to pace instruction
- Ability to ask effective questions
- Good attitude
- Ability to teach actively

IV. *Professional Traits of Teachers Based on a Survey: Views of Heads of Schools*

1. Accommodating
2. Caring
3. Confident
4. Enthusiastic
5. Fair
6. Honest
7. Interactive
8. Kind
9. Knowledgeable
10. Motivator
11. Patient
12. Positive
13. Practical
14. Respectful
15. Smiling
16. Static
17. Strict
18. Supportive
19. Trusting
20. Firm yet flexible
21. Trustworthy

V. Traits Included in the Character Curriculum of State Board of Education, Georgia

1. Character.
2. Courage
3. Patriotism
4. Citizenship
5. Honesty
6. Fairness
7. Respect for others
8. Kindness
9. Cooperation
10. Self-respect
11. Self-control
12. Courtsy
13. Compassion
14. Tolerance
15. Diligence
16. Generosity
17. Punctuality
18. Cleanliness
19. Cheerfulness
20. Professional pride
21. Respect for authority
22. Respect for the creator
23. Patience
24. Creativity
25. Sportsmanship
26. Loyalty to the ideals
27. Perseverance
28. Virtue

6.4 SIGNIFICANT TRAITS ATTACHED WITH EACH LETTER OF THE WORD TEACHER

Each letter of the word signifies some traits or values of the teach.

T stands for — Tact, Tolerance, Truth, Training, Technology
E stands for — Efficiency, Enthusiasm, Ethics, Etiquette, Energy
A stands for — Accuracy, Adaptability, Affection, Alertness, Appearance
C stands for — Character, Clarity, Cooperation, Constructiveness, Creativity, Concern for others
H stands for — Hard work, Humility, Honesty, Humour, Human Relations
E stands for — Eagerness, Efficiency, Emotional Stability, Expressiveness
R stands for — Rationality, Relationship, Resourcefulness, Reliability

Notes: 1. There is no unanimity regarding the traits of a teacher.
2. Some scholars tend to equate the professional characteristics of a teacher with his professional traits.

6.5 ROLES OF THE TEACHER

Total development of the child as his primary responsibility—In the words of Dr. E. A. Pires: "He (teacher) has to concern himself with the total development of the child and not only with one or two aspects. He must be-friend him and help him in his emotional and social development. He must be a philosopher illumining the way of his intellectual and spiritual progress. He must be his guide in his moral and aesthetic advancement. In fact, he must be 'all things' to all his pupils—a physician concerned about their physical health, a mental hygienist leading them carefully to sound mental health, a philosopher guiding them painstakingly in their search for truth, a moralist assisting and encouraging them to acquire goodness, an artist helping them to find beauty. In fact, he must be a minister ministering to their every need. Such a ministry calls for educated services."

The teacher is expected to play the following roles:

1. *Provider* of effective instructional output.
2. *Manager* of teaching-learning process.
3. *Facilitator* of learning.
4. *Counsellor* of students.
5. *Parent Surrogate* (parent substitute). A teacher is expected to act as a parent of the students and treat them with affection and care.
6. *Ego-supporter.* He is expected to build up and maintain a healthy and strong 'ego' and 'self-concept' among children.
7. *Helper.* The teacher is expected to be a helper to students by way of providing them academic and personal guidance.
8. *Resource person.* He is expected to play the role of a resource person who possesses knowledge of the subject-matter and skills better than the pupils.
9. *Detective.* He acts as a detective in detecting offences and rule breakers.
10. *Facilitator of learning.* He is expected to promote significant learning among his students.
11. *Limiter or reducer of anxiety.* He is expected to assist students to control their impulses and reduce anxiety about conduct and performance in different problematic situations.
12. *Referee.* He is expected to settle disputes among students in an objective and fair manner.
13. *Group leader.* He is expected to act as a leader in developing suitable climate and cohesion in the class as a social group.
14. *Inspirer and exemplar.* He is expected to behave in a manner whereby the traits exemplified by him may be emulated by the students.
15. *Judge.* He is expected to evaluate the academic and other performance of the students in an impartial manner.
16. *Confidant.* He is expected to win and share the confidence of the students.
17. *Friend and Philosopher.* He is expected to play the role of a friend, philosopher and guide to the students.
18. *Upholder of the norms and values.* He is expected to uphold the norms and values of the society.
19. *Moral educator.* He is expected to inculcate the attitudes and moral values cherished by the society among the students.
20. *Democrat.* He is expected to play the role of a democrat.
21. *Rationalist.* He is expected to play the role of a rationalist by basing his actions on reason.
22. *Secularist.* He is expected to play the role of a secularist by having an open mind on the beliefs of all religions.
23. *Initiator.* He is expected to play the role of an initiator by exploiting the new technology to the best advantage of the students and the purposes of education. He should play the roles of a planned organiser of curricular innovator of educational ideas, practices and systems, writer of Radio and TV lessons and programmes, user of video-tapes and computers etc.
24. *Reformer.* In a country like India, where conservatism and superstitions prevail, a teacher is expected to play the role of a social reformer.

25. *Equaliser*. He should act as equaliser by working for minimising inequalities in the educative process and by building up an egalitarian, secular and socialist society.

Note: All the roles overlap.

Teacher's Role Towards Parents

Close cooperation between the parent, who is the first teacher, and the teacher, who is the second parent, is the very foundation on which rests the fruitfulness of the training imparted in our institutions.

Following are the important roles of the teachers towards parents:

1. Participating in parent-teacher and similar activities.
2. Participating in community affairs.
3. Making himself available to parents at scheduled times to discuss pupil progress and behaviour.
4. Evincing a sympathetic, helpful and understanding attitude towards parents and their children's schooling problems.
5. Reporting and discussing with parents, pupil progress, problems and needs.
6. Assuring through personal behaviour in the community that the school staff-image in the community is favourable.
7. The teacher should encourage the parents of the pupils to visit the school frequently.
8. He should see that parents are cordially received when they visit the school.
9. He should regularly inform the parents of the progress of their wards.
10. He should encourage the parents to consult the teachers as well as him on special problems of their wards.
11. He should visit the homes of the pupils and should suggest to the teachers also to do the same.
12. He should organize parents-study-groups from time to time.
13. He should provide adequate facilities for the organisation and proper functioning of the Parent-Teacher Association in the school.

Teacher's (includes Head) Role Towards Community

1. The teacher should plan school programme with reference to the needs of the community.
2. He should encourage the use of community resources for vitalising class-room instruction through excursions, field trips, study of local history etc.
3. He should encourage and organise social service programmes to render public service.
4. He should allow the community to use school facilities and services like school building, library, and dispensary seeing at the same time that the work of the school does not suffer.
5. He should organise social and cultural activities in the school to interpret the school programme to the community.

6. He should actively participate in the social and cultural functions of the community.
7. He should be above politics and religion in organising school programmes.
8. He should not allow the school to become a tool in the hands of any pressure group.
9. He should not allow his political beliefs to influence his administration of school.

6.6 INSTRUCTIONAL INPUT

Broadly speaking an effective instructional input includes:

1. Curriculum Development and Implementation.
2. Adjustment to Individual Differences and Development.
3. Dynamic Techniques of Instruction.
4. Use of Technology of Teaching.
5. Evaluating and Discussing Pupils' Performance.

(1) Curriculum Development and Implementation—This implies:

1. Participation in grade level or subject-matter study of existing curricula and in the development of improved expanded curricula.
2. Determining the object, scope and methods of the grade and subjects to be taught.
3. Devising assignments, when necessary, in order to enrich the teaching programme for the pupils.
4. Correlating his subject-matter curriculum with the curriculum of other subjects.

(2) Adjusting to Individual Differences and Development Levels—This calls for:

1. Drawing upon and applying basic knowledge of the psychology of the child in order to establish readiness for learning.
2. Making an effort to know as much as possible about the background and out of school environment of each child, in order to improve the teaching learning process.
3. Developing in each pupil a sense of personal growth and value.
4. Maintaining discipline by being consistently friendly, fair and firm.
5. Handling behaviour problems in a controlled manner.

(3) Dynamic Techniques of Teaching (Effective teaching-learning)— This includes:

1. Selecting materials, teaching aids and methods which will facilitate the learning process and stimulate the desire for further learning.
2. Meeting the needs, backgrounds and capacities of the children, being taught.
3. Teaching by using a suitable variety of lectures, discussions, demonstrations, visual and oral presentations, recitation, directed group effort, experimentation, special projects and field trips.
4. Analysing and evaluating the effectiveness of various teaching techniques in order to improve the learning process.

5. Endeavouring to obtain and maintain pupil interest and attention so that teaching is done in a receptive atmosphere.
6. Endeavouring to assure that material taught is applied in such a manner as to develop a pattern of understanding for future use in other areas.
7. Encouraging and guiding critical thinking by pupils.
8. Developing desirable work and study skills and habits.
9. English pupil participation in the lesson planning process.
10. Developing broad outlines and objectives to be attained within prescribed limits, for a subject or skill area based upon the needs and interests of a specific group of pupils.
11. Making suitable lesson plans.

(4) Use of Techniques of Teaching—This relates to:

1. Use of blackboard.
2. Use of charts, models, graphs, etc.
3. Use of new technology, i.e., computer, radio and T.V.

(5) Evaluating and Discussing Pupils' Performance—This comprises:

1. Devising and administering appropriate tests to measure the level and quality of pupil learning.
2. Interpreting test results and related findings to pupil progress in order to improve the teaching-learning process.
3. Reporting pupil achievement and progress to parents by means of progress reports.
4. Discussing pupil achievement with the parents individually, in groups and conference.
5. Cooperating and enlisting the cooperation of school specialist in the process of evaluation.

Instructional Input and Teaching Skills

While talking of teaching skills, it must be remembered that there is no watertight compartment as regards skills at different stages. These are classified for the sake of convenience, otherwise they are interrelated. A particular skill cannot be confined to one teaching stage only.

1. *Teaching Skills at the Planning Stage*
   (i) Writing instructional objectives
   (ii) Selecting the content
   (iii) Organising the content
   (iv) Selection of audio-visual aids and their procurement
2. *Introductory Stage Skills*
   (i) Creating set induction—preparing the minds of the students
   (ii) Introducing the lessons
3. *Presentating Stage*: *Teaching Skills*

(i) Questioning Skills
   (a) Structuring class-room questions
   (b) Fluency in asking questions
   (c) Probing question
   (d) Question delivery and distribution

(e) Higher order questions
(f) Divergent questions
(g) Management of answers

(ii) Content Presenting Skills
(a) Pacing of the lesson
(b) Lecturing
(c) Illustrating with examples
(d) Demonstrating
(e) Explaining
(f) Discussing

(iii) Audio-Visual Aids Skills
(a) Using teaching aids
(b) Stimulus variation
(c) Silence and non-verbal cues
(d) Reinforcement

(iv) Managerial Skills
(a) Promoting pupil involvement and participation
(b) Recognising attending behaviour
(c) Class management

4. *Closing Stage Skills*
(i) Planned recapitulation
(ii) Evaluating pupil progress
(iii) Diagnosing learning difficulties of the pupils and taking remedial measures
(iv) Giving assignments

6.7 TEACHER AS A MANAGER AND FACILITATOR OF INSTRUCTION

Traditional Role of the Teacher as Information Giver	*Modern Role of the Teacher as Manager and Facilitator of Instruction*
1. Works on the formulated objectives.	1. Formulates clearly defined objectives based on the needs of students.
2. Focuses in the presentation of content, facts and information.	2. Focuses on the process of learning—learning how to learn.
3. Assumes the responsibility for deciding what the students need.	3. Involves the student's actively in assuming the responsibility of their own learning.
4. Decides what the students need and provides it through lectures etc.	4. Assists the students to learn to be active information seekers and makes use of all available resources.
5. Stresses memorisation as a method of learning.	5. Motivates the students to learn by discovery and exploration, asks questions, formulates problems.
6. Emphasises group performance.	6. Emphasises individual achievement in relation to the student's own needs and objectives.

Traditional Role of the Teacher as Information Giver	*Modern Role of the Teacher as Manager and Facilitator of Instruction*
7. Promotes competition with peers for achievement, recognition, grades and other rewards.	7. Promotes group work on problem-solving activities and learning effectively.

6.8 TEACHER AS A COUNSELLOR

Teacher—*A First-Hand Source in Guidance and Counselling.* The teacher is directly and intimately involved in all the class-room activities and guidance. As expressed by L.L. Bojkin, "The principal area of student personnel work is teacher-student relationship, not occasional interviews with specialised counsellors."

The teacher's guidance viewpoint must be incorporated in the teaching and interpersonal relationship with students. As stated by Gordon, "The major task of the teacher is the study of student." Bojkin states, "Good teaching has emotional and moral as well as intellectual objectives. It aims at the growth of the whole person as well as the mastery of the subject in hand."

Teachers are a powerful group of men and women who have studied he nature of individual growth, who have become acquainted with the new techniques of teaching and who deal with people while they are still in the process of 'becoming' and can play an active role in guidance work.

Areas of Guidance Work by the Teacher

1. The teachers as teachers are primarily concerned with the problems and needs of their students.
2. The teachers should try to detect the emerging maladjustment of pupils.
3. They should provide situations for the maximum development of the pupils.
4. They should implement in right earnest the decisions made as a result of the pupils' contacts with counsellors.
5. They should make use of every opportunity of acquiring information and many insight about pupils and their experiences.
6. They should find opportunities of developing contacts with parents and community agencies. These contacts have many possibilities in the overall guidance programme.
7. They should develop personal contacts with students.
8. They should construct and administer tests in their regular academic courses.
9. They should guide their students in the taking of notes.
10. They should guide students in giving short talks.
11. They should guide students in the proper use of the school or college library.
12. They should acquaint the students with the fields in which their subjects are related to.

13. They should report to the school counsellor about students who are experiencing special difficulties.
14. They should assure responsibilities for the organisation of the co-curricular activities which are closely allied to their subject-matter fields.

How to Play this Role?

There are five important aspects in this regard:

1. *To gain understanding of every pupil in his class.* Through daily observation, listening to what pupils say, talking with them and their parents, and sometimes visiting their homes. Since a teacher cannot keep all this information about each child in his mind, he should use some form of cumulative record which he can also pass on to the next teacher to give him background in understanding each new class.

2. *To accept children as they are and to look for the best in them.* For example, when a boy gets up to recite and gives a confused answer, instead of calling on some other student, the teacher, by asking a few questions and comments should help him to think through the question more clearly himself. And when he had done this successfully, the teacher says, "I knew you could do it, if you kept on trying."

3. *To provide the experiences each child needs.* (a) schoolwork that is meaningful to him, in which he can succeed with reasonable effort, (b) friendly relations with teachers and other pupils that give him social experiences, and (c) encouragement to study at home on his own initiative. As the child grows older, he should have work experiences in school and outside of school that help him to discover what he can do best and what he likes to do.

4. *To guide as he teaches, being constantly sensitive to the individuals and their interaction in the group.* For example, when a pupil gives the wrong answer, the guidance-minded teacher, instead of merely saying "Wrong" and calling on someone else to answer the question, is more likely to ask: "How did you get that idea?" This helps the teacher to understand children's misconceptions and to show them how to correct them. It also prevents a child from experiencing another failure; instead, he gains a little more self-confidence as a result of the teacher's emphasising whatever is positive in what he says and does.

5. To help the child make educational and vocational plans in line with his abilities, aptitudes and interests.

6.9 TEACHER AS A COMMUNITY LEADER

There is a paragraph in the McNair Report on the Training of Teachers which says, "It is a truism to say that every teacher in, however humble a capacity he or she may be serving, is directly and vocationally involved in moulding the shape of things to come." "If that truism be true", observes Prof. W.O. Lester Smith of the London University, "the unsettled times in which our young citizens are going to live their lives make it necessary that those who aspire to the teach should have thought and should continue to think about the problems of society with all the intelligence at their work."

Prof. Ottaway thinks that teachers in the schools can have the most powerful influence in the community; teachers' professional organisations and unions are among the orthodox pressure groups and they can bring their views before the public opinion and government.

An American educationist, Edmund W. Gordon, has pointed out: "It is the task of the teacher to educate—to educate for change—to educate through change—to educate for orderly planned revolution. It is necessary to educate through more disruptive revolutionary action".

A teacher can convey, disseminate and develop knowledge, attitude, skills and values to the students through the following ways:

1. Direct teaching.
2. Providing opportunities to the students to practice the values of democracy, secularism and socialism.
3. The teacher himself becoming a model embodying the desired values.

Limitations of the teacher in social change—Shri S.P. Ruhela and K.C. Vyas pose this question in the context of Indian situation: "How can they (teachers) be so (effective) when the occupation of school teachers has so far not been able to emerge as a profession in the strict sense of the term due to their effective unenlightened and key and strategic decision-making positions contraposed to another class of the elite equipped with education in vernaculars, occupying a subordinate position in the hierarchy of offices. This latter stratum is increasingly deprived of the opportunity of serving national positions demanding advanced knowledge of English."

7

Class-room Management

7.1 MEANING AND CONCEPT OF CLASS-ROOM MANAGEMENT

Class-room management is a very broad concept. It includes all the activities of the teacher that he undertakes for the creation of such an environment that allows the best display of student's abilities in the teaching-learning process. The environment involves the maximum involvement of the students in the class-room activities. The teacher and the students are full of enthusiasm. The environment is based on mutual goodwill and trust. The teacher gives due regard to the individuality of the students and the students in turn show spontaneous regard for the teacher. The teacher in the true sense is the friend, philosopher and guide to the students.

Class-room management implies creating an environment in the class where students working together under the leadership of the teacher are able to perform effectively towards the attainment of instructional goals. Management is needed in every activity and everywhere. Class-room is no exception. It brings order and system in the work. Appropriate class-room management means providing motivation to the learners. It means to ensure that the learners take full interest in the teaching-learning process. It implies creating democratic class-room climate so that the three types of behaviour, i.e., cognitive, conative and psychomotor of the students are developed to the maximum. It means that discipline should take the form of 'self-discipline' and 'social discipline.'

7.2 SIGNIFICANCE OF CLASS-ROOM MANAGEMENT

Class-room management is one of the most important elements of the school programme. It is not without reason that the Education Commission (1964-66) observed: "The destiny of India is being shaped in her class-rooms. This, we believe, is no more rhetoric." The Commission has given so much importance to this element that the report begins with these remarks.

The students spend most of their time in the class-room and likewise most of the work a school undertakes is done in the class-rooms. The environment of class-rooms has a great influence on the many-sided development of the personality of the student. The better the class-room management, the better the performance of the students. There is no doubt that the standard of management of the class-rooms determine the standard of the school.

Importance of the Class-room as a Social Group

It has been observed by Kuppuswami that class-room as an instructional group helps its members to satisfy their needs and achieve goals. Class-room group has a special significance in the school programme on account of the following functions:

1. Improvement in the behaviour of the students.
2. Development of mental process through intellectual activities.
3. Development of feeling of service.
4. Preparation for social life—present as well as future social life.
5. Exciting sympathy of members.
6. Developing qualities of leadership.
7. Acquiring more knowledge.
8. Development of the feeling of co-operation.

7.3 FOUR-FOLD PROCESS OF CLASS-ROOM MANAGEMENT

K. Davis has given the four-fold process of class-room management.

1. Planning
2. Organising
3. Leading and motivatng
4. Controlling

Planning—Before taking up the classwork, the teacher analyses the content or topic into elements and arrange these in logical consequences. He then formulates his teaching objectives in behavioural terms. Thereafter he selects the appropriate strategies.

Organising—This is the second step of managing teaching-learning process. The teacher organises the learning resources for the achievement of his objectives efficiently, speedily and successfully. The teacher creates a suitable learning environment in the class. He decides about the teaching-learning strategies to be adopted.

Leading and motivating—The primary task of the teacher is to motivate the students. The key-note of this step is to enable the student to learn how to learn through his own efforts. The teacher encourages the students to participate actively in the teaching-learning process. He provides maximum opportunities to the students for participation in the class-room activities.

The teacher makes use of his creativity, experiences and constructive imagination in providing appropriate activities relating to learning.

Controlling—This involves three major activities, namely (1) Observing the learning system, (2) Evaluating the teaching-learning system, and (3) Modifying the teaching-learning system.

7.4 PRINCIPLES OF CLASS-ROOM MANAGEMENT

1. Principle of professional competence of the teacher.
2. Principle of involvement of the students.
3. Principle of social discipline.
4. Principle of effective class-room routine.
5. Principle of effective psychological environment.

6. Principle of healthy social environment.
7. Principle of healthy physical environment.
8. Principle of motivation of the learners.
9. Principle of overall effective environment.

7.5 INFLUENCING FACTORS OF CLASS-ROOM MANAGEMENT

The primary responsibility of class-room management rests with the teachers. However, some of the elements of effective class-room management do depend on the provision of various types of physical facilities which are provided by the management. The overall management skills and efficiency of the head of the school also have a bearing on the class-room management.

Here we are basically concerned with the role of the teacher in managing the actual class-room teaching and the allied issues.

Important, influencing factors are as under:

1. Overall environment of the school.
2. Psychological environment of the class-room.
3. Physical environment of the class-room. This includes:
   (i) Proper class-room size.
   (ii) Provision of seating appropriate arrangement.
   (iii) Appropriate furniture.
   (iv) Sufficient light and air.
   (v) Necessary facilities for the teacher, i.e., teacher's table, chair, blackboard, etc.
   (vi) Cleanliness of the class-room.
   (vii) Arrangement of the time-table.
4. Personality of the teacher.
5. Teaching-learning process.
6. Teacher's behaviour towards students.
7. Class-room routine, i.e., taking roll-call etc.
8. Disciplinary standard, Code of behaviour.
9. Involvement of the students in the lesson.
10. Behaviour of the teacher towards students.
11. Reinforcing attending behaviour of the students, i.e., ensuring students' attention in the class-work.
12. Reinforcing accepting student behaviour of the students – mode of students' entering the class, standing while questioning and answering, observation of proper etiquette.
13. Social environment of the class-room.
14. Appropriate standard of group behaviour.
15. Personality traits of the teacher.

Important Elements in the Class-room Management

- Management of Normal Class-room Routine
- Teaching Methods, Techniques and Skills
- Teaching Skills
- Class-room Discipline Appropriate Student Behaviour
- Effective Group Dynamics
- Teacher's own Motivation
- Personality of Teacher
- Desirable Teacher Behaviour in the Class-room

7.6 TECHNIQUES OF CLASS-ROOM MANAGEMENT

Class-room Routine Management

1. Learn the names of the students quickly.
2. Learn carefully the seating plan of students.
3. Keep the class-room neat and tidy.
4. Keep class-room well-ventilated and lighted.
5. Take the roll-call and enquire about the absentees.
6. Insist on correct postures.
7. Be always punctual.
8. Stand throughout the great part of the class period.
9. Impress upon the students the importance of respect for school property.
10. Have a definite system for collecting and distributing material to avoid confusion.

Teaching Procedures and Methods

1. Keep everything ready to start class-work.
2. Be sure you get the attention of every member of the class.
3. Use a variety of teaching aids.
4. Make assignments definite and clear.
5. Word questions clearly so that the students know what you are expecting from them.
6. Teach the whole class and not a few students sitting on the front benches.
7. Distribute questions evenly.
8. Put questions to inattentive students also.
9. Do not often repeat your questions.
10. Do not put questions hurriedly.
11. Allow reasonable time to the students to answer your questions.
12. Encourage students to answer questions rather than having doing all the talking yourself.
13. Encourage students to report on anything of current interest to them in the class which pertains to the course.
14. Provide opportunities for all students to participate in the lesson.
15. Avoid being side tracked.
16. Stop trying to teach students something which they cannot learn.
17. Check the written work of the students carefully.
18. Make necessary explanations about corrected assignments.
19. Avoid difficult assignments in the beginning.
20. Allow supervised study time.
21. Vary methods of teaching and learning; use dramas, panel discussion, debate, etc.
22. Make your blackboard writing legible.
23. Keep the students always busy in doing some worthwhile work.
24. Make every pupil feel that he is essential to the success of the lesson.
25. Do not leave anything in disorder when you leave the class.
26. Rub off the blackboard when you leave the class-room.
27. Prepare plan of your daily work systematically.

28. Train your students to keep themselves busy when you are not in the class-room.
29. Do not embarrass pupils before other pupils.
30. Show consideration for bashful pupils.

7.7 TEACHING SKILLS

Teaching skills of the teacher greatly influence motivation. It is not easy to give an exact number of teaching skills involved in motivating students in the class. Commonly identified skills in the teaching-learning process may be listed as under:

1. Skill in introducing the topic.
2. Skill in putting questions.
3. Skill in dealing with pupils' answers.
4. Skill in stimulus variations.
5. Skill in the use of blackboard or the chalk-board.
6. Skill in handling teaching aids and other equipment's.
7. Skill in non-verbal cues.
8. Skill in reinforcement.
9. Skill in the use of illustrations and examples.
10. Skill in exposition of lecturing.
11. Skill in explanation.
12. Skill in encouraging group discussion.
13. Skill in planned repetition.
14. Skill in drawing out conclusions from students.
15. Skill in teacher liveliness.
16. Skill in the closure of the lesson.
17. Skill in using appropriate methods of teaching.

Teacher's Own Motivation and Interest in Teaching

The teacher must be interested in what he is teaching and in the children whom he is teaching. If he is not interested in the work himself, he can never motivate the class. It may be said that a teacher who has been teaching the same subjects to the same classes for years tends to lose interest. But this is not the fact. The subject-matter may be the same but the children are not the same. Even the subject-matter is changing and developing. Moreover, with experience the teacher will discover new approaches and methods of teaching even the same subject-matters.

7.8 CLASS DISCIPLINE: CODE OF BEHAVIOUR

1. Base your discipline on do's rather than don'ts.
2. Insist on good conduct or manners and high standards of work.
3. Be sympathetic and understanding in your dealings with students.
4. Be firm and consistent in your dealing with students.
5. Do not allow students to wander around.
6. Maintain a certain reserve and be friendly rather than 'chummy'.
7. Try to adopt this philosophy, "I like you even though, I do not like what you do."

8. Be just and fair.
9. Avoid telling the class to keep order.
10. Do not use abusive anger.
11. Avoid sarcastic remarks.
12. Avoid threats.
13. Attend to minor problems before they become major ones.
14. Encourage honesty.
15. Make every effort to solve your own disciplinary problems and seldom approach the head for the purpose.
16. Do not discuss your family problems in the classroom.
17. Do not discuss matters relating to your colleagues with the students.
18. Do not narrate your experiences too often in the class.

7.9 EFFECTIVE GROUP DYNAMICS

Origin

The phrase group dynamics came into being in 1944 when Curt Lewin set up the Research Centre for Group Dynamics to meet the need of making a scientific approach to the understanding of the dynamics of group.

Definitions of Group Dynamics

In the words of Cartwright D. and Zhander A.: "Group dynamics should be defined as a field of inquiry dedicated to advancing knowledge about the nature of groups, the laws of their development, and their interrelations with individuals, other groups and larger institutions."

According to Good's Dictionary of Education, "Group dynamics implies an interactive psychological relationship in which members of a group develop a common perception based on feelings and emotions."

Kretch and Crutchfield view group dynamics "as changes that place within the group."

In the words of Otlo Klineberg: "It is not easy to define or limit the important area of group dynamics. From one point of view it represents a field of enquiry, a series of inter-related problems; from another it includes a set of techniques; from a third, a theory, of the groups and of interaction within groups."

The focal point of all the above mentioned definitions is 'interrelation' or 'interaction' among the members of the group.

Group Dynamics in the Class-room

Gates, I.A. is of the view that group dynamics offers the best means available for the development of three types of skills namely (i) skills essential for democratic living, (ii) skills essential for better social understanding, and (iii) skills for preparing the individual members of the group for democratic leadership.

According to Segal, D., group dynamics is the process by which one must consider other individuals in a group, and a problem at the same time, and it not only tends to increase understanding to the problem, but also creates a solution which the individual practises in bringing about emotional balance.

A wise teacher can make his class-room teaching easier and effective if he can direct group dynamics into constructive paths. Through group discussion and activity methods, the teacher would give the individual student a chance to participate actively and to contribute to group work in the class.

A teacher is expected to understand the various forces working in the class-room so that he makes use of the forces in his teaching.

The teacher must know how adolescents form groups and what is the structure of groups in general. He must understand the pattern of friendship or preferences of the members of the various groups. The teacher must detect 'stars', as well as the 'isolates' in the group to take appropriate action for adjustment.

The teacher must ensure that groups are not formed on the basis of caste, creed or religion, etc.

If the teacher is well-equipped with the basic knowledge of group dynamics, he would be in a better position to improve the emotional and social climate in the class.

Group dynamics is also influenced by sympathy, suggestion and imitation.

Sympathy enables the member of a group to perceive the psychological state of the other member. He begins to feel as others feel.

Suggestion plays a big role in influencing the group behaviour. The suggestions put forward by the leader of the group are readily accepted.

The behaviour of the leader of the group is imitated by the members of the group.

It would be desirable for a teacher to throw some light on the qualities of leadership so that students choose their leaders wisely and the teacher is able to influence the class through its leaders. However it must be stressed, that teacher must remain neutral in the selection of leaders.

The recent studies have made it clear that for bringing about changes in the individual, we must bring about changes in the characteristics of the group. The teachers, therefore, should adopt group methods in the class and through these influence the attitudes of the members of the group. Group training is better than individual training.

Some specific group technique which could be utilised for improvement of the group process are:

(i) Buzz session in which a small group of five or six students participate, is organised for purposes of stimulating discussion.

(ii) Role playing, in which problems of handling a situation are dramatised for the benefit of the group.

(iii) Brain storming, in which a group is organised for stimulating discussion.

(iv) Catharsis, in which a planned group expression of problems of concern to the group is provided.

(v) Recreational experiences in which opportunities are provided for participation in dramatics, picnics, parties, etc., to improve the morale of the group.

Personality Traits of the Teacher

1. Be punctual in your programme.

2. Do not use loud voice.
3. Avoid mannerism.
4. Be always cheerful.
5. Handle controversial topics skilfully.
6. Be humorous.
7. Use polite and proper language.
8. Avoid sarcastic remarks.
9. Be well-mannered.
10. Show sincere interest in students, school activities and co-workers.
11. Be frank to admit, "Don't know all the answers."
12. Cultivate initiative and resourcefulness.
13. Be true to the ethics of the teaching profession.

7.10 VARIOUS WAYS OF CODIFYING STUDENT'S BEHAVIOUR: ACCEPTABLE STUDENTS BEHAVIOUR

1. Honest behaviour.
2. Appropriate postures of the students:
   (i) While standing
   (ii) While sitting
   (iii) While moving
3. Appropriate mode of addressing the teacher and students.
4. Observing courtesy.
5. Entering and leaving the class-room with permission.
6. Not speaking or answering in unison.
7. Observing discipline when the teacher is not in the class.
8. Keeping the class-room clean.
9. Speaking only when asked.
10. Keeping note books neat and tidy.
11. Bringing text-books and note books according to time-table.
12. Paying attention to the work.
13. Observing good manners.
14. Maintaining good relationship with classmates.
15. Not using other's article without permission.

'A' to 'Z' of Effective Teacher and Effective Class-room Management and Instruction

A 'A' is for alertness on the part of the teacher to the multifarious needs of the learners. Alertness is very helpful in taking appropriate decisions and timely corrective measures.

B 'B' is for business like attitude. It is to be ensured that every learner in the class, remains busy in realising the goals set.
'B' is for balanced behaviour.

C 'C' stands for cooperative teaching-learning. The learners must be made active partners.
'C' is for clarity of purpose. The teacher and the learners must be clear about the goals for the achievements of which they are working.
'C' is for clarity of the subject-matter taught. A teacher must make all

possible efforts to make his lesson clear. Difficulties of the learners must be appreciated and clarified.

D 'D' stands for democratic class-room environment.

'D' is for discovery. Children should be guided to find out new facts, ideas and principles. It helps children in becoming independent and resourceful learners.

'D' stands for democratic discipline.

E 'E' stands for expectancies. Each learner should be expected to learn. No learner should be considered without any potential.

'E' stands for enthusiasm. The teacher himself must demonstrate enthusiasm for his work.

F 'F' is for feedback. Feedback helps the teacher and the learners to take timely corrective measures for the completion of the task.

'F' stands for faith of the teacher in himself.

G 'G' is for goal-setting. Appropriate goals should be set for the learners. They should also be made clear about the suitability of goals. Efforts may be made to associate the learners with the setting of goals.

H 'H' is for hard work on the part of the students as well as teachers.

'H' is for humour. Humour on the part of the teacher releases fatigue and tension.

'H' stands for human touch.

I 'I' stands for involvement of all the learners in class-room activities and experiences.

'I' stands for impartial attitude.

'I' stands for inspirational teaching-learning.

J 'J' stands for just attitude.

'J' stands for judicious rewards and punishments.

K 'K' stands for knowing children's abilities, aptitudes and interests.

'K' stands for the knowledge of the sub-matter.

L 'L' stands for linking present, past and future knowledge.

'L' stands for leadership qualities.

M 'M' stands for motivation.

'M' stands for management of the class.

N 'N' stands for needs of the learners and their satisfaction.

O 'O' stands for open-mindedness.

'O' stands for out of class activities.

'O' stands for objectivity in approach.

P 'P' stands for praise. Verbal and non-verbal praise of children can motivate them to hard work.

'P' stands for personal contact with every learner.

Q 'Q' is for quiz. From time to time, quiz competitions may be arranged in the class.

'Q' stands for quality teaching.

'Q' stands for question-answers.

R 'R' stands for review of the lesson.

'R' stands for relationship.

'R' stands for resourcefulness.

S 'S' stands for success experience. Success motivates the learner to achieve more.
'S' stands for scientific temper.
'S' stands for self-analysis and self-control.

T 'T' stands for technology of teaching.
'T' stands for tutoring which involves removing difficulties individually or in small groups.

U 'U' stands for undivided attention to teaching.
'U' stands for unbiased attitude to the treatment of controversial issues.

V 'V' stands for visual aids.
'V' stands for variety of experiences.
'V' stands for voice-modulation.
'V' stands for variation in the presentation.

W 'W' stands for welcoming attitude.
'W' stands for warmth towards students.

X 'X' stands for X-ray of the teaching process. It implies finding out of the difficulties and potentials of the students.

Y 'Y' stands for yardstick, i.e., same standard basis of making a judgment on the performance of the students.
'Y' stands for you, implying that you (student) are the most important element in the teaching-learning process.

Z 'Z' stands for zeal and zest for work.
'Z' stands for zenith or excellence.

8

An Overview of Teacher's Roles, Functions and Status: Views of Eminent Thinkers

8.1 GREAT THINKERS ON THE SIGNIFICANT ROLE AND STATUS OF THE TEACHER

Traditionally, in view of the significant role played by the teacher in the all-round development of the students, a teacher has been paid very high tribute by thinkers of East as well as of the West. Here some of such views are given.

1. "The teacher is a maker of man."

   —*Adams, John,* (Second US President, 1735-1826)
2. "A teacher affects eternity; he can never tell where his influence stops."

   —*Adams, Henry Brooks,* (American Man of Letters 1838-1918)
3. None can teach admirably if not loving his task.

   —*Alcott, Amos Bronson* (American Educator, 1799-1888)
4. The true teacher inspires self-trust. —*Alcott, Amos Bronson*
5. The true teacher defend his pupils from his personal influence.

   —*Alcott, Amos Bronson*
6. To know how to suggest is the art of teaching.

   —*Amiel, Henri Federic* (Swiss Philosopher, 1828-1881)
7. Teachers who educate children deserve more honour than parents.

   —*Aristotle* (Greek Philosopher, 384-322 B.C.)
8. And through thee I believe
   In the noble and the great who are gone;
   Pure souls honour'd and blest
   By former ages, who else
   Such, so soulless, so poor,
   In the race of men whom I see
   Seem'd but a dream of the heart,
   Seem'd but a cry of a desire
   Yes I believe that there lived
   Others like there in the past
   Not like the men of
   Who all-round me to-day
   Bluster of cringe, and make life
   Hideous, and arid, and vile;
   But souls temper'd with fire,

Fervent, heroic, and good,
Helpers and friends of mankind...

—*Arnold Mathew* (English Educator, 1822-1888)

9. He is wise who can instruct us and assist us in the business of daily virtuous living. —*Carlyle, Thomas* (English Essayist, 1795-1881)

10. Each teacher should realise the dignity of his calling; that he is a social servant set apart for the maintenance of proper social order and the securing of the right social growth.

In this way the teacher always is the prophet of the true God and the usherer in of the true kingdom of God.

—*Dewey, John* (America Educator in 'My Pedagogic Creedy', 1859-1952)

11. The more a teacher is aware of the past experiences of students, of their hopes, desires, chief interests, the better will he understand the force at work that need to be directed and utilised for the formation of reflective habits.

—*Dewey* (How We Think)

12. The teacher is a guide and director, he steers the boat but the energy that propels it must come from those who are learning. —*Dewey*

13. Of all the different factors which influence the quality of education and its contribution to national development, the quality, the competence and character of teachers are undoubtedly the most significant.

—*Education Commission* (1964-66), 3.01, p. 46

14. It is the supreme art of the teacher to awaken joy in creative expression and knowledge. —*Einstein, Albert* (A Swiss Physicist, 1879-1955)

15. The spirit can only teach.

—*Emerson, Edward Waldo* (American Educator, 1844-1930)

16. The secret of education lies in respecting the pupil.

—*Emerson, E.W.*

17. The whole art of teaching is only the art of awakening the natural curiosity of young minds for the purpose of satisfying it afterwards.

—*France, Anatole* (French novelist, 1844-1924)

18. You cannot teach a man anything; you can only help him to find it within himself. —*Galilei, Galileo* (Italian Astronomer, 1564-1642)

19. Woe to the teacher who teaches one thing with the lips and carries another in the heart. —*Gandhi, M. K.* (*To Students*, p.16, 1869-1948)

20. The politician may succeed in his purpose even though he lacks character, but a people's teacher cannot do without character. If he lacks he will be like salt without its savour. —*Gandhi. M.K.* (*True Education*, p.161)

21. The exercise of the spirit entirely depended on the life and character of the teacher. The teacher had always to be mindful of his P's and Q's whether he was in the midst of his boys or not. —*Gandhi M.K.* (*Towards New Education*, p.19)

22. If I were to be their real teacher and guardian, I must touch their hearts. I must share their joys and sorrows, I must help them to solve the problem that faced men, and I must take along the right channel, the surging aspirations of their youth. —*Gandhi, M.K.* (Autobiography, p. 417)

23. A cowardly teacher would never succeed in making his boys valiant as a stranger to self-restraint could never teach his pupils the value of self-restraint.

—Gandhi, M.K. (*Towards New Education*, p. 19)

24. I have always felt that the true text-book for the pupil is his teacher. —*Gandhi, M.K.* (*Autobiography*, p. 411)

25. We must procure the best teachers for our children whatever it may cost. —*Gandhi, M.K.* (*True Education*, p.44)

26. It is possible for a teacher situated miles away to affect the spirit of the pupils by his way of living.—*Gandhi, M.K.* (*Towards New Education*, p.19)

27. The teacher's is a high office and it enables him to exercise great influence upon the boys and girls in his charge. They regard what he says as gospel truth. —*Gandhi, M.K.* (*True Education*, p. 77)

28. There is no school equal to decent home and no teacher equal to honest virtuous parents. —*Gandhi, M.K.* (*To Students*, p. 15)

29. I have found that boys imbibe more from the teacher's own lives than they do from the books that they read to them or the lectures that they deliver to them with their lips —*Gandhi, M.K.* (*To Students*, p.15)

30. If they (teachers) impart all the knowledge in the world to their students but indicate not truth and purity among them, they will have betrayed them, and instead of raising them set them on the downward road to prediction. —*Gandhi, M. K.* (*The Task Before Indian Students*, p. 14)

31. When it is remembered that the primary aim of all education is, or should be, the moulding of the character of pupils, a teacher who has a character to keep need not lose heart. —*Gandhi, M. K.* (*The Task Before Indian Students*, p.77)

32. Everyone of us has good inherent in the soul, it need to be drawn out by the teachers and only teacher can perform this sacred function whose own character is unsullied, who are always ready to learn and to grow from perfection to perfection. —*Gandhi, M. K.* (*The Task Before Indian Students*, p.78)

33. I have felt the teachers' work lies more outside than the inside the lecture room.... Unless the teachers are prepared to give all their time outside the class-room to their students, not much can be done. Let them fashion their hearts rather than brains. —*Gandhi, M. K.* (*To the Students*, p.7)

34. The teacher leads you to the threshold of your own mind. —*Gibran, Khalil* (1883-1931)

35. A teacher who can arouse a feeling for one good action, for one single good poem, accomplishes more than he who fills our memory with rows and rows of natural objects, classified with name and form. —*Goethe, Johann Wolfgang Von* (German Writer 1749-1832)

36. The same persons telling to the same people the same things about the same things. —*Greek Proverb*

37. To hold my teacher— equal to my own parents. —*Hippocrates* (Greek Physician, 460-400 B.C.)

38. One who makes two ideas grow where only one grew before. —*Hubbard, Elbert* (American Essayist, 1859-1915)

39. The teacher is indeed the architect of our future. Society can neglect him at its own peril —*Husain, Zakir* (Head of the National Committee on Basic Education 1937, President of India, 1967-1969, (1897-1969)

40. A teacher whose soul is wrinkled and whose heart is atrophied, who is devoid of energy and enthusiasm, capacity and character and who simply marks time, his eyes fixed on the calendar, is a disgrace to the profession and curse on society. A teacher must not regard himself as a mere wage-earner whose job begins at 10 a.m. and ends at 5 p.m. when he can shake the dust off his feet and walk out of the bread-giving factory. No, he is a spiritual alchemist charged with the sacred work of creating cultured citizens.

—*Joshi S. Balakrishna* (Recipient of National Awards for Teachers, *Education in Practice*, p. 32, 1955)

41. The teacher has therefore to instruct, inspire and illumine.

—*Joshi S. Balakrishna* (*Education in Practice,* p. 100, 1955)

42. Without good teachers, even the best of systems is bound to fail. With good teachers even the defects of a system can be largely overcome.

—*Kabir, Humayun* (Indian Educationist, 1902-1969)

43. They are literally the arbiters of a nation's destiny. It may sound a truism, but still it needs to be stressed that the teacher is the key to any educational reconstruction. —*Kabir, Humayun*

44. If you neglect the teacher, you neglect the child, and if you neglect the child, you neglect the future of that country to which that child belongs.

—*Kabir, Humayun*

45. The school which has good teachers needs little more and the school without good teachers is little for anything else.

—*Locke, John* (English Philosopher, 1632-1704)

46. For him the teacher's chair becomes a throne.

—*Longfellow, Henry Wordsworth* (American Scholar, 1807-1882)

47. The best teacher of children, in brief is one who is essentially child-like. —*Mencken, H.L.* (American Journalist, 1880-1956)

48. A tutor should not be continually thundering instruction into the ears of his pupils, as if he were pouring it through a funnel, but after having put the lad, like a young horse, on a trot before him, to observe his paces, and see what he is able to perform, should according to the extent of his capacity, induce him to taste, to distinguish, and to find things for himself, sometimes opening the way, at other times leaving it for him to open.

—*Mntaigne, Michel Eyquem De* (French Philosopher, 1533-1592)

49. I do not teach, I only tell. —*Mntaigne*

50. Instead of facility of speech she has to acquire the power of silence, instead of teaching she has to observe, instead of the proud dignity of one who claims to be infallible, she assumes the vesture of humility.

—*Montessori, Maria* (Italian Educator, 1870-1952)

51. Teacher partly doctor, partly scientist and wholly religious.

—*Montessori*

52. The broader the teachers' scientific culture and practice in experimental psychology, the sooner will come for her the marvel of unfolding life, and her interest in it. —*Montessori, Maria*

(*The Advanced Montessori Method, Vol. 1*, p. 128)

53. We underscore that the prime task of the teacher is concerned with man-making, namely the making of the Indian of tomorrow.

—*National Commission on School Teachers,* 1983-85

54. Teacher is an agent of change. —*National Commission on Teachers for Higher Education*, 1983-85

55. The status of the teachers reflects the socio-cultural ethos of a society; it is said that no people can rise above the level of teachers.

—*National Policy on Education*, 1986

56. A teacher does not live for himself, but his pupil and for the truth which he imparts. His aim is to be a colourless medium through which that truth may shine on opening minds. How can be this if he is continually interposing himself and saying, "instead of looking at the truth, my children, look at me, and see how skilfully I do my work. I thought I taught you admirably today. I hope you thought so tool?"

—*Palmer, G.H.* (American Educator in the *Ideal Teacher*, 1842-1933)

57.I think one of the most difficult things for a teacher to learn or to acquire – let's put it that way is to be a learner.

—*Parkhurst, Helen H.* (*Education in the Dalton Plan*, 1922)

58. While books can teach, only personality can educate.

—*Parkhurst*

59. The teacher's part in the process of instruction is that of guide, director or superintendent of the operation by which the pupil teaches himself.

—*Payne, Joseph* (English Educator, 1803-1876)

60. It is like the art of the gardener under whose care a thousand trees blossom and grow. He contributes nothing to their actual growth; the principle of growth lies in the trees themselves. He plants and waters, but God gives the increase.... So with the educator; he imparts no single power to men. He only watches lest any external force should injure or disturb. He takes care that development runs its course in accordance with its own law.

—*Pestalozzi, Johann Heinrich* (Swiss Educator, 1746-1827)

61. The first condition of a good teacher is that he shall be trained as a teacher and not brought to serve other profession. —*Pettison Mark*

62. If a nation's teachers are C_3, the nation itself cannot but be C_3. And let there be no doubt about this — If we wish to be an A_1 nation, our teachers will have to be A_1. —*(Dr.) Pires, E.A.* (Indian Educator)

63. Do not train boys to learning by force and hardness; but direct them to do it by what amuses their minds, so that you may be better able to discover with accuracy the peculiar bent of the genius of each.

—*Plato* (Western Educational Philosopher, 427-347 B.C.)

64. Let such persons teach others who themselves excel.

—*Pope, Alexander* (English Critic, 1688-1744)

65. Their (Teachers') own character should be such that there is no difference between what they say and do. When we act upon this ideal, then alone we can be sure of a bright future for our own country.

—*Rajendra Prasad* (First Indian President, 1951-1962)

66. Let him have towards his pupils the benevolent disposition of a parent and consider himself as holding the place of those who have entrusted him

with his charge. He must neither be vicious himself, nor countenance vice; austere though not harsh; mild though not familiar; let the first generate hatred, the second contempt. Let him talk frequently of virtue. The oftener he advises, the seldomer he will be obliged to punish. Let him be plain and simple in his manner of teaching; patient in labour; rather punctual in making his scholars comply with their duty, than, too exact in requiring more than they can do.

—*Quintilian, Marcos Fabius, Quintilianus* (Roman Rhetorician) 42-118 A.D.

67. The function of the teacher is of vital importance. He must be a committed man, committed to faith in the future of man, in the future of humanity, in the future of this country and the world. He must work with this implicit confidence in the power of humanity, in the recuperative power which it has and by which it can cleanse and purify itself. Unless he has faith in that, he will never be able to advance higher.

—*(Dr.) Radhakrishnan, Sarvapalli* (*Speeches and Writings*, 1965, p. 203)

68. Teachers, according to our tradition, have been sovereign over themselves and servants of the people. They maintain absolute control over their own feelings and try to help humanity to the extent possible. That has been the tradition. The greatest teachers of our country have been those who have made our civilisation live.

—*(Dr.) Radhakrishnan, Sarvapalli* (*Speeches and Writings*, 1965, p. 204)

69. We in our country look upon teachers as gurus, acharyas. What do these words indicate? 'Acharya' is one whose 'achaar' or conduct is exemplary. If he is a victim of 'durachaar', then he is not an 'Acharya'. He must be an example of 'sadachaar', of good conduct. He must inspire the pupils who are entrusted to his care with love of virtue and goodness and abhorrence of cruelty and violence. —*(Dr.) Radhakrishnan, Sarvapalli*

70. '*Andhakar*' is not merely intellectual ignorance but spiritual blindness. He who is able to remove that kind of spiritual blindness is called a guru. Are we deserving of that noble appellation of an 'acharya' or a guru? That is the first thing that everyone of us will have to realise.

—*(Dr.) Radhakrishnan, Sarvapalli*

71. The teacher's place in society is of vital importance. He acts as the pivot for the transmission of intellectual traditional and technical skills from generation to generation, and helps to keep the lamp of civilisation burning. He not only guides the individual, but also so to say, the destiny of the nation.

—*(Dr.) Radhakrishnan, Sarvapalli*

72. A true teacher always goes down to the level of the taught. A teacher who can never let himself down, to the level of the taught is not a true teacher.

—*Swami Ramakrishnananda* (*For Thinkers on Education*, 1948, p. 209)

73. The true aim of everyone who aspires to be a teacher should be not to impart his own opinions, but to kindle minds.

—*Robertson, Fredrik William* (English Writer, 1816-1853)

74. The teacher is like the candle which lights others in consuming itself.

—*Ryburn, W.M.* (Indian Educator)

75. The severity of the Master is more useful than the indulgence of the father. —*Sadi* (Persian Scholar, A.D. Gulistan, 1258)

76. Self-analysis on the part of the teacher is a necessary equipment.
—*Saiyidain, K.G.* (Indian Educator, 1904-74)

77. You do not have to think hard when you talk to a teacher.
—*Salinger, J.D.* (*The Catch in the Eye*)

78. We are, however, convinced that the most important factor in the contemplated educational reconstruction is the teacher—his personal qualities, his educational qualifications, his professional training and the place that he occupies in the school as well as in the community.
—*Secondary Education Commission* 1952-53

79. The reputation of a school and its influence on the life of the community invariably depend on the kind of teachers working in it.
—*Secondary Education Commission*

80. They will not look upon their work as an unpalatable means of earning a scanty living but as an avenue through which they are rendering significant social service as well as finding some measure of self-fulfilment and self-expression. —*Secondary Education Commission*

81. The good teacher, in our reorganised school, will endeavour to win the love and confidence of his children and establish his prestige on sincerity, integrity, hard work and a sympathetic handling of their problems.
—*Secondary Education Commission*

82. While we teach, we learn.
—*Seneca, Lucius Annaeus* (Roman Philosopher, 4 B. C.-65 A.D.)

83. Teachers should be held in the highest honour. They are the officer of legislators. They have agency in the prevention of crime, they aid in regulating the atmosphere, whose incessant action and pressure cause the life blood to circulate, and to return to pure heart of the nation.
—*Signourney, Lydia Huntlay* (1791-1865)

84. He that governs well, leads the blind; but he that teaches gives him eyes. —*South, Robert* (English Divine; 1634-1716)

85. Whoe'er excels in what we prize.
Appears a hero in our eyes:
Each girl, when pleased with what is taught.
Will have the teacher in her thought.
—*Swift, Jonathan* (English Satirist, 1667-1745)

86. I have found that little children learn more quickly from the attitude of the teacher than from the knowledge imparted by him.
—*Tagore* (*Jivan Smriti*, p. 16-17)

87. Man can learn only from a man. Just as a water tank can be filled only with water and fire can be kindled only with fire, life can be inspired only with life... In our social organisation we are searching for a guru who will give peace to our life; in our educational system we are searching for a guru who will emancipate our mind from its imprisonment.
—*Tagore, Rabindranath* (Indian Philosopher, Poet, 1861-1941)

88. If the teacher does not himself possess learning how can he impart it to others? He is like a lamp lighting other lamps. But a lamp cannot put light into other lamps if it does not itself burn and shed light. The teacher who merely repeats bookish knowledge mechanically can never teach anything

and can never inspire, and without proper inspiration independent creative faculties can never develop. —*Tagore* (*Siksa, 1342 B.S. ed., p. 264*)

89. In teaching, the guiding spirit should be personal love. Have more faith in the principle of life, in the sanctity of the human soul than in the mere methods of teaching.

90. Communication of life can only be through a living agency. And culture, which is the life of mind, can only be imparted through man to man.

—*Tagore*

91. The essence of the thing is that the teacher needs to be a real person with a full life of his own, a background of vivid personal experience, a conviction about the purpose of education and the kind of society which he want to help bring about.

—*Tomlinson, Henry Major* (English Novelist, 1873-1958)

92. If there is any profession of paramount importance I believe it is that of the school master.

—*Tyndall, John* (English Natural Philosopher, 1820-1893)

93. The right kind of teacher is one who possess a vivid awareness of his mission. He not only loves his subject, he loves also those whom he teaches.

—*University Education Commission*, 1948-49

94. No teacher who is not a master of the field, who is not in touch with the latest development in his subject and who does not bring to bear upon his duties a free and untrammelled mind will never succeed in inspiring youth with the love of truth which is the principal object of all higher education.

—*University Education Commission*

95. Knowledge may be gained from books but the love of knowledge is transmitted only by personal contact.

—*Van Dyke, Henry* (American Essayist, 1852-1933)

96. Teacher is the 'Brahma', the 'Vishnu' and the 'Maheshvara'.

—*Vedic Prayer*

97. The true teacher is he who can immediately come down to the level of the student, and transfer his soul to the student's soul and see through and understand through his mind. Such a teacher can really teach and none else.

—*Vivekananda, Swami* (Indian Social Reformer, 1863-1902)

98. The teacher is the real maker of history.

—*Wells, Herbert George* (Historian, 1866-1946)

99. The teacher has a double function. It is for him to elicit the enthusiasm by resonance from his own personality, and to create the environment of a larger knowledge and a firmer purpose.

—*Whitehead, Alfred North* (Prof. of Philosophy, Harvard, 1861-1947)

8.2 A FEW EPITHETS ABOUT TEACHERS

1. The vanity of teaching often tempted a man to forget he is block-head.

—*Halifax Lord,* (English Statesman, 1866-1959)

2. He is awkward and out of place, in the society of his equals. He comes like Gulliver from among his little people, and he cannot fit the stature of his understanding to yours. —*Lamb, Charles* (English Essayist, 1775-1834)

3. The average schoolmaster is and always must be essentially an ass, for how can one imagine an intelligent man engaging in so purile an avocation.

—*Manckeen, H.L.* (in *Prejudices*)

4. He who can, does. He who cannot, teaches.

—*Shaw, George Bernard* (English Writer, 1856-1950)

5. Everybody who is incapable of learning has taken to teaching.

—*Wilde, Oscar* (Irish Dramatist, 1854-1900)

6. He is either dead or teaching school.

—*Zemobius* (Greek Sophist A.D. 117-138)

Ideal Teacher

A poor teacher tells
An average teacher explains
A good teacher demonstrates
And a great teacher inspires.

8.3 RESPONSIBILITIES OF THE TEACHERS AS PER H.P. CODE (2001)

The Code prescribes the responsibilities of the teacher in the following areas:

1. Adherence to the ideals of the profession.
2. Responsibilities towards students.
3. Responsibilities towards colleagues.
4. Responsibilities towards authorities.
5. Responsibilities towards non-teaching staff.
6. Responsibilities towards guardians.
7. Responsibilities towards society.

1. Responsibilities to the Ideals of Teaching Profession

Whoever adopts teaching as a profession, is under an obligation to conduct himself in accordance with the ideals of the profession. A teacher is constantly under the scrutiny of his students and society at large. Therefore, every teacher should see that there is no incompatibility between his precepts and practice. The national ideals of education which have already been set forth and which he/she should seek to inculcate among students must be his/her own ideals. The profession further requires that the teachers should be calm, patient and communicative in temperament and amiable in disposition. Teachers should:

(i) adhere to a responsible pattern of conduct and demeanour expected of them by the Community;
(ii) manage their private affairs in a manner consistent with the dignity of the profession;
(iii) strive for continuous professional growth through study and research;
(iv) express free and frank opinion when participating in professional meetings, seminars and conferences;
(v) maintain active membership of professional organisations and strive to update their knowledge through them;
(vi) perform their duties in the form of teaching, tutorials, practical and seminar work conscientiously and with dedication;

(vii) cooperate and assist in carrying out functions relating to the educational responsibilities of the schools, the Board of School Education such as: assisting in appraising application for admission advising and counselling students as well as assisting in the conduct of Board and School examinations, including supervision, invigilation and evaluation; and

(viii) participate in extension, co-curricular and extra-curricular activities including community service.

2. Responsibilities of the Teachers towards Students

Teachers should

(i) respect the right and dignity of the student in expressing his/her opinion;

(ii) deal justly and impartially with students regardless of their religion, caste, political, economic, social and physical characteristics;

(iii) recognise the differences in aptitude and capabilities among students and strive to meet their individual needs;

(iv) encourage students to improve their attainments, develop their personalities and at the same time contribute to community welfare;

(v) inculcate among students a scientific outlook and respect for physical labour and ideals of democracy, patriotism, and peace;

(vi) be affectionate to the students and not behave in a vindictive manner towards any of them for any reason;

(vii) pay attention to only the attainment of the students in the assessment of merit;

(viii) make themselves available to the students even beyond their class hours and help and guide students without any remuneration or reward;

(ix) aid students to develop an understanding of our national heritage and national goals; and

(x) refrain from inciting students against other students, colleagues or administration.

3. Responsibilities of the Teachers towards Colleagues

Teachers should

(i) treat other members of the profession in the same manner as they themselves wish to be treated;

(ii) speak respectfully to other teachers and render assistance for overall professional betterment;

(iii) refrain from lodging unsubstantiated allegations against colleagues to their higher authorities; and

(iv) refrain from allowing considerations of caste, creed, religion, race or sex to influence their professional working.

4. Responsibilities of Teachers towards Authorities

(i) discharge their professional responsibilities according to the existing rules and adhere to procedures and methods consistent with their profession in initiating steps through their own institutional bodies and/or professional organisations for change of any such rules detrimental to the professional interest;

(ii) refrain from undertaking any other employment and commitment including private tuitions and coaching classes which are likely to interfere with their professional responsibilities;

(iii) cooperate in the formulation of the policies of their institution by accepting various offices and discharge the responsibilities which such offices may demand;

(iv) cooperate through their organisations in the formulation of policies of the other institutions and accept offices, as necessary;

(v) cooperate with the authorities for the betterment of the institutions keeping in view the overall interest and in conformity with the dignity of the profession;

(vi) give and expect due notice before a change of position is made; and

(vii) refrain from availing themselves of leave except on unavoidable grounds and as far as practicable with prior intimation, keeping in view their particular responsibility towards the completion of the academic schedule.

5. Teachers and Non-teaching Staff

(i) Teachers should treat the non-teaching staff as colleagues and equal partners in a cooperative undertaking, within every educational institution; and

(ii) Teachers should help in the functioning of the Joint Staff Councils covering both teachers and the non-teaching staff.

6. Teachers and Guardians

Teachers should try to see through teachers' bodies and organisations that institutions maintain contact with the guardians of their students, send reports of their performance to the guardians whenever necessary and meet the guardians in meetings convened for the purpose for mutual exchange of ideas and for the benefit of the institution.

7. Teachers and Society

Teachers should:

(i) recognise that education is a public service and strive to keep the public informed of the educational programmes which are being provided;

(ii) work to improve education in the community and strengthen the community's moral and intellectual life;

(iii) be aware of social problems and take part in such activities as would be conducive to the progress of society and hence the country as a whole;

(iv) perform the duties of citizenship, participate in community activities and shoulder responsibilities of public offices;

(v) refrain from taking part in or subscribing to or assisting in any way, activities which tend to promote feeling of hatred or enmity among different communities, religious or linguistic groups but actively work for national integration.

Note: Regarding Tailoring/Knitting/Embroidery and bringing/use of help books. The Government has imposed a complete ban on the following activities in the offices/institutions vide letter No. Shiksha-IIGA(10) 1/94 dated 8-11-94.

1. Bringing of Tailoring/Knitting/Embroidery material and allied work.
2. Use of help books/keys to text-books in all its institutions.
3. Use of Radio/Transistor in the offices and institutions is completely prohibited.
4. Teaching Staff will not perform any tuition work either before or after the school hours.

SECTION III

9

Educational Administration in the State of Himachal Pradesh

9.1 INTRODUCTION

Till 1976, education subject to some provisions relating to higher education and a few other areas, was a state subject, under the Constitution of India. In 1976, education become a concurrent subject, i.e., the responsibility of the Central Government and the State Governments. Nevertheless the primary responsibility in education remained with the State.

The National Policy on Education (1986 and as amended in 1992) paid emphasis on decentralisation of education. It also envisaged establishment of State Advisory Boards of Education on the lines of Central Advisory Board of Education. The State Governments play a predominant role in almost all dimensions of education. Accordingly, its educational and management system is Secondary Education, by and large is the concern of the State Government. Of course it is expected to work under the guidance of the Central Government, Ministry of Human Resources Development, Department of Education and it has to carry out policies under the broad framework of the policy formulated.

Education Codes Serve as Guidelines for All those Engaged in Education.

The Minister of Education of a State is not responsible for the entire education of the State. General education is his responsibility but other Ministers and Departments have under their control educational institutions pertaining to their specialised fields like agricultural schools.

9.2 EDUCATIONAL ADMINISTRATIVE STRUCTURE OF A STATE

In all States, the Education Secretary/Commissioner is the administrative head of the Secretariat. He is directly responsible to the Minister of Education. Often he belongs to the Indian Administrative Service. He is assisted by one or two Additional Secretaries, Deputy Secretaries, Under Secretaries and other Secretariat Staff. In bigger States like Uttar Pradesh, there is a Special Secretary.

The Secretary keeps liaison between the Directorate of Education or Directorate of Public Instruction and the Secretariat.

The Directorate executes the policies of the Government which is usually framed in the Secretariat.

The Director of Education/Director of Public Instruction runs the Directorate of Education or the Department of Education.

In bigger States, there are separate posts of Directors for looking after higher education, secondary education and primary education.

The Director is assisted by a number of officers.

For the purpose of administration, management of education, a State is divided into regions, divisions, districts or circles etc.

9.3 PYRAMID STRUCTURE OF EDUCATIONAL ADMINISTRATION AND MANAGEMENT

The educational structure is usually in a pyramid shape. The broad base of the structure indicates that at the lower level the number of individuals tend to be very large. The structure tapers to a point in the upward direction because at each successive higher level, an increasing amount of leadership, planning and other administrative responsibilities are performed. These activities involve greater responsibilities but are concentrated in a small number of persons. For instance, in some States the topmost levels consist of special Secretary Education, Secretary of Education/Commissioner Education. Below are the Director of Education or Director of Public Instruction, Director Secondary Education, Director College Education, Director Primary Education, etc.

9.4 BROAD PATTERN OF THE ADMINISTRATION SET-UP OF THE STATE DEPARTMENT OF EDUCATION

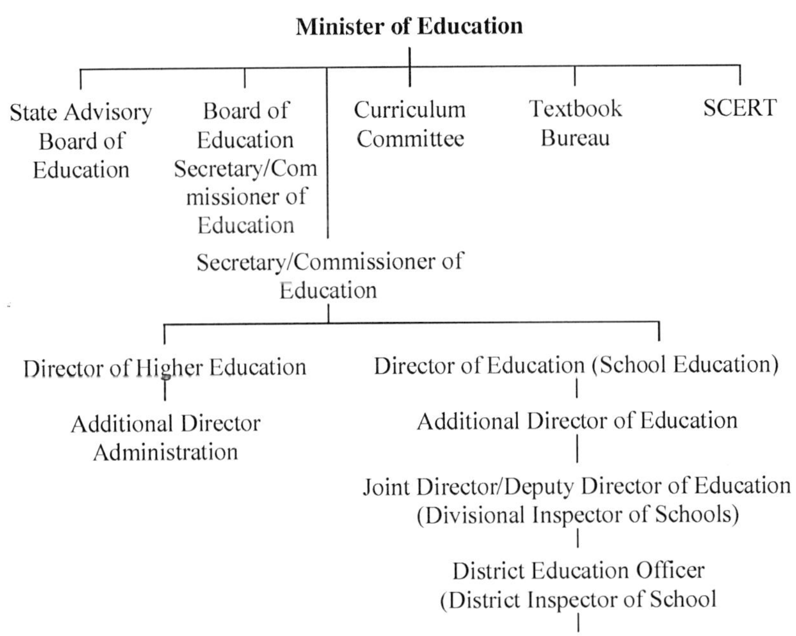

Fig. 9.1: Administrative Set-up of a State Department of Education

Note: All States do not have identical administrative set-up. Sometimes Minister of Education is assisted by Minister of State or Deputy Minister

9.5 ACTS AND CODES PROVIDING LEGAL FOUNDATION TO THE ORGANISATION, ADMINISTRATION AND MANAGEMENT OF EDUCATION IN HIMACHAL PRADESH

The following Acts and Code have provided legal basis to education:

1. The Himachal Pradesh Compulsory Education Act, 1953.
2. The Himachal Pradesh Board of School Education Act, 1968.
3. The Himachal Pradesh University Act, 1970.
4. The Himachal Pradesh Education Code, 1985.
5. The Himachal Pradesh Prevention of Malpractices at University, Board of Secondary Education or Other Specified Examinations Act, 1984.
6. The Himachal Pradesh Universities of Agriculture, Horticulture and Forestry Act, 1986.
7. The Himachal Pradesh Panchayati Raj Act, 1994.
8. The Himachal Pradesh Education Code, 2001.

9.6 NUMBER OF EDUCATIONAL INSTITUTES IN THE STATE OF HIMACHAL PRADESH (2003-2004)

1.	Primary Schools	=	110013
2.	Middle/Senior Basic Schools	=	2076
3.	High/Higher Secondary Schools	=	820
4.	Colleges of General Education	=	69
5.	Professional Education	=	2
6.	Universities/Deemed Universities/Institutes of National Importance/Research Institutes	=	7

Source: Economic Survey 2005-2006, Ministry of Finance, Government of India)

9.7 EXPANSION OF SCHOOL EDUCATION (SCHOOLS) IN HIMACHAL PRADESH (1993 AND 2002)

Category of School/Year	*1993*	*1992*	*% Increase*
Primary Schools	7721	10868	40.76
Upper Primary Schools	1108	1902	71.66
Secondary Schools	1025	1320	28.78
Senior Secondary Schools	241	807	234.85

Source: '*Seventh All India School Education Survey: Provisional Statistics*' as on September 30, 2002, NCERT, 2005

9.8 STRUCTURE OF EDUCATION IN HIMACHAL PRADESH

The structure of education in Himachal Pradesh follows the national pattern of education, popularly known as 10+2+3. It is explained as under:

Age	*Classes*	*Stage of Education*
6-11	Primary	I-V
11-14	Upper Primary	VI-VII
14-16	Secondary	IX-X
16-18	Senior Secondary	XI-XII

Growth of Secondary and Senior Secondary Schools in Himachal Pradesh (1996-97 to 2003-2004)

Year	*Secondary Schools*	*Senior Secondary Schools*	*Total*
1996-97	1168	421	1589
1997-98	1169	462	1631
1998-99	1028	497	1525
1999-2000	1040	523	1563
2000-2001	1183	649	1832
2002-2003	1320	808	2128

Sources: 1. *Selected Educational Statistics, Department of Education, Government of India.*
2. *'Seventh All India Educational Survey', Provisional Statistics as on September 30, 2002, NCERT, 2005.*

Note: The Economic Survey 2005-06, Ministry of Finance, Government of India mentions only 820 institutions under the head 'High School/Higher Secondary/Intermediate and Junior Colleges' (Table S-113).

9.9 ORGANISATIONAL SET-UP OF EDUCATION DEPARTMENT OF HIMACHAL PRADESH

The Education Department is under the charge of Education Minister. All policy matters and major administrative decisions are generally taken by Education Minister who is assisted by Education Secretary who enjoys full administrative and financial powers such as sanctioning of various schemes and projects, etc. All schemes of expansion of education, Plan and Non-plan are approved by Education Secretary, and then submitted to Planning Department for approval. Education Secretary, in addition is overall head of the Education Department for all purposes.

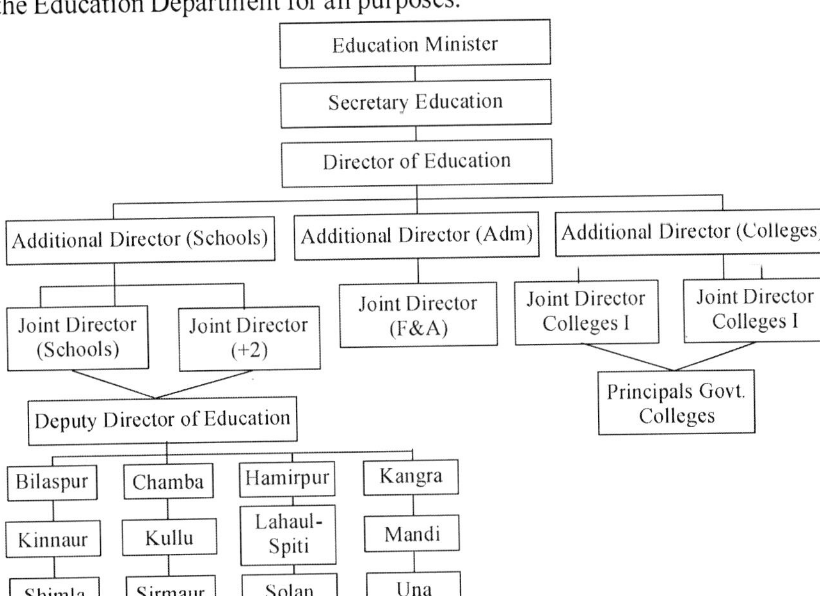

Fig. 9.2: Hierarchical Chart of Education Department

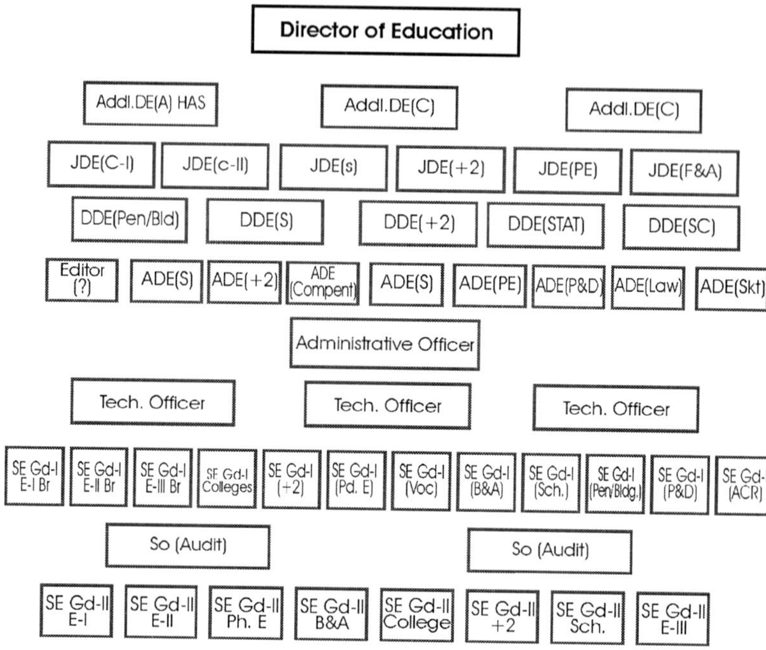

Fig. 9.3: Organisational Chart of Himachal Pradesh Directorate of Education

Functions of the State in Education

The Minister of Education of the State looks after education. The Minister is also responsible to the State Legislature of which he is a member.

The State runs the entire programme in the provincial educational domain, through a separate department known as the Education Department which is under the charge of the Director of Public Instruction/Director of Education.

The State opens various educational institutions catering to the different needs of the people.

The State gives grants-in-aid to various private bodies running educational institutions and thus wields a good deal of control over them.

The State has a considerable control over the affairs of the Universities located within the territory.

The State sends visiting bodies to look into the working of these bodies from time to time.

The State supervises all the institutions started by private bodies.

The State appoints commissions and committees to go into the various phases of education in order to suggest steps to improve the same.

The State passes legislation to control all aspects of education in the State.

The State frames rules and regulations regarding payment to teachers and other staff.

9.10 HIMACHAL PRADESH EDUCATION CODE

Administrative control of education is exercised as per Education Code. For the first time, the Himachal Pradesh Education Code came into force w.e.f.

w.e.f. 28th July, 1985. Earlier, education in Himachal Pradesh was controlled and organised in accordance with the provisions of the Punjab Education Code.

The 1985 Code was replaced by the Education Code 2001. The regulations in this Code apply to all the Government, Government aided, the Educational Institutions affiliated to the Himachal Pradesh Board of School Education and those institutions recognised (prior to 15.7.96) by the State Government.

9.11 HIMACHAL PRADESH STATE BOARD OF SCHOOL EDUCATION

Constitution of the Himachal Board Education

The H.P. Board of School Education came into existence in 1969 through an Act of 1968. The Board had its headquarters at Shimla. Subsequently, it shifted to Dharamshala in Kangra District in 1983. Prior to the establishment of the H.P. Board of School Education, the Punjab University, Chandigarh, was conducting public examinations in respect of secondary and senior secondary schools and connected therewith. The demand of setting up Himachal Pradesh Board of School Education was felt on account of increase in the number of schools. Moreover, the State wanted its own control in matters of education also.

Primary Aim of the Board

The aim of the Board is to improve, maintain and coordinate the standards of secondary education in the State.

9.12 FUNCTIONS OF THE HIMACHAL PRADESH BOARD OF EDUCATION

The Board performs the following functions:

1. Prescribes syllabi.
2. Publishes text-books for school education.
3. Arranges for the preparation, writing, compilation, printing, publishing and sale of text-books, other educational material and undertakes the publication of any other educational work, books or periodicals.
4. Arranges for regular revision of text-books and other books.
5. Adopts measures to promote the cultural, moral, physical and social welfare of students in recognised institutions.
6. Organises and provides lectures, demonstrations and educational exhibitions, seminars and symposiums, and takes such other measures as necessary to raise and promote the quality of school education in Himachal Pradesh.
7. Takes necessary steps with regard to the modernising of school curricula, strengthening of science and mathematics education, work experience and vocationalisation.
8. Organises research on matters concerning education.
9. Affiliates schools and other institutions.
10. Prescribes courses of instruction in schools.

11. Prescribes standards that the schools and other institutions seeking affiliation with the Board ought to fulfil in terms of teachers and their qualifications, curriculum, equipment, buildings and other educational facilities.
    (i) Middle Standard Examination and Middle Standard Supplementary Examination;
    (ii) Matriculation Examination and Matriculation Supplementary Examination;
    (iii) Senior Secondary Certificate Examination (Ten Plus One) and Senior Secondary Certificate Supplementary Examination (Ten Plus One);
    (iv) Senior Secondary Certificate Examination (Ten Plus Two) and Senior Secondary Certificate Supplementary Examination (Ten Plus Two);
    (v) Junior Basic Training: J.B.T. Part-I Examination and J.B.T. Part-I Supplementary Examination;
    (vi) J.B.T. Part-II Examination, J.B.T. Part-II Supplementary Examination;
    (vii) J.B.T. Condensed Course Examination and J.B.T. Condensed Course Supplementary Examination;
    (viii) Oriental Title/Language Teacher: O.T./L.T. Examination and O.T./L.T. Supplementary Examination;
    (ix) Pre-Vocational Training Course: P.V.T.C. Examination & P.V.T.C. Supplementary Examination;
    (x) Teacher's Training Certificate: T.T.C. (Anglo Indian) Examination.

Nearly 4.5 lakh candidates annually appear in the examinations conducted by the Board.

Medium of Examination

(i) Medium for English is English except for a passage of English, which is translated into Hindi;
(ii) Medium for the paper of Sanskrit is Hindi;
(iii) Medium for the papers in other languages is the language concerned;
(iv) Medium for Senior Secondary Classes for the subjects of Mathematics, Biology, Chemistry and Physics is English.
(v) Medium for all other examinations and subjects is Hindi or English.

Syllabi in Subjects of Examination

The syllabus in each subject for the examination setting out the detailed courses of study and scheme of examination is prescribed by the Board from time to time.

9.13 RECOMMENDATIONS FOR STRENGTHENING THE FUNCTIONING OF THE BOARD

Dr. Manju Narula of the NIEPA, New Delhi, conducted a study on the functioning of 4 Boards namely of Himachal Pradesh, Madhya Pradesh, West

Bengal and Andhra Pradesh. The study dealt with the issues of managing quality of these Boards.

The functioning of the Himachal Pradesh School Education Board was considered satisfactorily with reference to the relevant Act. However, the study observed that the following recommendations could be considered for enhancing quality and change.

1. The Board should be fully autonomous in discharging its functions and duties.

2. Strong coordination with Directorate of Education for monitoring of school education needs to be developed.

3. The need of the hour is the total personality development of children. Therefore, purpose of education is to shoulder the responsibility of judging the extent to which the multifaceted objective has been realised. In the evaluation process, the coverage of both scholastic and non-scholastic aspects, of pupil development has to become an important component of the scheme of evaluation. In non-scholastic aspects evaluation of personal and social qualities, interests, attitudes, proficiency in literacy, scientific and cultural activities, etc., needs to be incorporated.

4. The Board needs to be changed from an examination Board to an education Board.

5. There is a need for regular training programmes for evaluators, so that re-evaluation/re-checking cases can be reduced.

6. To improve the quality of schools, training of teachers is very essential. Therefore the need is introduction of large-scale programmes of in-service teacher education for updating their knowledge of content and upgrading their skills of objective-based teaching.

7. There is need to create awareness in the students about the evil effects of copying.

8. Need for strong research wing is felt in the Board for improving the quality of secondary education, so that functional research programmes can be planned for further improving the content and process of examinations and the practices and procedures of the Boards.

9. In the present era when national boundaries are disappearing, the Board has to think regarding curriculum not only in the context of national level but also from the point of view of international level.

10. E-connectivity helps in having better network between the schools and the Board. There is a need to go further in this direction in a state like Himachal Pradesh, where physical barriers exist; e-education can overcome this problem.

Source: Narula, Manju, '*Quality in School Education: Secondary Education and Education Boards*'. NIEPA, Shipra, 2006, New Delhi.

10

Co-Curricular Activities

10.1 CONCEPT OF CO-CURRICULAR ACTIVITIES

Co-curricular activities are those activities, which are undertaken side by side with the curricular activities, i.e., instruction of various subjects. They supplement curricular activities and prepare the students in the 'Art of Living and Working Together'.

In the past, co-curricular activities were mainly organised after school hours and, therefore, were called extra-curricular. But now they are treated as integral part of the activities of the school as its curricular work and their proper organisation needs just as much care and forethought". The Secondary Education Commission remarks: "Given a clean, pleasant and well-maintained school building, we would like the school to see if it can provide a richly varied, pattern of activities to cater to the development of their children's entire personality. It has to formulate a scheme of hobbies, occupations and projects that will appeal to, and draw out the powers of children of varying temperaments and aptitudes."

These activities are as old as education itself though their sphere was not so vast as it is today. Monitor system was one of the important institutions of the ancient Indian system of education. The Gurukulas of old were residential institutions providing opportunities of social contacts on a large scale.

In Athens and Sparta, student participation in organising activities like athletics and music was very common.

Types of Co-curricular Activities

Broadly speaking co-curricular activities may be categorised under thirteen heads, although there are no water-tight compartments as the activities overlap.

Chart Sharing Types of Co-Curricular Activities

(1) Academic Development Activities
(2) Aesthetic Development Activities
(3) Cultural Development
(4) Emotional Development Activities
(5) Leisure Utilisation Activities
(6) Literacy Development Activities
(7) Moral Development Activities
(8) Physical Development Activites
(9) Productive Activities
(10) Social Development Activities
(11) Scientific Temperament Development Activities
(12) Spiritual Development Activities Vocational Oriented Activities
(13) Vocational Oriented Activities

Academic Development Activities

- Preparation of Charts, Models, etc.
- Subject Clubs, e.g., Economics Clubs, Geographical Clubs
- Projects
- Symposiums
- Surveys
- Quiz

Aesthetic Development Activities

- Sculpture
- Dramatics
- Drawing
- Exhibitions
- Fancy Dress
- Music
- Painting
- School Decoration

Citizenship Training Activities

- Visit to Assembly and Parliament
- Cooperative Store
- Students Council
- Youth Parliament
- Social Service

Cultural Development Activities

- Dancing
- Drawing and Painting
- Celebration of Festivals
- Visits to Cultural Places

Emotional and Integration Development Activities

- Camps
- Celebration of National and International Days
- Educational Tours
- Speeches

Leisure Time Activities

- Album making
- Coin Collecting
- Photography
- Stamp Collecting

Literacy Development Activities

- Brain trusts
- Declamation contests
- Debates
- Recitation
- Library work
- Public speaking

Moral Development Activities

- Celebration of birth-days of great men
- Lectures
- Morning assembly
- Social service

Productive Activities

- Card board work
- Clay work
- Embroidery
- Craft work
- Leather work
- Kitchen gardening
- Soap making
- Toy making

Physical Development Activities

- Athletics
- Cycling
- Mass drill
- NCC
- Swimming
- Yogic
- Indoor and Outdoor

Social Value Development Activities

- Girl guiding
- Scouting
- Labour week
- First Aid
- Red Cross
- Community Service

Scientific Temper Development Activities

- Science clubs
- Science quizes
- Science fairs
- Visits to places of scientific importance
- Science models

Multipurpose Activities and Projects

- Beautification & cleanliness of school campus
- Social service
- Social surveys
- Tree plantation
- Adult education
- Community service and awareness

Importance of Co-Curricular Activites

All-roundness is the theme of the modern education which recognises that when the child comes to the school, he comes for mental, physical, social, spiritual and vocational education and as such he must be educated and nourished in all of them. According to the modern concept of education, the three traditional Rs should be replaced by 7Rs, i.e., Reading, Writing and Arithmetic (denoting school subjects in the old concept of education), Rights, Responsibilities Recreation and Relationships (new 4 Rs in the context of democratic values). This can be achieved only by providing a well-organised and supervised programme of co-curricular activities along with curricular programme.

The remarks of the Secondary Education Commission (1952-53) on the role of co-curricular activities are worth noting: "The school is not merely a place of formal learning whose main concern is to communicate a certain prescribed quantum of knowledge but rather as a living and organic community which is primarily interested in training its pupils in what we have called the 'gracious art of living'. Knowledge and learning are undoubtedly of value, but they must be acquired as a by-product of interested activity because it is only then that they can become a vital part of the student's mind and personality and influence his behaviour. 'Art of living' is much more comprehensive concept than the acquisition of knowledge, however intelligently planned. It includes training in the habit and graces of social life and the capacity for cooperative group work. It calls for patience, good temper, sincerity, fellow-feeling and discipline. These objectives can only be cultivated in the context of the social life and the many co-curricular activities must find a recognised place in any schools."

The Indian Education Commission (1964-66) stressed the importance of co-curricular activities in these words: "We conceive of the school curriculum as the totality of the learning experience that the school provides for the pupils through all the manifold activities, in the school or outside, that are carried on under its supervision. From the point of view, the distinction between curricular and extra-curricular work ceases to exist, and a school camp and games are curricular or rather co-curricular activities."

Changes in the philosophical and psychological ideas have now given a new direction to the school curriculum.

Philosophical ideas have brought about a change in the concept of education. The crying need of the hour is the 'education for democracy' and hence education must aim at producing those individuals who can intelligently and amicably participate in the various activities of life. Traditional curriculum has failed to meet the demands of the changing concept of education. The co-curricular programme is a convenient tool by which an inadequate curriculum may be modified.

A consideration of psychological factors urges upon us the necessity of giving more and more attention to understand the individual differences of the children and of providing proper outlets for the flow of the energies of the children. These activities are very helpful in this regard.

'Learning by Doing', 'Learning by Living' and 'Learning without Tears' are the main characteristics of new education.

The educational values of co-curricular activities are many as well as varied. Some of the important values derived from these are detailed here.

1. *Academic Development and Growth:* The teaching of civics, composition, history, geography, etc., can be greatly supplemented. Election to the students council would give them a picture of Central and State elections. Excursions to historical, geographical and industrial places enrich the experience of the students. Writing for the school magazine supplements the teaching of languages. Similarly there are many practical activities which afford opportunities to supplement class-room work.

2. *Development of Aesthetic Values:* It is common knowledge that aesthetic sensibility cannot be taught but it is taught and developed through real

programmes. Participation in dances, dramatics, fancy dresses, flower shows, etc., by the students provide them opportunities to appreciate and develop aesthetic values.

3. *Civic Training:* The school should be a training ground for democracy. It should be organised and administered on democratic lines. The introduction of self-government provides experience of the life of a democratic society. In this, pupils determine the policies and the programmes. They plan and present assembly programmes. The individual pupil learns how to conduct a meeting in an approved parliamentary style. It gives him an opportunity to exercise his vote. While working together, the students learn that rights involve responsibilities. They get valuable lessons in cooperation which can be learnt by practice. In order to retain his position as a member in a Students Council, Athletic team, etc., a student has to learn to cooperate.

4. *Community Relations:* Social service activities bring closer the school and the society. Students also earn appreciation of the society for the good work done by them.

5. *Cultural Values:* Activities like visits, celebrations of community festivals, dance, drama, etc., enable the students to appreciate cultural heritage and develop cultural values.

6. *Dignity of Labour:* In activities like camps and social service, students develop the value of dignity of labour.

7. *Disciplinary Values:* Discipline becomes self-discipline. The students remain busy and different kinds of activities develop their talents in different directions. They make laws for the various societies and come to realise the need for showing respect to other school laws.

8. *Followership Qualities:* By participating in student government, students learn that folowership and leadership go hand in hand. Both are complementary and supplementary.

9. *Guidance and Counselling:* Students get opportunities to know their assets and liabilities. The teachers and especially the school counsellor come to know them better and accordingly suggest programmes for their development.

10. *Pleasurable Instruction :* Pleasure and interest combined with instruction and guidance sugarcane the pill of learning and experience.

11. *Leadership qualities:* Many programmes have to be organised. Many situations have to be faced in the running of various societies. All these inculcate in the students the virtues of initiative, clear thinking, originality, resourcefulness, good judging power, tolerance, patience, enthusiasm, self-confidence and reliance which are very essential in a leader.

12. *Learning and Earning:* Many activities provide opportunities to the students to earn also.

13. *Loyalty:* The more the students run the school affairs, the more they feel that the school belongs to them and they belong to the school. During the labour week, cleaning of the school by the students themselves develops the ideas: 'This is my school because I have made it with the sweat of my brow.' Tournaments and activities like school functions also foster this sentiment.

14. *Moral Training:* Students get opportunities of social contact. They also get opportunities of doing social service. This teaches them the lesson of

morality. They acquire the virtues of honesty, sympathy and good etiquettes.

15. *Physical Development:* Games, N.C.C., Physical Drill, etc., contribute to the physical development of the individual.

16. *Self-Expression:* Someone has a talent for writing, another for speaking, a third for music and so on. These activities bring out these qualities and develop them. This self-discovery and self-knowledge will tell them in what direction they should turn their ability and talent to advantage and help them to make wise vocational choice.

17. *Recreational Interests:* Education for leisure is as important as education for work. If recreational interests are developed during school life, they prove to be very beneficial in the leisure hours of adult life and make life fuller and richer.

Mohi-ud-din has described the recreational value of these activities as "Provision in the school of a programme of free and creative activities, by way of crafts and hobbies, give direction to youthful enthusiasm and training for healthy occupation... The last, but certainly not the least important function of extra-curricular activities is thus to convert the leisure in after-school life from a curse into blessing, from a burden into an opportunity for a fuller, richer and nobler life."

A good deal of educative work can be accomplished through recreation. In the opinion of G.D. Sondhi: "So wide is the field of recreation that there is no school, no teacher, no student that cannot find something of interest in it. If there are no playgrounds, yet there are school courtyards and school-rooms where some form of recreation can be introduced—be it group dancing, play-acting, clay modelling, paper cutting, painting, group-singing, carpentering, spinning, weaving and the like. Opportunities for joy-giving will be provided and boredom eliminated and invention, initiative and emotional control developed."

"Then there are outdoor activities like camping and hiking, gardening and even cycling and mountaineering which build up some of the basic requirements for success in life—the spirit of service, observation, grit, determination and courage." He further observes: "Pleasure and interest combined with some instruction and guiding, sugar-coat the pill of learning and of discipline."

The fundamental point that these activities are means and not ends, should not be lost sight of.

Knowledge and learning are acquired as a by-product of interesting activity.

18. *Psychological Values:* Co-curricular activities provide the children a psychological compensation from the usual dull, routine like and monotonous class-room environment in the following manner:

(a) The co-curricular activities provide much needed channels or outlets for sublimation.
(b) These activities play a significant role in training the emotions of students.
(c) They cater to the various aptitudes and interests of the students.
(d) They are a potent means of developing and ensuring mental health.

19. *Social Training:* Co-curricular activities are very useful in giving

training in 'Art of Living.' According to the Secondary Education Commission, the 'Art of Living is a more comprehensive concept than the acquisition of knowledge, however, intelligently planned. It includes training in the habits and graces of social life and the capacity for cooperative group work it calls for patience, good temper, sincerity, fellow-feeling and discipline. These can only be cultivated in the context of the social life and the many curricular and co-curricular activities that must find a recognised place in every good school. By participation in co-curricular activities pupils learn valuable lessons in practical cooperation and the habits of team work. They realise the relation of the society to the individual and of the individual to the society.

Mohi-ud-din states that these activities have a social appeal: "By reason of the social appeal of extra-curricular activities, their cooperative method, their spontaneity and their intrinsic interest, they are a significant social medium for the civic training of the young".

To be a good member one must sacrifice one's immediate interests if need be, for the welfare of the group. It is well-known that boys and girls in the process of maturity, move from sheer individualism to social awareness.

20. *Sublimation of Instincts:* Gregarious instinct in the adolescent is very predominant. This tendency expresses the desire of the growing boys to behave socially. If no opportunities are provided to them, they will form their own groups. This grouping may be harmful to them and the society also and may take the shape of gangs, etc. Their energies will be misdirected and they will indulge in anti-social acts. Without proper guidance, they are likely to develop wrong scales of social values that will be harmful and even disastrous to them and to society at large. Various co-curricular activities, e.g., self-government, social service league, scouting, etc., will be very conducive to sublimate this instinct by providing them a field for doing something socially worthwhile through group activities. Similarly, their other instincts of self-assertion, sex and self-abasement will be sublimated.

21. *Team Spirit:* In the beginning every player wishes to carry the ball himself and does not realise that he must depend upon others to realise the goal. But with the passage of time an individual discovers that one must play in a team if one is to win anything worthwhile. Thus a team spirit develops in him. Spirit of 'give-and-take' takes the place of selfishness.

22. *Vocational Development:* Through participation in several co-curricular activities like craft work, dramatics, dance, music, gardening, photography, etc., students develop vocational interests which greatly help in career planning.

10.2 PRINCIPLES OF ORGANISING CO-CURRICULAR ACTIVITIES

1. *Principle of Variety of Activities.* A wide variety of activities should be planned in order to meet the different needs of a large number of students.

2. *Principle of Organising Activities During School Hours.* As far as possible, activities should be organised in school time.

3. *Principle of Equal Opportunity to Students.* All the students should have equal opportunity to be a member of school club.

4. *Principle of Gradual Growth of the Programme.* Activities should be started in a small way and developed gradually.

5. *Principle of Careful Consideration.* Every careful consideration should be given when a new society is to be started. Normally, when once an activity is organised and scheduled, it should not be allowed to die.

6. *Principle of Framing Activity Time-table.* An activity time-table and a calendar for activities may be prepared.

7. *Principle of Guidance by Teachers.* The co-curricular programme should be organised under the guidance of teachers.

8. *Principle of Considering Teacher as an Adviser.* The teacher should not play the role of a dominator rather that of an adviser.

9. *Principle of Providing Facilities to Teachers.* Some credit either in the form of less teaching periods or in the form of extra-payment to teachers should be given.

10. *Principle of Participation of a Large Number of Teachers.* As far as possible, each member may remain in-charge of a particular activity of his interest.

11. *Principle of Maintaining Records.* Record of the various activities must be kept by every society.

12. *Principle of Reasonable Expenditure.* Activity should be less expensive as far as possible.

13. *Principle of Provision for Funds.* Sufficient funds to meet the expenditure involved on various activities should be raised by the society concerned.

14. *Principle of Balanced Stress.* Funds should not be spent on a few stars (a few players or debaters etc.).

15. *Principle of Allotting Regular Time.* Regular time should be devoted to these activities.

16. *Principle of Evaluation.* Provision should be made for periodic appraisal of the services and value of these activities.

17. *Principle of No Show Work.* These activities may not be started merely for 'show work'.

18. *Principle of Publicity.* Publicity should be given to the activities of these societies and the community should be well-informed.

19. *Principle of Means not Ends.* Co-curricular programme must be organised and considered as a means to the educative process.

20. *Principle of Appointing Activity Director or Coordinator.* To make the activity programme effective, the head would do well to appoint a teacher as an activity director or coordinator. His teaching load must be so reduced that he may give sufficient time to the planning and execution of various activities in the school. His duties would be:

(i) To plan the schedule of the year's activities to; set dates of special activities, such as concerts parents days, school dances, etc.

(ii) To secure a list of clubs that the teachers desire to offer.

(iii) To take care of special discipline cases during club periods.

(iv) To coordinate with transport service to take students to various places.

(v) To issue bulletins of club activities.

(vi) To select only those activities which are by and large related to the school curriculum and community needs.

(vii) To make the programme as inexpensive as possible.
(viii) To ensure that each student of the school participates in one activity at least according to his interest.

10.3 ROLE OF A TEACHER IN CO-CURRICULAR ACTIVITIES

Teachers should take an active interest in organising co-curricular activities as an integral part of the school programme. They should participate enthusiastically in this programme.

In the teaching of subjects, they get innumerable opportunities to suggest a variety of activities. The scope of activities is very fast.

The language teachers can organise essay competitions, handwriting competitions and debates, spelling competitions, etc.

Social studies teachers can take up projects on the lives of great historical figures. Several types of maps could be prepared. Excursions to places of historical importance may be organised. Social surveys could be undertaken.

The science teachers can take up activities as mentioned in the beginning of this chapter.

As a matter of fact, scope of organising co-curricular activities is unlimited.

Causes of Lack of Due Interest among the Students in the Co-curricular Programme

1. Interference with studies.
2. Inconvenient hours of activities.
3. No credit in the examinations.
4. Inadequate provisions regarding these activities.
5. Lack of suitable play-grounds in the crowded cities.
6. More emphasis on intellectual development of the child and very little emphasis on his other developments, e.g., physical, moral, aesthetic, social etc.
7. Poor economic conditions of a number of students compelling them to work in their homes after school hours and thus leaving very little time at their disposal for participating in the activities which are organised after school hours.
8. Indifference of parents rather discouragement sometimes.

Causes of the Lack of Interest among Teachers in Organising Co-curricular Activities

1. No extra pay or credit is usually given to them for organising such activities.
2. Teacher's teaching hours are not reduced.
3. A majority of the teachers do not possess the proper training for organising such activities.
4. Some of the teachers do not see any good coming out of these activities as they do not fully realise that they should aim at the all-round development of the personality of the student.
5. Due to the rigid outlook of the teachers and the Heads, the idea of the self-government is not allowed to creep into the minds of the students of the school. They feel that the students are not sufficiently mature

and may misuse power invested in them.

6. The vain idea of superiority among the teachers checks them from allowing the students to share responsibility with them.

Limitations of a Co-curricular Programme

1. *Disregard of Institutional Conditions.* Many schools undertake activities simply because other schools have started these. They do not take into consideration their assets and limitations.
2. *Lack of Accommodation.* Some schools do not have playgrounds; no space for indoor games; no space for mass drill.
3. *Lack of Funds.* Some schools lack finances for purchasing equipment for sports, craft work, hobbies, workshop material, etc.
4. *Lack of Variety.* Some schools organise a few activities only with the result that students with diverse interests do not get opportunity to participate.
5. *Lack of Adequate Staff.* The number of teachers who can provide effective guidance to student in this field is limited.
6. *Conservative Attitude of Authorities.* Many heads and teachers do not find any good coming out of a co-curricular programme and they are rather indifferent to it.
7. *Over-emphasis on Academic Work.* Generally speaking no regular time is allotted to the organisation of these activities and undue stress is laid on academic achievements.
8. *Overemphasis on Co-curricular Activities.* Some schools follow the extreme course. They over-stress this programme.
9. *Heavy Load on Teachers.* These activities put a heavy load on the teachers and they feel over-burdened.
10. *No Credit in the Annual Examination.* Usually very little consideration is shown to students' performance in these activities while promoting them.

Concluding Observations

Harry C. Mckown has very aptly observed: "A school with only extra-curricular activities (co-curricular activities) would be as absurd as a school without them". In other words an ideal balance has to be struck between the curricular and co-curricular programme.

10.4 DESCRIPTION OF VARIOUS CO-CURRICULAR ACTIVITIES

I. Clubs in the School or School Clubs

Clubs may be constituted for undertaking different co-curricular activities in the schools. Every club must have its constitution. Its specific aim must be clear. It must meet the needs of the students. Johnson and Faunce give the following objectives of the school clubs:

1. They provide opportunities to the students for learning experiences based on their interests. Students are attracted to a club because of their enthusiasm for the programme it offers.
2. They supplement the curricular work. Visits to places of historical or

scientific importance, etc. can be organised by these clubs.

3. They provide opportunities for the development of pupil abilities.
4. Clubs are very helpful in making the constructive use of leisure time.
5. Clubs may help in the exploration of occupational interest of the students.
6. Clubs provide opportunities for the practice of group planning and decision.

Leadership of the Sponsors or the Teachers-in-Charge of the Club

Leaders or sponsors must possess the following qualities:

1. They should be able to enlist the cooperation of the students.
2. They must be able to offer constructive suggestions for activities of the club.
3. They must be able to guide without dictation.
4. They must have the ability to plan systematically.
5. They must be willing to give time and thought in making the work of the club a success.
6. They must be democratic in spirit.
7. They must possess a sense of humour.
8. They must have the necessary talent and skill so that their performance is higher and better than their pupils and they look up to them as a model.
9. They should help the clubs and societies to make a wise choice of office bearers indicating what qualifications are necessary in an office bearer but should do nothing to force their choice in favour of any individual student.
10. They should make as careful preparation for participation in co-curricular activities as they do for their teaching work.

Clubs may be organised for a variety of activities and school subjects.

II. Dramatics or Dramatisation

Meaning. Dramatisation has been described as "a synthetic art, involving the purposive coordination and control of the delicate organs of speech and muscles of the body combined with a sense of rhythm, with a view to give free and intelligent expression of emotions and ideas."

Values of Dramatisation

(i) Dramatic art affords innumerable opportunities for the correlation of a large number of subjects.

(ii) In the preparation of their roles, the students indirectly and unconsciously improve their speech habits and language.

(iii) A systematic study of historical events has to be made when pageants of the life of great persons are prepared, i.e., pageant on the life of Buddha, Chandragupta, Vikramaditya, Gandhiji etc.

(iv) Children prepare costumes suiting different ages and thus come to know about the dresses of the people during different periods of history.

(v) Dramatics also add to the geographical knowledge of the students.

(vi) Carpentry and other mechanical arts facilitate the work of construction of the stage. Dance and music add to the beauty of a drama.

(vii) Drama has its great social value. It is a cooperative enterprise and develops qualities of cooperation and social understanding.

(viii) It helps in fostering '*espirit de crops*' among the students. In various school functions, dramas form the chief items of the programme. For the honour of the school, every student works to the best of his capacity.

(ix) Dramatics afford the students many opportunities for training in team work.

(x) There are many activities in a drama and as such students of diverse aptitudes get chances to choose items for which they are best suited and satisfy their urges, e.g., self-expression through the various activities of a drama.

(xi) Dramatisation provides a healthy and rich entertainment.

(xii) From literacy points of view, it provides practical opportunities for improving speech, expression, intonation etc.

(xiii) It may prepare for a vocation.

(xiv) It provides attraction to the guardians of the students and other dignitaries to visit the school and promote it.

(xv) The staging of dramatic performance provides valuable experience to students in organising programmes.

Essentials for the Success of Dramatics

A number of rehearsals bring grace and success to the play when it is staged. Pupils should prepare as much stage material as they can.

Children should be encouraged to write their own plays. The usual participants in this activity should be given opportunities to play different roles. The same pupils as far as possible should, however, not be allowed to play the role of villain.

Selection of Play

1. Only competent teachers should undertake this programme.
2. Plays chosen should depict the evils of the social customs and promote social reforms.
3. A play should have a literary value.
4. The students should be able to understand and appreciate the play.
5. It should have also entertainment value.
6. It should be free from objectionable subject-matter.
7. There should be no vulgarity in the play.

III. Educational Excursions and Tours

Meaning of Educational Excursions: Educational excursions imply small journeys which are undertaken to agricultural, cultural, geographical, historical and industrial places which are not very far off from the educational institution. However educational tours may be, for far off places.

Significance of an Educational Excursions and Tour: W.M. Gregory evaluates school excursion in these words: "Education has been too far removed from the basic experiences of modern life. Many students are quite deficient in opportunities for some perception exploration and raw experiences. They need fewer words and more activities with things, situations, conditions and relations. For useful learning, pupils require experiences with the raw materials of life. A garden, a shop, a live animal collection, a trip to a farm, a mill, a store, a park, a museum—all must have a place in the modern school." Following are some of the main advantages of excursions:

(i) *They supplement class-work:* Visits to museums, forts, temples, caves, mountains, valleys, canals and fields help in supplementing the teaching of social studies by providing first-hand information. Industrial establishments and laboratories, etc., are very useful places for the students of science. Excursions to these places bring reality, clarity and vividness to the 'dead matter' of various subjects, and provide for valuable correlation of subjects.

(ii) *They introduce variety in the school programme:* These excursions infuse a new life and vigour in the children and give them some relief from the dull and monotonous life of the class-room.

(iii) *They develop qualities of leadership:* Excursions help in developing qualities of initiative and leadership in the students by affording them opportunities to make necessary arrangements. These also encourage a spirit of cooperation among the students.

(iv) *They acquaint the pupils with the environment:* Excursions enable the students to know intimately their environment by putting them in direct touch with the things, persons, organisations and institutions.

(v) *They develop self-activity among the students:* Excursions make pupils active agents rather than passive recipients. Students get opportunities to plan various programmes connected with excursions. Besides they get opportunities to develop keenness and accuracy of observation. All their senses are at work and they experience the joy of discovery.

(vi) *They develop the aesthetic sense of the students:* Excursions to natural settings and places of beauty create love for nature and develop aesthetic sense.

(vii) *They foster ideals of emotional and national integration:* The students come into contact with people of different races, regions and states. This enables them to appreciate the unity in diversity.

Proper Planning of Excursions: To derive the maximum benefit from excursions, it is essential that these should be properly planned. The teachers and the students may work out the plan of the excursion jointly. An excursion must be wisely conceived, properly planned and well conducted. It must be a result of careful thinking. The organisers would do well to obtain sufficient information before hand regarding the importance of places to be visited so that they may be able to give suitable replies to the various queries of the students.

The fact that the excursions are arranged for educational-*cum*-recreational purposes should not be lost sight of and therefore, if possible, student singers, titbit tellers and photographers should find a place in the party so that learning and laughing should go hand in hand.

The appointment of group leaders facilitates work to a considerable extent.

The group leaders should preferably be those students who have some knowledge of the locality or who know the technique of explaining things in a clear way.

The importance of maintaining discipline in an excursion can hardly be ignored and a sympathetic and resources teacher shall not find it difficult to do so.

IV. Labour Week

Regarding this type of work, K.G. Saiyidain writes: "I feel strongly that not only in this country, but in the whole world, we have to make an earnest and concentrated effort to give a new orientation to the social ideology of our children and youth particularly in the direction of inculcating a sense of the dignity of labour and cultivating the capacity to work together for constructive and socially worthy causes. I cannot think of any better method of doing so than by bringing all school children together into a fellowship of work and service where the meanest work will be undertaken in a spirit of adventure and comradeship because it is useful and provides healthy outlet for their energies and talents."

Following types of work may be done during a labour week:

(a) Cleaning and white-washing the school building.
(b) Decorating the rooms.
(c) Removing stones, iron nails, waste paper, etc. from the school compound, playground, lanes and streets.
(d) Filing pits in the streets and lanes, and cleaning roads.
(e) Organising first-aid centres for the public.
(f) Teaching adults.
(g) Improving drainage of selected localities and drying marshy land created by open drains.
(h) Turning school compounds.
(i) Propaganda amongst the public regarding the importance of personal cleanliness and social sanitation in order to ward off common diseases.

To make this programme a success, the teachers themselves should take an active part in activities stated above. This will give incentive and encouragement to the students.

V. Morning Assembly/School Assembly

Meaning: Flora T. Cook describes the morning assembly as: "The morning assembly is a common meeting ground to which each brings his offerings, the fruit of his observation and studies or music, literature, and art that delight him, a place where all cooperate for the pleasure and well-being of the whole."

Prof. Fretwell calls the assembly "Town meeting of the school."

In the words of W.R. Smith: "School assembly can serve as a focusing centre of all form of extra-curricular life."

Nature of Activities of the Assembly: Common activities of an assembly are:

(i) School prayer.
(ii) Singing of national anthem.
(iii) Singing of devotional song.

(iv) Roll call.
(v) Checking of cleanliness.
(vi) Checking of school uniform.
(vii) Short speech or some moral aspect by the head or the teacher or the student or the guest speaker.
(viii) Announcements.
(ix) Commendations.
(x) Mass drill.
(xi) Daily news.

Objectives, Purposes and Values of the School Assembly

(i) *To provide a solemn occasion:* The singing of morning prayer and devotional songs provides a very solemn and elevating occasion and makes a good beginning for school work.

(ii) *To develop devotion to God and Spirituality:* It can be used to create in the students an urge for prayer and meditation which also helps in emotional stability.

(iii) *To develop spirit of patriotism:* Singing of some patriotic song or narration of some patriotic event inculcates the sentiment of patriotism and love for the country.

(iv) *To celebrate festivals and days:* Some of the important national days and religious festivals can be celebrated.

(v) *To unify the school:* An assembly is very helpful in developing a community spirit among the students. They get occasions to see, feel and know the school as an organised group. An average student remaining in his class does not appreciate his relationship to the school as a whole.

(vi) *To serve as clearing house:* The school assembly serves as a clearing house for all school activities both curricular and co-curricular.

(vii) *To familiarise the students with the common rules and ideals of the school:* Every child must become a full-fledged citizen of the school. In a school assembly, the students should be told about the traditions, rules and ideals of the school.

(viii) *To develop correct audience habits:* To be socially efficient, every child must know how to behave in a gathering. Social etiquette demands that children must listen to the speakers with courtesy and patience. When and how to applaud is another quality that must be developed. The school assembly trains the students in this art.

(ix) *To give due recognition to worthwhile achievements publicly:* Prizes to the students for outstanding accomplishments of nature, curricular or co-curricular should be given before the entire school. This action will motivate other students to perform outstanding accomplishments.

(x) *To give opportunities to students to face the audience:* It gives training to a large number of students in effective appearance and expression before a critical audience. Students advanced in different spheres present their programmes and give stimulus to others to emulate their example.

(xi) *To widen interest:* Assembly experience deepens and widen student interests.

(xii) *To develop good habits:* Habits of punctuality and regularity are developed.

(xiii) *To motivate students:* Announcement and public recognition to outstanding performance of some students in academic and co-curricular programmes motivate other students to work hard.

(xiv) *To make general announcements:* Changes in the school schedule, preparation of any special programme can be announced in the morning assembly.

Edmonson and others expect the assembly to discharge the following functions:

1. To develop school unity.
2. To encourage school spirit.
3. To motivate curricular functions.
4. To stimulate extra curricular activities.
5. To motivate expression and overcome self-consciousness.
6. To develop proper habits and attitudes in audience.
7. To share information.
8. To influence public opinion.
9. To develop aesthetic sense.

Essentials for Ideal Assembly Programmes

1. All programmes should be carefully planned and executed.
2. Sufficient care should be exercised to ensure that the students observe disciplinary etiquettes.
3. The assembly should not be made a forum for saying unpleasant things.
4. One of the worst things a head would do in an assembly is to find fault openly with some staff member or to criticise the entire student population of the school. This unpleasant element should be avoided.

VI. National Cadet Corps (NCC)

The National Cadet Corps Directorate, Ministry of Defence, has enunciated the following objectives of the National Cadet Corps:

First, to develop character, comradeship, the ideal of service and capacity for leadership in young men and women;

Secondly, to provide service training to young men and women so as to stimulate interest in the defence of the country; and

Thirdly, to build up a reserve of potential officers to enable the Armed Forces to expand rapidly in a national emergency.

Membership: The membership of the N.C.C. is entirely voluntary and there is no liability for military service. It undertakes the training of the young between the age of 13 and 20. Free training is imparted to the cadets. Free uniform are issued to them and all expenses on account of messing and amenities for them during camps are met by the State Government.

Divisions. The National Cadet Corps consists of three divisions:

Junior Division. In the Secondary and Senior Secondary Schools and the Public Schools, Junior divisions have been raised. It comprises three units—Army, Navy and Air Force.

Senior Division. This is also composed of three wings—the Army, the Navy and the Air Force Wings. The maximum tenure of service for a cadet in the Senior Division is four years. This unit is raised in the colleges.

Girls Division. Though the present strength is not an encouraging one, yet it is hoped that more units will be raised before long as it is becoming increasingly popular.

VII. School Magazine

Significance and Values of School Magazine: A school magazine is the embodiment of the corporate life of an institution and affords suitable opportunities to the students for giving expression to their thought and ambitions.

In the words of Jacobson: "The school magazine offers great opportunities for those who participate in it. It is not uncommon to find that pupils and their parents consider the editorship of the school paper the most valuable experience which has come to a pupil, particularly when directed by a wise sponsor who make it a very purposive educative experience. All pupils who serve on the magazine secure some experience in creative writing; usually the form of their writing improves because a powerful incentive for correct form exists when the material is to be printed or mimeographed for public examination."

It serves as a link between the school and the parents as it reaches them through the students.

A school magazine supplements class work to some extent. The students learn to write their thoughts in an effective, clear and concise manner. Study habits are developed as the students consult some books or journals to write for their school magazine and make the best use of their leisure time.

Spears and Lawshe list the following functions of the school paper as an aid to the school:

1. To educate the community as to the work of the school.
2. To publish school news.
3. To create and express school opinion.
4. To capitalise the achievements of the school.
5. To act as a means of unifying the school.
6. To express the idealism and reflect the spirit.
7. To encourage and stimulate worthwhile activities.
8. To aid in developing right standards of conduct.
9. To promote understanding of other schools.
10. To provide an outlet for student suggestions for the betterment of the school.
11. To develop better inter-school relationships.
12. To increase school spirit.
13. To promote cooperation between parents and school.

Factors Essential for the Success of the School Magazine: Contributions from the students should be corrected before their publication. The school magazine should include a variety of articles. Not only short stories, essays, poems, titbits but current news, school news about curricular and co-curricular activities, photos, designs and cartoons, etc., should also find place in the school magazine. Student editors should be carefully appointed. Prize for the best contributions may be given to the students to give them an incentive to write. The teachers should not make the school magazine as their organ.

The teacher in-charge of the magazine should be a man of vision, of literary taste and well-versed with the current events.

In schools where the number of students is small and the financial position does not permit the publication of a full-fledged magazine, it will be advantageous to take resort to wall-magazine.

Blackboard or wall-magazine greatly help in the preparation of the printed magazine. News on boards may be written every day in the morning. Daily news should be illustrated with the help of a map. Important places where important events take place should be shown on the map. Other boards dealing with facts and figure regarding our natural resources, development projects, inspiring thoughts from religion, history or ethics may be prepared weekly or fortnightly as the case may be. The students should be made responsible for preparing these boards.

VIII. Scouting and Girl Guiding

Values of Scouting: Prof. Bertrand Russell has very beautifully commended the value of scouting: "The naturalist may praise it for its success in putting the boy close to Nature's heart, the moralist for its splendid code of ethics, the hygienist for its method of physical training, the parent for its ability to keep his boy out of mischief; but from the standing point of educator, it has marvellous potency for converting the restless, irresponsible, self-centred boy into the straight-forward, dependable, helpful young citizen. To the boy who will give himself to it, there is plenty of work that looks like play, standard of excellence which he can appreciate, rules of conduct which he must obey, position of responsibility which he must occupy as soon as he qualifies himself, in a word: a programme that appeals to boy's nature."

Another writer, Dr. L.D. Coffman writes: "Scouting gives us no lecture on vocational guidance, and yet it teaches the meaning, the importance of the dignity of work; it operates no bank and yet it teaches the meaning of thrift; it contains no jails and yet it teaches the meaning of self-control; it does not preaching and yet it teaches devotion to a cause and loyalty to a purpose; it is founded upon no religious creed or sectarian doctrine and yet it emphasises above all things the importance of religion. It is universal in appeal, natural in its methods, progressive in its outlines, strengthened and cemented by the bonds of fellowship and the idealism of the movement.

Following are some of the important contributions of scouting:

1. *Social Service Training:* Scouts render a very useful service in the fairs and gatherings. Anti-malaria work, flood relief work, adult literacy work and cleaning campaigns are the other fields of their activities.

2. *Good Fellowship:* A good deal of the sufferings of the world is due to the absence of fellowship feeling. If humanity is to survive, a spirit of good fellowship must be developed in the students who in a few years are expected to play an important role in the world. Scouting knows no barriers of caste,

creed and colour. Camp life and other cooperative activities are the means to develop this quality of brotherhood.

3. *Dignity of Labour:* It is an open secret that an average student shirks work. He does not take pride in doings things for himself. This movement is the best one to provide practical opportunities to the students to throw themselves with vigour and derive pleasure from work.

4. *Sublimation of Instincts:* Patrol contest and games take the place of gang fights. Sex instincts is sublimated through contact with nature. Self-assertion finds its outlets in producing patrol and troop leaders. Similarly, other instincts finds suitable channels.

5. *Love of Nature:* Various outdoor games, # life and excursions bring the students in close touch with nature and develop their aesthetic sense and engender in the minds of the students love for nature.

6. *The Spirit of Adventure:* Students are by nature restless and curious to know new things. They like to explore and face difficulties. The outdoor life provides worth-while opportunities to satisfy their lust for enterprise and discovery. "The outdoor life is the life blood of scouting." Writes F.G. Pearce.

7. *Practical Efficiency:* There are many activities like health training, first-aid, home nursing, rescue and emergency aid, swimming, riding, etc., which greatly increase the practical efficiency of the scouts.

History of Scouting: Sir Robert Baden Power (1857-1941) founded the Boy Scout Movement in 1908. However, in India, the movement was introduced in 1911 at Bangalore. Many rival organisations such as the 'Seva Dals', 'Bharat Youth Sangha', Seva Samiti, Boys Scout Association and finally, the Hindustan Scout Association, came into existence.

Badel Powell had served the army in India, Afghanistan and then in South Asia.

In India it was considered for long that the movement was alien in its character.

The movement has received a great setback with the starting of N.C.C. and other organisations.

The movement is non-political, non-official but voluntary.

How to Start a Scout Troop

(i) It should be started by a teacher who himself possesses the spirit of service and is really interested in scouting. 'Come on', and never 'Go on', should be his watchword.
(ii) There should not be more than thirty-two boys in a troop. This number can easily be managed by one scout master.
(iii) Generally speaking, a troop should not be instructed as a whole. The scouts are to be trained, through patrol leaders and directly by the scout master.
(iv) Right type of boys should be selected for scouting.
(v) Preliminary training should start with outdoor life. A picnic may be arranged and scouting may be talked about. Thus gradually the students should be made conversant with scout law, scout uniform and scout promise.
(vi) Twice a week, an hour and a half before or after school will suffice

for the training in scout tests (Tender Foot and Second Class Tests). Time should be adjusted in cooperation with other teachers.

(vii) Inter-patrol competitions should be held as these are very helpful in maintaining keenness and promoting efficiency.

(viii) Scouts should be motivated to take pride in their uniform from the very start.

(ix) A scout troop must have ropes, flags, bandages, compass, first-aid material, books and camping and picnic equipment.

(x) A suitable room in the school should be provided and known as scout room.

(xi) Practical opportunities should be provided to the scouts to do social service.

(xii) Camp fires should be organised.

(xiii) Records of the work of the troop should be kept.

(xiv) Too many rallies should be avoided.

(xv) Scout troop should not be started merely for the purpose of show or at the time of inspection.

(xvi) The scout master himself should follow the scout laws.

IX. Social Service and Community Development Activities

School as a Social Institution: School is set up by the Community/Society to serve its needs. One of the important ways to serve the community is to render social service by the students. There are several areas in which the students can render very useful service to the community.

The Education Commission (1964-66) laid a great emphasis on labour and social camps of the students. It suggested the following programme:

During the period of the camp, students should be expected to put in 8 hours of work per day and the general routine would be as follows:

2 hours—personal time in morning.
2 hours—rest and relaxation in the afternoon.
6 hours—manual work.
2 hours—intellectual work not connected with school studies.
2 hours—personal time in the evening.
8 hours—sleep.

Values and Advantages of Camps and Community Development Programmes

(i) They inculcate in students the spirit of community service.

(ii) They develop in the students the spirit of self-sacrifice.

(iii) They give children a scope for the exercise of initiative.

(iv) They build up an attitude of cooperation and fellow-feeling.

(v) They help to built an environment of cooperation in the home and the outside world.

(vi) They train students in leadership.

(vii) They give children training in citizenship and in the art of self-government.

(viii) They develop wider outlook.

(ix) These activities help in the many-sided development of the pupil—

physical, mental, moral, religious and social.

(x) These activities foster dignity of labour.

(xi) These directly and indirectly impart moral education.

In short, these activities develop virtues of give and take, cooperation, participation in social life, sharing responsibilities, cooperative endeavour, mutual adjustment, internal self-discipline friendly disposition, ideals of service, proper attitudes, etc.

Financial Aspects: A part of the funds for the programme could be obtained from the local Rural Works Programme. All the overhead charges—which will come to a very small amount—should be met by Government. The student should be required only to bear: (1) transport charges to the camp site and back, and (2) food charges during the stay at the camp. Even these could be subsidised to some extent on the basis of the work that the students put in. A student who holds freeship or half freeship should be given similar concessions in the camp. Adjustments could also be made by requesting the students to bring some articles of foodstuffs etc. from home. On the whole, an attempt should be made to keep the cost of this camp down to the minimum for each period. Moreover, camps for boys and girls will have to be organised separately; and there need not be much and girls will have to be organised separately; and there need not be much difference between the types or programmes undertaken for them.

(*See also Labour Weeks*)

10.5 STUDENT PARTICIPATION AND STUDENT SELF-GOVERNMENT

A school is considered to be an ideal place for training in citizenship and democratic values in student's participation in running some of administrative functions is also known as a sort of student self-government. Self-government on a large scale by the pupils is not possible even, in well established progressive schools in our country. There are nevertheless practical undertakings in the schools to train pupils for citizenship. The organisation of co-curricular activities offers a field in which student government to a considerable extent could function very effectively. The simple Council Types of self-government is easy to practise.

To start with, a school may have school Sabha. Each class or section elects one representative to the Sabha. Some talented students may be nominated by the head of the school in consultation with the staff adviser. The Sabha may have six committees under it and the members may be elected from among the elected representatives. One staff member may act as an adviser to each committee. The following activities may be undertaken by these committees.

(a) Games and sports Committee.

(b) Health and sanitation Committee.

(c) A committee for organising activities like debates, dramas, magazines, hobbies, etc.

(d) Discipline committee.

(e) Committee for social welfare activities like Adult Literacy Campaigns, Flood Squads, Labour Weeks, etc.

(f) School Cooperative Store Committee.

No rigid rules can be laid down for the range of activities to be undertaken by the Sabha. Every type of activity which has some educational significance may come under its purview.

H.C. McKown has given a list of 147 activities which can be undertaken by the Sabha or the Council. Some of these activities are given here:

1. To welcome new students.
2. To supervise and help in the maintenance of good sanitary conditions in the school.
3. To decorate the class-rooms and the school premises.
4. To visit sick students.
5. To meet and welcome the visiting teams.
6. To provide assistance to the weak and handicapped students.
7. To plan campaigns—courtesy, safety, punctuality etc.
8. To organise contests and competitions.
9. To publish school magazine and school bulletins.
10. To organise and manage a lost and found department.
11. To promote better lunch-room and cafeteria manners.
12. To promote good manners at athletic contests.
13. To look after library and reading-room.
14. To promote good behaviour at assembly, public, events, before and after school.
15. To arrange lectures.
16. To organise exhibitions.
17. To organise the school store.
18. To organise the school-bank.
19. To introduce students to new movements in education.
20. To promote and arrange inter-school visits.
21. To arrange inter-school sports tournaments.
22. To promote inter-home programme exchanges.
23. To hold academic contests.
24. To organise excursions and trips.
25. To provide for publicity of commendable school work.
26. To promote good dress and neat appearance.
27. To collect material for school museum.
28. To supervise ventilation.
29. To discourage smoking.
30. To discourage seeing bad pictures.
31. To look after the school garden.
32. To promote good habits.
33. To arrange medical aid for the needy.
34. To assist health and police authorities.
35. To organise health social service at various occasions.
36. To assist in community-fund drives.
37. To organise school functions.
38. To organise literacy campaigns.
39. To conduct campaigns to improve school spirit.
40. To plan and promote a "better manners campaign".
41. To visit other schools to gain new ideas.

SECTION IV

11

School Time-Table

11.1 CONCEPT OF SCHOOL TIME-TABLE

The school time-table is a chart which indicates all the activities undertaken by each member of the staff and the student in each class or on farm or workshop at a particular time of the day when the school is functioning. It is the school mirror which reflects the school programme. It is called the 'Second Clock' of the school on the face of which is shown the daily schedule of the school. In the words of H.G. Stead, "It is the time-table that supplies the framework within which the work of the school proceeds. It is the instrument through which the purpose of the school is to function."

Time-table is an outline of the day's work in a school which indicates:

1. Time of the beginning and ending of the school day.
2. Time of beginning and ending of each class period and the activity of the class.
3. Subjects and activities being undertaken by students in each class, in each period and by an each teacher.
4. Days on which every subject is taught.
5. Name of the teacher teaching a particular subject in a particular period and in a particular room.
6. Room or place where each activity is going on.
7. Recess Break or interval time.

Significance of the School Time-table: Spark Plug of the School

The time-table reflects the essence of the words of wisdom as said by Pitman, "Well arranged time is the surest mark of a well-arranged mind."

Dr. Jaswant Singh regards the time-table of the school as the "spark plug of the school which sets into motion its various activities and programme." Some educators regard it as the 'mirror' that reflects the entire daily schedule of the school.

Time-table is an indispensable document of the school. The main points of the significance and value of time-table are discussed below:

1. *Brings System in the School Life*: Without the time-table, there will be chaos and confusion all-round in the school. In the absence of the time-table, the school life will come to a standstill and become a free for all affairs.

2. *Eliminates Wastage of Time and Energy:* Undoubtedly all planned programmes eliminate wastage of time and energy and it is equally true in the

case of a school time-table. The entire school work is, by and large, equitably distributed among the members of the staff. It directs the teacher's and students energy and attention to one thing at a time by placing proper persons at their proper places at the proper time and in the proper manner.

3. *Ensures Due Attention to Every Subject or Activity:* In framing the time-table, due attention is given to every subject. Periods are allotted to different subjects according to their importance and their fatiguing nature.

4. *Develops Moral Values:* It helps to develop qualities like punctuality and regularity both in the teachers and the students by placing before them a set programme of activities.

5. *Ensures Regular and Even Progress:* Regular and even progress is ensured because time-table prevents laxity and shortages.

6. *Provides a Psychological Environment:* It has got a psychological value leading to the removal of fatigue which may occur due to prolonged hours of teaching and learning. It brings new motivation and stimulation to teachers and students.

7. *Ensures Equitable Distribution of Time to Different Subjects and Activities:* Time-table helps in avoiding the allotment of too much or too less work to any teacher.

8. *Develops Good Habits.* It helps in developing regular habits of work in students as well as teachers.

9. *Facilitates Advance Planning by the Teachers and Students:* Time-table helps in chalking out plans in a systematic manner.

10. *Ensures Efficiency:* There will be no looseness, duplication of effort and repetition of items and activities. Everybody in the school system knows what to do at a particular time.

11. *Helps in Maintaining Discipline:* Since the students are kept gainfully busy in desirable activities, they have little excuse to loiter about. When they are busy, they do not think and act in wrong directions.

12. *Facilitates Supervision:* The head finds it convenient to supervise the work of the teachers and students and offer appropriate guidance to them. He can have individual consultation with the teachers when they are not busy with their classes.

13. *Leads to Even and Regular Process:* It avoids imbalances and leads to even and regular process in all areas of school curriculum.

11.2 TYPES OR FORMS OF A SCHOOL TIME-TABLE

The form of a time-table depends upon the nature of activities carried on in a school. The more the number and variety of activities, the more types of time-tables. In an ordinary school four forms of time-table, i.e., consolidated time-table of the school, class time-table, teachers' vacant period time-table and teachers' time-table will serve the purpose. Time-table for co-curricular activities is coming into vogue in view of their importance in the field of education. Similarly in schools where games are properly organised, the need for games' time-table can hardly be stressed. The progressive schools maintains special room time-table. Time-table for homework is also maintained by some schools.

Ideally speaking there should be seven kinds of time-table.

1. Master time-table indicating the entire programme of the school.
2. Class time-table.
3. Teachers' time-table.
4. Vacant period time-table.
5. Games time-table.
6. Co-curricular activities time-table.
7. Home work time-table.

One copy of class time-table should be kept in the class-room concerned. A copy of the teachers' time-tables should be put in the staff room. One copy of each of the time-table should be kept in the Head's office so that he may know at a glance what work a particular class or teacher is doing at a given time.

11.3 PRINCIPLE OF SCHOOL TIME-TABLE CONSTRUCTION

The construction of time-table makes large demands on the ingenuity and skill of the Head. Framing of a time-table is a time absorbing task. Some of the chief factors which determine the construction of a time-table are:

1. Principle of following departmental regulations.
2. Principle of considering the type of school.
3. Principle of amount of time available.
4. Principle of relative importance of a subject.
5. Principle of incidence of fatigue.
6. Principle of justice.
7. Principle of variety.
8. Principle of free period for teachers.
9. Principle of play and recreation.
10. Principle of optimum utilisation.
11. Principle of local variation.
12. Principle of initiation.
13. Principle of elasticity.

1. *Principle of Following Departmental Regulations:* Generally, the State Department of Education issues directions regarding the number of working hours of a school, examination and evaluation schedule and holidays to be observed etc. It is obligatory for the schools to obey these regulations.

2. *Principle of Considering the Type of School:* The type of school, i.e., a boys' school or girls' school, urban or rural, infant school or school for girls, public or ordinary, will determine the nature of activities of the school and time-table will be framed accordingly. The double shift will call for shortening the duration of the school hours. Similarly, co-educational school will necessitate numerous changes so as to meet the specific needs of both the boys and the girls. In the higher grades of schools the duration of the periods will be longer than in the lower grades of schools.

3. *Principle of the Amount of Time Available.* The amount of time to be given to each subject or activity is determined by the total amount of time available at school. Generally speaking, the higher the grade of the school, the longer the school day. There are certain departmental regulations concerning school timings which have got to be obeyed. According to the

Punjab Education Code, the hours for opening and closing Government schools shall be fixed by the Inspector, and for other recognised schools by the Local Bodies or Managers concerned, after consideration of the season, locality and class of pupils and subjects to the restriction that the total weekly period of instruction (excluding the time allotted to drill and recess) does not exceed the following limits:

Class I	16 Hours
Class II and III	19 Hours
Class IV	24 Hours
Secondary Classes	30 Hours

Recommendations of the Education Commission (1964-66): The Commission made the following recommendations:

(A) The working hours per day should vary from four hours at the pre-primary stage to about six hours at the higher secondary stage.
(B) The total period does not include the time for co-curricular activities.
(C) The period includes the time for library period or the guided studies.
(D) At the lower primary stage the hours of instruction should be about 900 and at the higher primary and secondary stages they should be not less than 1,000 and preferably raised to 1,100 or even 1,200 if conditions are favourable.

4. *Principle of Relative Importance and Difficulty of Subjects:* There are certain social and economic considerations that determine the importance of a subject in the school curriculum and so the time is allotted to each subject in the school time-table accordingly. Subjects like English and Mathematics which are considered to be important and difficult are allotted more time.

5. *Principle of Incidence of Fatigue:* The element of fatigue influences the construction of the school time-table in a number of ways. Subjects requiring more brain-work are placed on the time-table when the brains of the students are quite fresh and when they are capable of doing hard and difficult work. Each part of the morning is considered better than the corresponding part of the afternoon. In other words, the middle or the morning is better than the middle of the afternoon although the middle of the afternoon is better than the end of the morning and the end of the morning is better than the end of the afternoon. It is a common feeling to think that mental freshness is the greatest in the morning. It gradually increases until it reaches its maximum about the middle of the morning. That is the case after recess. Mental freshness is greater not just after recess but in the second period after recess. The best periods for fatiguing subjects are, therefore, the second, and third periods in the morning and second period after recess. The order of subjects causing fatigue is as follows: Mathematics, English, Indian Languages, Science, Nature Study, Science Practical, Drawing, Crafts, Music, etc. The second and the third periods in the morning and the second in the afternoon are considered to be the best periods for the fatiguing subjects. English and Mathematics should, therefore, be placed as far as possible in these periods. The worst period is the last period in the afternoon and it may be given to manual work, science practical, physical exercises, etc.

The 'fatigue principle' is true of the days of the week also. Tuesday and

Wednesday are considered to be the best days in which maximum work could be done. The end of the week is like the end of the day and fatigue is the greatest.

The younger are quickly fatigued, and therefore, the duration of the period in the lower classes should not exceed thirty minutes and in the higher classes it should not exceed forty minutes. In the summer season, the duration of the period should be reduced.

Likewise teachers are not given four periods continuously to teach.

6. *Principle of Justice.* Work among the members of the staff should be equitably distributed. Unequal distribution of work causes frustration among them and hampers progress. Similarly, time should be allotted for different activities according to their importance in the school curriculum.

7. *Principle of Variety.* It should always be remembered that to keep the children sitting the whole day long at the same place is in no way a wise procedure. As often as possible and convenient, the classes should change place. It has been stated that "Change of room, of seat, of posture is an antidote against weariness." Change of occupation is one of the best forms of rest. This applies to both students and teachers. The children should not be kept at the same subject or type of subjects or at subjects which have high fatigue element. Variety can be introduced in the following manner:

(a) No subject except in case of science practical should be kept for two consecutive periods as it is likely to cause monotony in the class.
(b) Variation in the subject should be aimed at in order to avoid boredom, e.g. Ancient History should not be followed by Medieval History.
(c) The same class should not, as far as possible, sit in the same room for the whole day.
(d) As far as possible, the same teacher should not have consecutive periods in the same class, except in the primary classes.
(e) If a subject is taught only two or three times a week, the periods should follow the intervals.
(f) The drill period, science practical and craft work, all provide for a change of the nature just referred to above.

8. *Principle of Free Periods for Teachers:* Free periods for the teachers should be provided so as to increase their efficiency and also for correction work. The free periods of the teachers should be scattered all over the week as far as possible. The language teachers should be given more free periods as they have to do a lot of correction work. In the period immediately preceding the science and other practical periods, the teachers concerned should be kept free to enable them to make the necessary preparation for the work to be undertaken in the coming period. On an average, teachers should be allowed two vacant periods per day.

9. *Principle of Play and Recreation:* Attention is to be given to provide for rest and recreation. The children should not be deprived of play. It affords them a good opportunity for enjoying fresh air outside and mixing freely with each other besides giving them time to have something for replenishing their energy. The recess period provides for rest and recreation and its duration should not be less than half an hour.

Provision for Radio and Television Broadcasts should also exist wherever possible.

Provision for various co-curricular activities should also be made in the time-table.

10. *Principle of Optimum Utilisation of School Building and Equipment.* The number of students in a school, the number of teachers for various subjects the number of rooms, laboratory (arrangement and furniture etc.,) also affect the framing of the school time-table. The time-table of a single teacher school will be quite different from that of other schools having many teachers. Sometimes, due to paucity of rooms, two classes are held in the same room. In such cases time-table should be arranged in a manner that when one class is busy at writing work, the other should be doing reading work and the like.

11. *Principle of Local Variations:* The hours of work and the duration of recess may be marginally adjusted to suit local conditions, i.e., distance of the school especially in rural areas, train timings, rainy days etc.

12. *Principle of Initiation:* Interesting programmes in the beginning of the day provide motivation to work enthusiastically.

13. *Principle of Elasticity.* The time-table should not be kept rigid but flexible and fluid. In view of the various difficulties that are likely to crop up, a fluid time-table is always desirable. Sometimes specific needs of many children have got to be met and it becomes inevitable to make some variations. The transfer of teachers also necessitates to bring about variation in the time-table. It is not necessary that the time-table should show the time allowed for the sub-branches of a subject. If we allot 12-periods to English per week, it should be left to the teacher to decide how many periods he shall give to grammar, translation and composition and how many to text.

We should always remember that the time-table is a tool and not the master and as such it should never be allowed to dictate procedures and methods.

11.4 PROBLEMS IN THE CONSTRUCTION OF THE TIME-TABLE

The construction of school time-table is a very challenging and delicate task. There are several compelling, competing and conflicting interests which are to be reconciled and solved amicably to the maximum extent.

Following are the major practical problems which are usually faced in the construction of the time-table.

1. Adherence to departmental regulations.
2. Different types of schools having variety of activities.
3. Lack of the sanctioned staff.
4. Amount of time available for various activities.
5. Incidence of fatigue.
6. Equal distribution of work among the staff.
7. Allotment of number of periods to different subjects.
8. Free or vacant periods for teachers.
9. Periods for correction work.
10. Periods for individual contacts with teachers and students.
11. Limitations of the availability class-rooms.
12. Reconciliation of periods allocated to different subjects.

13. Late coming of staff.
14. Unforeseen absence of some staff members.
15. Adjustment of time-table according to local variation.
16. Lack of play facilities.
17. Lack of library facilities.
18. Shortage of furniture.
19. Shortage of instructional material.

11.5 TYRANNY OF THE SCHOOL TIME-TABLE AND MODERN PROTESTS: FLEXIBILITY OF TIME-TABLE

Many modern psychologists and educationists think of the curriculum in terms of activities instead of subjects. They advocate the abolition of the time-table and want to liberate the child from its limitations.

According to modern psychology, each individual is unique in certain respects. Each child has his own nature, his own preferences and his own rate and speed of working. When he is left to himself, he continues what he starts. He leaves it only when he loses interest or feels fatigued. If he is interested in his work, he is alert and active. This interest gives him psychological satisfaction. But when work is regulated by a rigid time-table, a child might have to stop at the time when he has begun to take interest in a subject due to ringing of the bell or the other way that is to feel fatigued with the subject before the period is over. Since the period is meant for a particular subject, he has to continue even though he is disgusted. It is for this reason that some educational reformers would like to abolish time-table altogether. According to them if a child is left to himself, he would give more time to those subjects in which he is interested and give up those in which he is not interested to come back at a more favourable time.

Several modern educationists do not prescribe any collective time-table as they think that education must cater to the individual needs of the students. The very fact that no two individuals are alike, necessitates that to meet the specific needs of many children, different methods will have to be devised and accordingly a new conception of time-table will serve the required purpose.

Usually the modern protest is due to the following defects in the rigid time-table:

1. The co-curricular programme hardly finds any mention in the time-table.
2. By dividing the school day into uniform chunks of 35 to 45 minutes, allocating certain hours per week to the study of individual subjects, the time-table places pupils and teachers in a kind of lock-up.
3. A rigid time-table militates against the integration of various experiences.
4. A rigid time-table is a great hindrance in the total growth of the pupil's learning experiences.
5. In the conventional time-table, there is hardly any coordination of the efforts of teachers.
6. The conventional time-table does not provide time for teacher-pupil conferences.

The present emphasis is on methods like the Dalton Plan, the Project Method and the like which are a great departure from the time-honoured time-table. 'Contract' is the important feature of the Dalton Plan. Class as a unit of organisation remains but as a unit of instruction vanishes. Child promises to do the given work in a specific period which is usually a fortnight and works according to his intellectual attainments. No collective time-tables are formed in such methods of education. During this time, the child is free to work in whatever subjects he wishes, when he wishes and as long as he wishes. The only condition is that he must complete all the work in his various subjects before another contract can be undertaken. In this way, each child can progress in the school at his own rate.

Many programmes have been evolved in progressive schools which provide flexibility and the common features are:

First, the instructional material is organised into larger meaningful units built round the needs and interests of the students.

Secondly, there is provision for some long periods for practical activities.

Thirdly, there are certain "unassigned" periods in which the students may engage themselves in some worthwhile hobby.

Finally, there is no rigidity and the teachers are at liberty to alter the daily programme according to the special circumstances connected with the needs and interests of the students. Of course this has to be pre-planned and in consultation with other teachers so that they may accordingly modify their programmes.

Summing Up

The task of a time-table framer is very delicate and challenging. It involves the interlocking or weaving of different subjects, teachers and classes into the school fabric.

The time-table maker should be a man of vision and must be open-minded. He should take into consideration the human factor. He should not try to 'boss' over other teachers. A good time-table maker makes the optimum use of men and materials.

11.6 ROLE OF THE TEACHER AND THE TIME-TABLE

The most important role of the teacher is to implement the time-table as faithfully as he can, wherever possible, he may give advance intimation of his leave from the school or the class. The teacher must reach his class in time. In case he is held up on account of some reason, he should inform the students and ask the monitor to keep the class busy. The teacher should not leave the class before the allotted time.

The teacher should prepare his own time-table for taking up different areas of his subject allotted to him and accordingly ask the students to bring books/stationery etc.

It helps the teacher to plan his work scientifically.

It helps the teacher to bring order and system in his instructional duties.

It helps the teacher to develop the habit of punctuality as he knows that if he reaches the class late, the students may also imitate him.

The teacher may can arrange his teaching aids systematically before the start of the period.

He should be broadminded and accommodating. He must fully appreciate that there is no full-proof time-table which can satisfy all the teachers. Some adjustments have to be made.

11.7 TIME-TABLE AND ALLIED MATTERS AS SPECIFIED IN THE HIMACHAL EDUCATION CODE

Time-Table: A class time-table of six hours daily teaching and 54 periods in a week, showing the routine of study for each day of the week, shall be displayed in each class-room and a general time-table showing the work of all the teachers and classes and time-table of each teacher will be similarly displayed in the Head's room and in the staff room.

Students Attendance Register: (i) The roll shall be called at the time when the school opens, and again at the beginning of the second meeting after recess. No blank shall be left and no pupil's attendance shall be marked after the roll has been called. When a pupil leaves the school due to sickness, or any other cause before he has completed 2 hours of secular instruction, his attendance for that school meeting shall be cancelled.

(ii) Correct admission number should be entered in each class attendance register to avoid complications while issuing School Leaving Certificate. This must be got checked once in a year by the Head of the Institution and every month by the checker of the register.

Fine for Absence: Fine for absence will be as per government instructions issued from time to time. In any government school, name of a pupil, who is absent without leave for ten consecutive school days or is continuously on sick leave for three calendar months, shall be struck off the roll and he shall not be readmitted without payment of re-admission fee as per rates applicable.

Late-Fee Fine: A late-fee fine at the rates as made applicable from time to time shall be charged from the students. If the dues remain unpaid for 10 consecutive school days, the student's name will be struck off the rolls for non-payment of dues.

Leave Application: Leave of absence may be granted by the Head of the Institution and also by the class teacher (subject to maximum of three days by class teacher) on written application signed or attested by the parents or guardian.

Monitor: One student in each class should be elected by that class/ nominated by the class teacher to act as a Monitor (representative) and definite duties should be assigned to him/her in connection with the discipline and proper working of that class. He/She should be given due regard.

Transfer of Certificate: (i) A pupil leaving one school may not be admitted to another without the production of a transfer certificate in the prescribed form, issued by the last school attended. The guardians of the ward may be guided to get the School Leaving Certificate(SLC) countersigned by the District Education Officer, if he/she intends to go out of Himachal Pradesh.

(ii) In case the SLC is not issued during the month in which the name of the student is struck off, late certificate fee at the prescribed rate will be charged.

(iii) When one SLC has been issued in favour of a student and a duplicate SLC is demanded the prescribed fee is to be charged.

The name of mother along with the name of father will be recorded in future in all educational documents, e.g., admission forms, examination forms and certificates to be issued.

Misbehaviour: Misbehaviour should be understood to include unpunctuality, irregular attendance, idleness, use of bad language and slovenly habits as well as breach of school rules and moral delinquencies.

(See also Chapter 5 for Allotment of Periods etc.)

12

School Records and Registers

12.1 INDISPENSABILITY OF SCHOOL RECORDS

Proper maintenance, accuracy and effective use of records go a long way in the efficient working of any institution or organisation and school is no exception. There is no doubt that the success of a school in each of its elements and its totality depends to a large measure on the scientific and systematic manner in which records are kept. On account of the importance of school records and its indispensability the school office is often called the "king-pin of the enterprise."

12.2 NEED OF SCHOOL RECORDS

Records are needed for the following purposes:

1. Legal Requirements. School records and reports are used to satisfy the legal requirements of the State Education Department, Examination Board, etc.

2. Relationships with Home and the Community. School is a social institutional answerable to the parents, the managing committee, the department and the public in general and the records kept by the school help to understand the problems and limitations of the school.

3. Records Essential for the All-round Growth of the Child. School is entrusted with the task of the all-round development of the personality of each child and to discharge this function it is absolutely essential to keep a record of his day-to-day growth and development.

4. Financial Requirements of the School. The school has to supply a variety of data to justify its financial needs. Financial grants are sanctioned for equipment, library books and furniture, etc., by the Education Department, Local Bodies and School Management Committee as the case may be.

5. Records and Grants-in-Aid. Sometimes certain conditions are laid down by the department for the payment of grants-in-aid to schools. This requires the supply of certain facts and statistics.

6. Educational Reform. Educational reforms can be undertaken only when the school records provide comprehensive data to those who are asked to shoulder the responsibility of educational reforms.

7. Assessment of an Institution. School records are helpful to assess the progress and needs of particular locality.

8. Cooperation of Parents. To make the parents interested in school work and in their wards, schools send progress reports from time to time. This helps in establishing closer contacts between the home and the school.

9. Examination and Evaluation Needs. Promotions of students are made on their performance which is reflected through the records of tests and examinations.

10. Guidance and Counselling. Records of performance of students on psychological tests and measurement prove very helpful in the counselling process.

11. Future Reference. It is only through records that the history of the school can be written. Past records may also help in improving the tone of the school and its performance also.

12.3 NEED OF SCHOOL RECORDS FOR THE SCHOOL, CLASS-ROOM TEACHERS AND PUPILS

L.M. Camberlain and L.W. Kidred give the following advantages of the school records:

Need of Records for the School

1. To locate each pupil quickly.
2. To make available the significant facts about each pupil.
3. To explain and remove undesirable conditions.
4. To find if all legal requirements are met.
5. To determine if any administrative or other changes are desirable.
6. To make important investigations and case studies possible.
7. To find if school funds are adequate and wisely expanded.
8. To reduce retardation and failure to a minimum.

Need of Records for the Class-room Teachers

1. To determine what work a pupil is capable of doing.
2. To provide learning activities suitable to each doing.
3. To formulate a basis for the intelligent guidance of pupils.
4. To explain the behaviour characteristics or unhappy conditions of any pupil.
5. To make possible the development of unusual capacities or exceptional talents.
6. To identify and make proper provision for the mentally slow children.
7. To make assignments to committee work.
8. To make periodic reports correctly and in time.
9. To be properly informed when conferring with parents and others about a pupil.
10. To make entries in the cumulative record card.

Need of Records for the Pupil

1. To receive fair consideration in his classification.
2. To do his best in making a good record.
3. To make progress in accordance with his ability.
4. To secure development of his natural capabilities.
5. To secure transfer of correct information to other schools when desired.
6. To receive proper adjustment and guidance.

12.4 MAINTENANCE AND ESSENTIAL REQUISITES OF SCHOOL RECORDS

1. Accuracy. All information contained in the school records should be accurate, well-organised, pertinent and justified solely on grounds of the contribution it can make either directly or indirectly to the welfare of the students.

2. Completeness. Data about a child should be gathered continuously, should be kept up-to-date and include information that reveals his true condition at any given time. In the case of his transfer from one school to another, his records should follow him.

3. Utility. Record system should provide for collecting and recording information that is relevant and useful in working with children.

4. Comprehensiveness. In view of the emphasis on the harmonious development of the child, different kinds of records will have to be kept. All members of the staff have a responsibility for keeping records peculiar to their field of activity.

5. Easy Maintenance. The records and reports should be easily maintained and should require a minimum of time and energy for making entries.

6. Systematic Maintenance. School records should be maintained and located where they will be used to the greatest advantage by staff personnel. Separate files or note-books should be kept for each separate record or report.

7. Availability. School records should always be available in the school premises and school not be removed from the school premises for the purpose of scrutiny.

A record system then should be designed carefully, kept efficiently, located strategically and should contain all information that is essential to the achievement of the aim for which it was established.

12.5 MODE OF KEEPING RECORDS

1. Prepare a stock list of registers maintained in the school.
2. Write distinctly the following particulars on the outer cover of each register.
   (a) The name of the school.
   (b) The serial number of the register.
   (c) The name of the register.
   (d) The number of volume.
   (e) The number of pages of the volume.
   (f) The opening and closing dates.
3. Number the pages consecutively either in the red ink or with a number machine when a register is opened.
4. Keep the register tidy. Avoid overwriting.
5. Make all the entries in ink.
6. Get each cutting attested by the Head.
7. Do not open a new volume of a register every year, if the previous volume contains some blank pages.
8. Fill up every column provided in a prescribed register and do not leave any blank space between entries.

School Office—As a general rule every higher secondary or senior secondary school must have one separate room for office. The office-in-charge must be a person trained for the type of work to be done in schools. The head must be relieved of the mechanical details of the office routine if he is to make the best use of his abilities and to discharge his functions of guidance and counselling and supervising. The school office should be spacious and well-ventilated.

12.6 BROAD CLASSIFICATION OR TYPE OF SCHOOL RECORDS

1. Accounts
2. Correspondence
3. Educational
4. Equipment
5. Financial
6. General or Miscellaneous
7. Service
8. Vocational or Productive

1. Accounts Registers. (i) Cashbook for daily receipts and expenditure, (ii) General Ledger or Classified Abstract of the monthly totals, (iii) Register of pay bill and (iv) Remittance register.

2. Correspondence. (i) 'From' and 'To' Registers, (ii) Peon Book, (iii) Memo Book, (iv) File of Departmental Orders and Circulars and (v) Register of Casual Leave Granted.

3. Educational. (i) Pupil's Attendance Register, (ii) Teachers' Attendance Register, (iii) Time-tables' Records, (iv) Examinations' Results Record, (v) Monthly Progress Register, (vi) Private Tuition Register, (vii) Public Examination Register, (viii) Register of Corporal Punishment, (ix) Teacher's Diaries, (x) Cumulative Records, (xi) Staff participation in Oriental Courses and (xii) Honours Roll.

4. Equipment. (i) Stock Book of Furniture and School Appliances, (ii) Library Catalogue, (iii) Accession Register, (iv) Issue Book, (v) Register of Newspapers and Magazines received, (vi) Stock and Issue Register of Sports Materials.

5. Financial. (i) Contingent Register, (ii) Acquittance Roll, (iii Contingent Order Book, (iv) Fee Collection Register, (v) Abstract Register of Fees, (vi) Bill Register, (vii) Register of Donations, (viii) Register of Scholarship, and (ix) Boys' Fund Registers.

6. General Records. (i) School Calendar, (ii) Log Book, (iii) Visitor's Book, (iv) Service Registers, (v) Admission and Withdrawal Register, (vi) Transfer Certificate Book, (vii) General Order Book, (viii) Casual Leave Register and (ix) Staff Meeting.

7. Service Matters. (i) Personal Files, and (ii) Service Condition rules, etc.

8. Vocational/Socially Useful Productive Work: (i) Craft Work, (ii) Farm Work, (iii) Producer's Register, (iv) Art Work Record, etc.

The list is no way a comprehensive and complete one. It includes only those registers which are commonly used. Additions will have to be made to suit the needs and requirements of individual schools. A few of the important school records, relating mainly to the educational aspect of school administration are described below:

12.7 DESCRIPTION OF SOME IMPORTANT SCHOOL REGISTERS AND RECORDS

Teacher's Diary

Meaning of a Teacher's Diary. By a teacher's diary, we mean the diary in which a teacher maintains the broad outline of the teaching-learning records of a year.

Contents of a Teacher's Diary. In general, following types of information is included in a teacher's diary.

1. Details of the syllabi of the subjects the teacher teaches in different classes.
2. Methodology of the teaching-learning adopted in each lesson he teaches daily.
3. Daily lesson notes or main points.
4. Students names and their addresses.
5. Significant details about children under his charge.
6. Names of the gifted children and their specific achievements and problems.
7. Particulars of weak students and steps taken to improve them.
8. Particulars of problem children.
9. Parents contacted.
10. Anything special.

Importance of Teacher's Diary

1. It is helpful to the teacher in planning his daily work.
2. It assists the teacher in bringing order in work.
3. It develops motivation in work.
4. It is helpful in making lesson effective.
5. It is a constant reminder to the teacher that the syllabus must be covered according to schedule.
6. It enables him to prepare aids before the lesson is taken up in the class.
7. It provides an opportunity to the head to provide guidance to the teacher after going through the diary.

The head can evaluate the day-to-day work of the teacher on this bases.

12.8 CUMULATIVE RECORDS

Meaning of Cumulative Records—Cumulative records are those records which relate to the progress and achievements of a student for a number of years. These records are usually kept in a cumulative record card which contains the results of different assessments and judgements held from time to time during the course of study of a student. A cumulative record is an account of the child's history in the school. It begins as soon as the child enters the school and continues till he leaves the school for good. Generally it covers three consecutive years. It contains information regarding all aspects of the life of the child—his physical, mental, social, moral and psychological. It seeks to give as comprehensive a picture as possible of the personality of a child. "Periodically the significant information gathered on students through the use of various techniques—tests, inventories, questionnaires, observations, interviews, case studies, case conferences and the like—should be assembled in summary form on a cumulative record", writes Jane Warters.

In the words of W.C. Allen: "The Cumulative Record is defined as a record of information concerned with appraisal of the individual pupil—usually kept on a card—kept in one place."

Need for School Record. The modern type of cumulative record was first made available in 1928 by the American Council on Education. The need of such a record was felt in view of the inadequate information that was contained in the various forms that were available. The Secondary Education Commission has made the following observation regarding the need for school records: "Neither the external examination nor the internal examination, singly or together, can give a correct and complete picture of a pupil's all-round progress at any particular stage of his education; yet it is important for us to assess this in order to determine his future course of study or his future vocation. For this purpose a proper system of school records should be maintained for every pupil indicating the work done by him in the school from day to day, month to month, term to term and year to year. Such a school record will present a clear and continuous statement of the attainments of the child in different intellectual pursuits throughout the successive stages of his education. It will also contain a progressive evaluation of development in other directions of less importance, such as the growth of his interests, aptitudes, and personality traits, his social adjustments, the practical and social activities in which he takes part. In other words, it will give a complete career".

Advantages of the Cumulative Record

1. A good record contributes to guidance work in general in the following ways: (a) By providing a sound basis for understanding the individual, (b) By showing the significant experiences of individual, (c) By indicating his readiness for new experiences, (d) By pointing out the routes to new goals, (e) By pointing out his strengths and weaknesses.

2. It helps curriculum revision by revealing the needs of the students.

3. It helps in the improvement of the methods of teaching by revealing the needs of the students.

4. It provides a helpful basis for educational and vocational placement.

5. It is an aid in the search for talent. It assists the teacher to find out students who are gifted in abstract verbal ability, science, the arts and social relations.

6. It helps the teacher to find out the slow learners and accordingly he suggests measures.

7. It serves as a link between the teacher and the parents. The teachers find it convenient to write letters of descriptive reports to the parents on the basis of the information contained in the record.

8. The school authorities can make suitable recommendations to the prospective employers and college admission officers.

9. The cumulative records help in furnishing sufficient data for reports to the various authorities engaged in the student welfare field.

10. At the time of the transfer of a student from one school to another it helps the new school authorities to know about the child and to avoid mistakes and to facilitate the adjustment of the child to the new environment.

Writing about cumulative record Jane Warters rightly says, "It aids teachers in the study of the individual by making it possible for them to understand his present through an analysis of his past, by furnishing clues regarding the cause of his behaviour difficulties and failures, and by disclosing his strengths and weaknesses".

Maintenance of the Record. The maintenance of the cumulative record card should begin when the student enters in school and should follow the student from class to class within a school and from school to school as he continues his progress.

The class teacher will maintain the cumulative record. In view of the fact that he spends much time with the students, he will be in a better position to judge the child from different aspects. He will maintain a diary or note-book in which he will note down from time to time his observations about his students. At the end of the year, he will make the necessary entries in the cumulative record card. It is very desirable that he consults his colleagues who also know the pupils. These entries should be made after careful consideration. All teachers should share in the work of collecting and reporting information on students.

Methods of Popularising this System. The use of cumulative record in our educational institutions is still in its infancy. It cannot be imposed upon the teachers. The teacher must be familiarised with the advantages of this system. Talks and refresher courses should be organised for this purpose. Faculty meetings should be organised to discuss the nature of the information that these cards should contain. It must be remembered that the maintenance of cumulative records is a cooperative affair in which administrators, counsellors, teachers, clerical staff, students and their parents must participate and all of these must be convinced of the importance of such records. Teachers and counsellors must be provided with time to make necessary entries. The records should be placed at a place where all may use them easily.

Forms of Cumulative Record Card. It is used in various forms such as card, sheet, printed folders, cards or sheets contained in an envelope, booklet or some combination of these forms.

Significance of the Cumulative Record

Writing about cumulative record, Jane Warters rightly says, "It aids teachers in the study of the individual by making it possible for them to understand his present through an analysis of his past by furnishing clues regarding the cause of his behaviour difficulties and failures, and by disclosing his strengths and weaknesses".

12.9 CONTENTS OF THE CUMULATIVE RECORD CARD

1. Personal data.
2. Schools attended.

3. Family history.
4. Physical data.
5. Medical report.
6. Attendance.
7. Psychological report.
8. Scholastic report.
9. Performance in co-curricular activities and sociability.
10. Position of responsibility held.
11. Vocational information.
12. Personality traits.
13. Specific remarks by the Head of the School.

A Specimen of the Cumulative Record Card

1. Personal Data

Name of Pupil .... Date of Birth ....
Father's Name .... Occupation ....
Guardian's Name .... Occupation ....
Relationship with the child Address ....

2. Schools Attended

Sl. No.	*Name of the School*	*Month and year of joining*	*Class of joining*	*Month and year of leaving*	*Class from which left*	*Reason for leaving*
1. 2.						

3. Family History

Year	*200...*	*200...*	*200...*
Type of family (whether joint or unitary) No. of members in the family Economic status of the family Child's position in the family (whether only child, eldest or youngest child, his number among the siblings) Any other significant factor			

4. Physical Data

Year	*Height*	*Weight*	*Chest Measurement*			*General Condition*
			Normal	*Expd.*	*Contrd.*	

5. Medical Report

		Any serious illness
200...		
200...		
200...		

6. Attendance

Year	*Possible*	*Actual*	*Nature of long absence, if any, with reasons*
200...			
200...			
200...			
200...			

7. Psychological Report if any and Results of Intelligence and Aptitude Tests

200...	
200...	
200...	

8. Scholastic Achievement

Subjects	*Class........*		*Class.................*		*Class.............*	
	Year..........		*Year.................*		*Year.............*	
	Half yearly	*Annu-ally*	*Half yearly*	*Annu-ally*	*Half yearly*	*Annu-ally*
English						
Hindi						
Sanskrit						
Mathematics/Arith and domestic science						
Physics						
Chemistry						
Economics						
History						
Geography						
Commerce						
Drawing						
Art						
Craft						
Physical Education						
Agriculture						
Practicals						

(Contd.)

(*Contd.*)

Subjects	*Class........*		*Class.................*		*Class.............*	
	Year..........		*Year.................*		*Year.............*	
	Half yearly	*Annu-ally*	*Half yearly*	*Annu-ally*	*Half yearly*	*Annu-ally*
Totals						
Position in the class						
No. of students in the class						

9. Performance in Co-curricular Activities

Activities	*Average grade of the child for each performance throughout a year*		
	200...........	*200.........*	*200...........*
Sports and Games			
Personal Hygiene			
Literacy Activities			
Cultural Activities			
Social Service			

10. Position of Responsibility Held or Merits Obtained, if any

Activities	*Year............*	*Year............*	*Year............*
Studies			
Games			
Bal Sabha			
Scouting			
Social Service			
Any other			

11. Vocational Information

Year	*Vocational Ambitions of the student*	*Counsellor's Report*
200.... 200.... 200....	....	....

12. Personality Traits

Traits	*200.........*	*200.........*	*200.........*
Truthfulness			
Honesty			
Courtesy			
Cooperativeness			
Industry			
Self-confidence			
Emotional stability			
Initiative			
Leadership			
Sociability			
Reliability			
Signature of the class teacher			
Signature of the Head			

12.10 CHARACTERISTICS OF A CUMULATIVE RECORD

1. Validity. The facts recorded must be authentic. It is better not to write any information than to give untrue information.

2. Comprehensiveness. A cumulative record should contain as complete and comprehensive information as possible.

3. Accuracy. The information in the record should be accurately recorded from original sources.

4. Objectivity. Personal opinions and judgements should be reduced to the minimum.

5. Economy of Space. The criterion of a good cumulative record form is that the maximum possible information is contained in the space available.

6. Recency. Any piece of information should be recorded as soon as it is obtained.

7. Outcome of a Cooperative Enterprise. It should be the result of group thinking.

8. Evaluation. It should be evaluated every year so as to know how far does it serve the purpose.

Problems in the Maintenance and Uses of Cumulative Record Cards

1. Who Should Maintain the Records?

(a) *Functions of the Class Teacher.* The records may be kept by the class teacher and he should be responsible for getting the necessary entries made. Class teacher's responsibility is greater as he will not only ensure correct and up-to-date entries but also act as a liaison between the pupil and the subject teachers, and between the pupil and the parents.

(b) *Function of Special Teachers and Teacher In-charge of Various Activities.* Their function is to assess the child's attainment from time to time, to record the same and to pass it to the class teacher.

2. Where to Keep Them?

This is a very formidable problem. Arrangements will have to be made so that is easily accessible to the teachers. If possible, it may be kept by the class teacher in the safe custody otherwise it may be kept in the Principal's Office. However, in either case, its contents should remain confidential.

3. When to Fill-up This Card?

Entries in the card should be made at the time of a particular event or test. It is advisable that every teacher should have a small notebook to record his observations at the time of the incident about a particular pupil. He may record the significant entries according to his convenience. As a rule, other teachers may not record the entries on the card itself. They would pass on the entries to the class teacher. This would enable the class teacher to maintain the records neatly and scientifically. Too many hands may spoil the beauty and the neatness of the card.

4. How to Check the Maintenance?

The Principal should check after every three months that the entries are regularly made and the records kept up-to-date. He may assign this work to one of his colleagues but must sign the record himself.

5. What should be the Design of Record Card?

Usually three types of card are being maintained in schools.

(a) Folder type,

(b) File type, and

(c) Envelope type.

6. The Problem of New Admissions and Migrations

The record should move with the student in case he is transferred from one school to another. It should go with the pupil from class to class and from school to school.

7. How to Help the Teacher in Discharging the Function?

(i) Adequate importance should be given to these records in internal assessment.

(ii) The employers may also give due consideration to these records.

(iii) Teachers should be trained in the maintenance of these records.

(iv) The state authorities should get prepared model forms of records for the schools.

(v) This work should be done by the teachers on the last working day of the month. There may not be any teaching work on that day. If we do not give adequate time to the teacher to fill up these cards, they will fill up these mechanically.

(vi) Adequate provision should be made for the safe custody of these cards.

(vii) The supervisor should inspect the maintenance of these records at the time of the annual inspection of the school.

Teachers' Attendance Register. This register shows the daily attendance of the teachers in a school, their time of arrival and departure, leave taken by them, holidays and their nature. It is generally placed in the Head Office. Every teacher must sign this register everyday when he comes into the school in the morning and leave at the termination of the school day.

Pupils' Attendance Register. Each class has its own register showing the names of the pupils on the rolls of a class. As far as possible, only one attendance register should be kept by any one teacher. Attendance should be marked both for the beginning of the school day in the morning and its end towards the evening. Ink or ball pen should be used for marking attendance. No blanks should be left. It is also not a good practice to put dots. The students are to be marked as 'leave' or 'sick' only when their leave applications are sanctioned by the competent authority. Holidays should be indicated in red ink. The name of a student may be struck off the rolls by the head of the school on account of (a) Non-payment of fees and other dues for 20 days after the last day for payment. This is not applicable in case of students of Class VIII and below, studying in government or aided schools or in schools run or aided by the appropriate authority except where such students have attained the age of fourteen years, (b) Continued absence without leave for six consecutive days by a student who has attained the age of fourteen years. (c) In the case of absence of any student who has not attained the age of fourteen years, from a school without leave for six consecutive days, the head of the school shall intimate such absence to the parents or guardian of such student.

Notes—(1) The above mentioned rules are contained in Delhi School Education Act and Rules.

(2) There may be different rules in States.

The reason for this action should be given in the remarks column against the name of the boy or girl and the necessary information should be given to the school clerk. The entries thus made should be got signed by the Head simultaneously both in the attendance register and withdrawal register. On the last working day of each month, the summary at the end of each page in the register should be carefully prepared and the register got checked by the teacher deputed for this purpose and then got countersigned by the Head. All amounts received by way of fees and funds must be entered in the register immediately on their receipt.

Truants should be noted particularly and their cases reported to the Head and the parents concerned.

Leave application for long sick periods should be supported by medical certificates.

12.11 ADMISSION AND WITHDRAWAL REGISTER

This is one of the most important school registers. The head of the institution is personally responsible for its sanctity. According to departmental rules, it is to be kept permanently, and therefore, it should be specially got bound and arrangements made for its safe custody. Entries should be made as soon as a pupil is admitted or at any rate before the close of the day. Every admission or re-admission made in any part of the year should be entered in it. Successive numbers should be given to the pupils on admission. Each child should retain this number as long as he remains in the school. A new entry should be made if a pupil leaves a school and rejoins it with a leaving certificate issued by another school. This register contains the following information: (a) The number of the child in the register. (b) Date of admission or re-admission. (c) Name of the child in full. (d) The exact date of birth of the child. (e) Name and address of the parent or guardian. (f) The class to which admitted. (g) The date of leaving and the class in which the child was at that time.

Special care is to be taken in recording the date of birth of every child. The entry once made should not be altered unless authorised by competent authority and that too in writing. The entries are to be made both in words as well as in figures. The exact day of birth is very important as it is also required as evidence in important matters.

12.12 STOCK OF NON-CONSUMABLE ARTICLES

All items of a more or less permanent nature bought and received in the school are entered in the property register. It contains the name of the article, its price and the ordering authority for its purchase.

The Head should get the stock of equipment checked once a year. Room-wise property list facilitates the work of checking. Proper checking of the equipment has a very good advantage. It helps the Head to know which article of equipment or furniture stands in needs of repairs or is missing.

Nothing should be struck off the register without the permission of the Head who is generally competent to do so.

Ledger. It is a necessary complement of the cash-book. All entries made in the cash-book are carried to the ledger in their respective accounts. It facilitates the preparation of monthly and annual accounts. It is also helpful in controlling future financial commitments.

Contingency Register. Every Head is generally provided with a contingency advance money which is spent for day-to-day expenses on petty items such as purchase of office stationery, postage, repairs to building and furniture etc. Details of such expenditure are entered in the contingency register. All entries in this register are supported by proper receipts which are placed in a separate file.

Boys' Fund Register. The Head of an institution is the sole in-charge of the boys' funds. He is responsible for keeping a regular account of the same and rendering it to the departmental auditors and the inspecting staff.

All income and expenditure pertaining to boys' fund should be entered regularly in the Boys' Fund Register.

It will not be out of place to mention that most of the problems in our educational institutions owe their origin to the use of these funds. Undue funds charged from the students lead to indiscipline. Wrong use of funds leads them to suspect the integrity of the authorities. Unfortunately the present trend is to use funds for all sundry purposes. A wise head will make a very judicious use of these funds. He will take his students into confidence and spend these funds through their committees working under the guidance of teachers.

12.13 ACCOUNTS AND FINANCIAL RECORDS

Cash-book. It contains a record of all money transactions that are being carried through from day-to-day in the school. The credit side of the cash-book shows all the monies received by the school from different sources, e.g., donations, grants-in-aid, fees, boys' funds etc., and its debit side indicates all the payments made, e.g., salaries paid, deposits made in the post office or bank, contingent expenditure incurred, etc.

Cash-book should be well-bound and the pages should be carefully numbered in print.

Cash-book should be written up daily. The entry relating to each item of receipt and expenditure should be made immediately at the time of transaction.

As far as possible, the cash balance should be immediately deposited in the post office or bank. Daily balancing of the cash-book avoids chances of errors.

12.14 MISCELLANEOUS RECORDS

Service Register. The register contains the record of the official life of every employee working in the institution. On the basis of this record matters concerning promotions, leave, superannuation, etc., are determined. It is therefore very important to make correct and complete entries in it. The entries in the service register should tally with other records. The date and the number of the appointment order should be noted in the case of the first appointment and in the case of transfers. No change in the date of birth is permissible except with the permission of the competent authority. All cases of suspension, or other punishment should be noted along with the reasons and the authority awarding the punishment. All questions relating to previous service should be settled immediately. Service registers should not be handed over to the persons concerned on their transfer from one school to another but should be sent to the officer responsible for the custody of the registers. Every Head should make it a point to ensure that the registers are free from faults of omission and erroneous insertions.

School Calendar. The school calendar is very conducive to the better and more systematic organisation of school activities. It is drawn up at the beginning of each school session. If possible all schools in the same area should have a uniform school year so that the migrating children are not handicapped and put to troubles. It should contain the following items of information:

(i) All types of holidays.

(ii) Dates for the submission of monthly, quarterly, half-yearly and annual reports and returns.

(iii) Dates of public and school examinations.

(iv) Dates of Meeting of School Committees, Teachers' Associations, Local Excursions, School Tournament, etc.
(v) Schedule of monthly tests.

The Log Book. In our schools it is devoted to the remarks of the inspecting staff in relation to the school and the members of the school staff.

Progress Report. A Progress Report serves three important purposes as given below:

(a) A Progress Report helps the parents to know about the progress of their children in the curricular as well as co-curricular work and thereby enables them to take necessary steps to improve the performance of their children.
(b) It serves as a link between the home and the school which is very important for the progress of the children.
(c) It has a psychological effect on the children who have a natural desire to please their parents. They try to put forth consistent and strenuous efforts to show good results and to secure the appreciation of both the parents as well as the teachers.

12.15 RECORDS AND REGISTERS AS PRESCRIBED BY THE HIMACHAL EDUCATION CODE

Record Keeping. Every school must keep proper records in the form of registers, files and charts to determine how well the school is contributing to students welfare and for preserving educational information. The following types of registers shall be maintained:

1. (A) Cash Registers:

(i) Cash-book [T.R.4 Treasury Rules 77(i)].
(ii) Register of contingent charges (T.R.29 Tr. Rules 299).
(iii) FR-4 Register (Expenditure Register).
(iv) Bill (Control) Register (Form T.R.28-A).
(v) Permanent Advance Register (Rule 90 of GFR & T.R. 502).
(vi) Register of Advance and Recoveries.
(vii) Register of Festival Advance.
(viii) Events Register.
(ix) Treasury Challan Register.
(x) Register of Income Tax Recoveries.
(xi) Telephone Rent Bill Register.
(xii) Telephone Trunk Call Register.
(xiii) Stamp Account Register.
(xiv) Acquittance Roll Register (sometimes records of acquittance are mentioned in the office copy of the bill concerned).
(xv) G.F.R. Ledger Book.
(xvi) Budget Control Register.

1. (B) Other Cash Registers:

(i) Amalgamated Fund Register.
(ii) Building Fund Register.
(iii) Fine Fund Register.
(iv) Fees/Funds Accounts Register.
(v) Medical Reimbursement Register.
(vi) T.A. Bill Register.

2. Establishment and Class Registers, etc.:

(i) Establishment Check Register.
(ii) Staff Attendance Register.
(iii) Staff Casual Leave and Earned Leave Account Register.
(iv) Order Book.
(v) Log Book Remarks Register.
(vi) Staff Meeting Minutes Register.
(vii) Faculty Meeting Minutes Register.
(viii) Institution Calendar Register.
(ix) Diary Register.
(x) Dispatch Register.
(xi) Peon Book.
(xii) Form of application for admission of students in school.
(xiii) Admission and Withdrawal Register.
(xiv) Class Attendance Register.
(xv) Terminal & Final Assessment/Examination Register.
(xvi) School Leaving Register/Transfer Certificate Book.
(xvii) Pupils Scholarship Register.
(xviii) Prize Distribution Register.
(xix) School Statistics Register.
(xx) General Stock Register (Consumable Articles).
(xxi) General Stock Register (Non-consumable).
(xxii) Science Articles Stock Register (Non-consumable).
(xxiii) Science Articles Stock Register (Consumable).
(xxiv) Sports Articles Stock Register.
(xxv) Library Books Register.
(xxvi) Misbehaviour, Conduct Register.

Note: Relevant Registers/Records from among these shall be kept by all middle schools also.

12.16 SPECIMEN OF SCHOOL RECORDS

1. Specimen of Simple Progress Report

Name of the School ....

Month ....

Student's Progress Records for the Term

Students name.. Class..

Admission name .... Date of birth..............................

Father's Name .... Address of Parent/Guardian ....

Academic

Subject	*Max Marks*	*Marks obtained or Grade*	*Position*	*Subject Teacher's Remarks*
Regional Language				
Second Language				
English				
Elementary Maths				
General Science				
Social Studies				
Art/Domestic Science				
Craft Training				
Work Experience				
Diversified Courses				
1.				
2.				
3.				
4.				
5.				
Total				

Co-curricular Activities and Citizenship

Practical Activities	*Remarks*
Games and Sports	
Social Behaviour	
Cleanliness	
Attendance	
Conduct	
Hand-Writing	
Home Work	
Health	

Class Teacher's Signature Principal/Headmaster's Signature

Guardian/Parent's Signature

(*Note:* Type of progress report depends on the nature of activities in the school.)

SPECIMEN OF REGISTERS

2. ADMISSION AND WITHDRAWAL REGISTER

Date of Admission	Admission No.	Name of the Students	Father's/ Guardians Name	Mother's Name	Date of Birth (In Words and Figures)	Enrolment No./ Registration No.	Occupation	Present Residential Address	Tele-phone No.	Tribe or Caste	Class to Which Admitted	Grade or Tuition Fee	Caution Money Taken	Class of Withdrawal	Date of Withdrawal	Remarks

3. DAILY CLASS ATTENDANCE REGISTER

Sl. No.	Admission No.	Class ……………. Section…………… Name of Scholar	DAYS OF THE MONTH																											
			1		2		3		4		5		6		7		8		9		10		11		12		13		…		31	
			M 1	A 2	M 1	A 2	M 1	A 2	M 1	A 2	M 1	A 2	M 1	A 2	M 1	A 2	M 1	A 2	M 1	A 2	M 1	A 2	M 1	A 2	M 1	A 2	M 1	A 2	…	…	M 1	A 2

No. of Scholars at the beginning of the month …………..
No. of Scholars at the close of the month …………..
No. of Scholars struck of the rolls …………..
New Admissions …………..
No. of School Meetings during the month …………..
No. of School Meetings from 1st April …………..
Total No. of attendances during the month …………..
Average daily attendances during the month …………..

Total No. of Students on roll …………..

Sch. Cast……… OBC ……… Others …… …..

FEE STATEMENT	BOYS	GIRLS	TOTAL	AMOUNT(Rs.)
Scholar 1st Grade	…………	…………	…………	…………
" 2nd Grade	…………	…………	…………	…………
" Half Rate (Poverty)	…………	…………	…………	…………
" " for Other causes	…………	…………	…………	…………
" Free (Poverty)	…………	…………	…………	…………
" Free (Teacher's Son)	…………	…………	…………	…………
" Free for other causes	…………	…………	…………	…………
Sc.Fee Half/Full Fee	…………	…………	…………	…………
Phy./Chem.Ha./Full F.	…………	…………	…………	…………
Biology Half/Full Fee	…………	…………	…………	…………
Music Half/Full Fee	…………	…………	…………	…………
Painting Half/Full Fee	…………	…………	…………	…………
SUPW Half/Full Fee	…………	…………	…………	…………
D.Sc./Scout H./F. Fee	…………	…………	…………	…………
Others Half/Full Fee	…………	…………	…………	…………
TOTAL	…………	…………	…………	…………

SUBJECT-WISE DETAILS	NAME OF TEACHER	NO. OF SCH. ON ROLL
English	………………	………………
Hindi	………………	………………
Mathematics	………………	………………
Phs. Education	………………	………………
Sanskrit	………………	………………
………………	………………	………………
………………	………………	………………
………………	………………	………………

.... School FOR THE MONTH OF ....

4. TEACHER'S ATTENDACE REGISTER

NAME																								
DESIGNA - TION																								
DATE	ARR.	SIGNA.		DEP.	SIGNA.		ARR.	SIGNA.		DEP.	SIGNA.		ARR.	SIGNA.		DEP.	SIGNA.		ARR.	SIGNA.		DEP.	SIGNA.	

LEAVES TAKEN

	Sick	Casu.	Priv.	Ear. L	H/P. L.	Total	Sick	Casu.	Priv.	Ear. L	H/P.L.	Total	Sick	Casu.	Priv.	Ear. L	H/P.L.	Total	Sick	Casu.	Priv.	Ear. L	H/P. L.	Total
This Mon.																								
Previous																								
TOTAL																								
Balance																								
TOTAL																								
Tea's.Ini.																								
Special L.																								
Principal's Remarks																								

5. TEACHER DIARY REGISTER

Week Date	Forecast	Amount Taught	Class & Subject	Notes & Observation by the Teacher	Remarks by Principal or Inspector
Date	Home Task for the Week				

6. STOCK REGISTER (FOR CONSUMABLE ARTICLES)

Name of the Institution .... Page No. ....

Name of the Article ....

Date of Receipt	Quantity of Number	Value (Rs.)	Progressive Total	Quantity Consumer	How Consumed	Signature of the receiving authority	Balance	Signature of the Head of Institution	Remarks

7. STOCK REGISTER
Non-Consumable

Name of the Institution .... Page No. ....

Name of the Article ....

S. No.	Date of Receipt	Quantity Received	Description of Articles nclu. specification and make	Condition old or new	Value (Rs.)	Progressive Total	No. Disposed	Manner of Disposal	Amount realised (Rs.)	Balance Qty.	Signature of Head of Institu.	Remarks

8. DESPATCH REGISTER

Name of the Institution .... Page No. ....

S. No.	Date	Name & Address	Place	Subject	File Head./No.	Stamps Received (Rs.)	Stamps Affixed (Rs.)	Stamps Balance (Rs.)	Remarks

9. CASH BOOK

RECEIPTS For the month of _____ PAYMENTS

Date	Particulars	Ledger Folio	Cash (Rs.)	Bank (Rs.)		Date	Particulars	Ledger Folio	Cash (Rs.)	Bank (Rs.)

10. LEDGER

Date	Particulars	C.B. Folio	Debit Rs.	Credit Rs.	Dr. or Cr.	Balance Rs.

....School

11. AQUITTANCE ROLL/PAY BILL

for the Month of ....

S. No.	Name	Designation	Monthly Pay		No. of Days	Basic Pay		Stagnating Pay/Personal Pay		D.A.		H.R.A.		C.C.A.		Interim Relief		Teaching Allowance		Medical	
			Rs.	P.		Rs.	P.	Rs.	P.	Rs.	P.	Rs.	P.	Rs.	P.	Rs.	P.	Rs.	P.	Rs.	P.

Washing Allowance		Total		DEDUCTIONS										Total Deductions		Balance Paid		Cheque No.	Payee's Signature with date	Remarks
				I. Tax		G.P.F.		T.B.S.		L.I.C./G.I.C.		Loan								
Rs.	P.	Rs.	P.	Rs.	P.	Rs.	P.	Rs.	P.	Rs.	P.	Rs.	P.	Rs.	P.	Rs.	P.			

12. REGISTER OF DAILY ATTTENDANCE OF THE STUDENTS

Std. .... Section .... Daily Attendance for the month of ....

S. No.	Name	1		2		3		4		...	31		No. of attendance for the month	No. of attendance brought forward	Total	Remarks
		1st meetings	2nd meetings	1st meetings	2nd meetings	1st meetings	2nd meetings	1st meetings	2nd meetings		1st meetings	2nd meetings				
1.																
2.																
3.																
4.																
5.																
6.																
7.																
8.																
9.																
10.																
...																
...																

Total:

Number of students on the Rolls at the beginning of the month:
Number of students on the Rolls at the end of the month:
Number of school meetings during the Month:
Number of school meetings from April:
Total of Attendances:
Average daily attendances:

Class Teacher

Principal

(Note: Schools have different types of Student Attendance Registers)

13

Supervision and Inspection

13.1 NOMENCLATURE OF THE WORD 'SUPERVISOR,' 'EDUCATION OFFICER,' 'INSPECTOR,' 'ADVISER' AND 'CONSULTANT'

Authors have used these terms interchangeably. However, the present trend is to minimise the use of the term 'Inspector' as it tends to denote the element of authority whereas this element is missing in other terms. Now the emphasis is on human relationships and mutual cooperation and the term 'Education Officer' is preferred.

Here we present the views of Commissions and some educators to throw more light on the issue.

The Secondary Education Commission 1952–53 has remarked, "In our view the true role of an inspector—for whom we would prefer the term Educational Advisor—is to study the problems of each school, to take a comprehensive side view of all its functions and help the teachers to carry out his advice and recommendations."

Prof. S.N. Mukherji thinks, "Perhaps the very selection of the term 'inspector' was unfortunate especially in the Indian context. The term seems to be closely associated with the corresponding rank in the police service which has to deal with the criminals. Perhaps in England where for long time the police has been looked upon as the servant and friend of the people, the term did not cause much harm. The conditions in India were different. The policemen here have been agents of foreign imperialism and as such were dreaded by the people. The police-officers on the other hand worked with a certain amount of suspicion and their attitude to general public was anything but that of service. It was associated with this connotation that school inspectors came, and there is no doubt that the attitude with which they looked upon the schools, and the attitude with which the teachers looked upon them was closely akin to the attitude of the people towards the police of those days."

Similarly Prof. Mukherji thinks, "Perhaps much can be gained, if the very term 'Inspectors' which seems to have a bad connotation being associated with Police Inspectors be changed into 'School Advisers' or 'School Visitors.' But more effective remedy would be to separate the administrative functions of the inspectorate from inspection work and entrust the same to two different agencies."

Prof. V.S. Mathur is of the opinion that under the present context "The term inspector is the only term that fits in our environment. The nearest to this is what we now have in the Punjab 'Education Officer' although the word 'officer' sounds a bit out of tune."

The present tendency among educationists seems to 'expel' the word 'Inspector' from the educational vocabulary in favour of 'Supervisor' or 'Education Officer.'

The 'Inspectors,' less frequently as officials or civil servants composing this staff are usually known as 'Inspectors,' less 'Councillors' (Germany, U.S.A.); 'Superintendents' (Australia, Canada, Philippines, etc.); 'Superintendents' (Cuba, Dominican Republic, etc.); 'Supervisors' (Canada, Panama, U.S.A. etc.) and 'Inspector' (U.K.). In some instances, different designations are used in one and the same country.

Summing Up

What matters is not what is, what people are called, but what functions they perform and more especially in what spirit they perform them. It is firmly held that supervision stands for a complex of attitudes and activities all directed towards the improvement of what goes in schools, and that in their varied degrees all who work in and for schools have supervisory responsibilities. Whether, there should be special categories of people called 'Supervisors' or advisers or officers, or organisers, or consultants or resource persons or counsellors or by other current catch phrase, or whether inspectors should be left to enjoy their traditional title, matters little.

Two things do matter everywhere: that the people should do the jobs whatever they are, and in the right way; and that these jobs should be clearly understood.

13.2 CONCEPT OF SUPERVISION

Here an attempt has been made to analyse the views of the educational administrators and thinkers with regard to the nature and scope of supervisory practices in the schools. An analysis of the 'Key Words' indicating the dimensions and facets of supervision will enable us to view the values in varying degrees in any scheme of school supervision and also the changing concept of the role and function of the Education Officer/Inspector from time to time.

1. *Noble-Dynamic-Considerate-Creative.* At its best, supervision is the most noble and dynamic of all educational endeavours. It is the most noble because it is the most creative. (Ayer, Fred C. *Fundamentals of Instructional Supervision.* New York: Harper and Brothers Publishers, 1954).

2. *Improvement of Instruction.* "The function of educational supervision is the improvement of instruction." (Adams, Harold P. and Dickey Frank, *Basic Principles of Supervision.* New York: American Book Company, 1953, p. 5, Preface).

3. *Improvement of Teaching-Learning.* "The function of supervision is the improvement of teaching. Improved teaching will improve learning. Since schools exist in order that learning opportunities—better than those elsewhere available—may be enjoyed by boys and girls, it is clear that supervision and supervisor to a higher degree determine the nature and quality of the educational programme in local communities." (Ayer, C. Fred, *Fundamentals*

of Instructional Supervision, New York: Harper and Brothers Publishers, 1954, Editor's Introduction by John Guy Fowlkes, p. 4)

4. *Stimulating Leadership.* "Undoubtedly, stimulating professional leadership from fair and sympathetic administrators and supervisors is one of the most important ingredients in the satisfaction of class-room teachers and other staff members." (American Association of School Administrators. *Thirty-third year book: Staff Relationships in School Administration*, Washington: 1955, p. 20.)

5. *Help and Encouragement.* "The chief duty of an inspector is to inspect schools. He must do this sympathetically and tactfully and give advice based on his own knowledge and experience which will help the teachers to make their schools enlightened and humanise institutions. He should feel free and of course be qualified to praise or to criticise; but his criticism should be calculated to encourage and not to intimidate. *Abbot-Wood Report*, New Delhi: Government of India, 1954, p. 30.)

6. *Improvement of Teaching.* "The aim of supervision is the improvement of teaching." Barr. A.S., Burton, W.H. *Supervision and Improvement of Instruction.* New York: Appleton—Century—Crafts, 1922, p. 10.)

7. *Teacher of Teachers.* "Supervision is an aspect of administration—specifically, the aspect with the face-to-face control of personnel. Since all supervision is essentially instructional in nature, a school supervisor could well be designated a teacher of teachers." (Bartky, John A., *Administration as Educational Leadership*—California, Stanford University Press, 1956.)

8. *Development Growth.* Good supervision is always concerned with the development of the teacher, the growth of the pupil, and the improvement of the teaching-learning process. Bartky, John A., *Supervision as Human Relations.* Boston and Company, 1955, p. 15.)

9. *Cooperative Effort.* "Supervision is a shared-relationship job—true supervision must be a cooperative effort." (Brown, Edwin J., Secondary School Administration. Boston, Houghton Mifflin Company, 1938, p. 136.)

10. *Expert Technical Service.* "Supervision is an expert technical service primarily concerned with studying and improving the conditions that surround learning and pupil growth." Barr, A. S., Burton, W.H. and Bruecker L.I., *Supervision*, New York: Appleton—Century Crafts 1947, p. 11.)

11. *Improvement of Teaching.* "Supervision is the foundation upon which all programmes for the improvement of teaching must be built." (Barr, A.S., and Burton, W.H., *The Supervision instruction*, New York: Appleton—Century—Craft, 1926, p. 1.)

12. *Coordinating-Stimulating—Directing.* "In general supervision means to coordinate, stimulate and direct the growth of the teachers in the power to stimulate and direct the growth of every individual pupil through the exercise of his talents towards the richest and the most intelligent participation in the civilisation in which he lives." (Briggs, T.H. and Justman, *Improving Instruction Through Supervision*, New York: The Macmillan Co., 1952, p. 12.)

13. *Educational Advancement and Improvement.* "The modern forward

looking school inspector fills the roles of liaison officer and human engineer as well as educator by interpreting the problems of principals, teachers and higher school authorities to each group and by working cooperatively with them for educational advancement and improvement." (*School Supervision*. Central Institute of Education, Department of Extension Services, Delhi, 1960, p. 25.)

14. *Leadership.* "Supervisor is a leader—or administrator—with special skills in the area of curriculum development and improvement." (Campbell, Road F., Corbally, Johan E. and Romesyer, Johan A., *Introduction to Educational Administration*. Boston: Allyn and Bacon, 1962, p. 395.)

15. *Growth.* "Any effective programme of instructional supervision is very directly concerned with the nature and quality of pupils' learning experiences in the schools. Although the ultimate purpose is growth, it is very largely achieved through processes involving teacher growth." (Cooper, Shirely and Fitzwater and Charles O., *Country School Adminis-tration*, New York: Harper and Brothers Publishers, 1954.)

16. *Professional Growth:* "The modern view-point calls for a Supervisor who looks his role as one of helping teachers better to accomplish their common purposes. His prime function is to provide friendly and professional guidance and help to teachers in service." (*Innovastion and Research in Education Administration.* Extension Services Department, Central Institute of Education, Delhi; 1961, p. 14.)

17. *Stimulating—Coordinating—Guiding.* "Supervision is the effort to stimulate—Coordinate and guide the continued growth of teachers, both individually and collectively in better understanding and more effective performance of all the functions of instruction, so that they will be better able to stimulate and direct each student's continued growth toward a rich and intelligent participation in society. The whole purpose of supervision is the development of better education for youth." (Douglass, Harl R; Bent, Rudy and K., and Boardman, Charles W., *Democratic Supervision in Secondary Schools.* Boston, Houghton Miffin Co., 1961, p. 6.)

18. *Promotion of Professional Growth.* "Instructional supervision, therefore, has the large purpose of improving the quality of instruction primarily by promoting the professional growth of all teachers and secondarily and temporarily by correcting deficiencies of preliminary preparation for teaching by the training of teachers in service." (Dun, F.W. *What is Instructional Supervision*, Proceedings of the National Educational Association. Vol. 61, 1923, p. 763.)

19. *Promoting Sound Development of the School System.* "The name Inspector is being changed to Education Officer, in recognition of the enlarged scope of the functions that an inspecting officer has now to discharge and of the new context in which he views his tasks in relation to the schools. While inspection is and remains a function of the Department's Officers it is only among many ways in which they exercise their influence in promoting sound development of the school system." (*Delhi Education Code*, Directorate of Education, Delhi, the Manager of Publications, Delhi, 1956, p. 95.)

20. *Resource Consultant.* "The role of principals and supervisors should be largely that of resource consultants, their chief responsibility being to facilitate and enrich the experiences of the class-room teachers." (Elshree, Willard S., and Reutter, E.E. Danund. *Staff Personnel in the Public School*, New York, Prentice-Hall, Inc. 1954, p. 252.)

21. *Encouraging.* "The Inspector's role is a quasi parental one, and accordingly his aim must be to encourage each individual teacher in his or her own growth to maturity." (France Louis, *The Inspection of School in France*, New Era, November 1955, p. 174.)

13.3 CHARACTERISTICS OF SUPERVISION

On the basis of the above concept of supervision, following characteristics of supervision may be mentioned:

1. Supervision is advising.
2. Supervision is assisting.
3. Supervision is collaboration.
4. Supervision is considerate.
5. Supervision is consultancy. (Service)
6. Supervision is cooperative (efforts).
7. Supervision is coordination.
8. Supervision is creative.
9. Supervision is development.
10. Supervision is discovering.
11. Supervision is disseminating.
12. Supervision is dynamic.
13. Supervision is encouragement.
14. Supervision is experimental.
15. Supervision is growth.
16. Supervision is guidance.
17. Supervision is helping.
18. Supervision is improving.
19. Supervision is inspiration.
20. Supervision is leading.
21. Supervision is noble.
22. Supervision is promoting.
23. Supervision is scientific.
24. Supervision is service.
25. Supervision is stimulation.
26. Supervision is suggestive.

13.4 TYPES OF SUPERVISION AND INSPECTION

1. Authoritarian: Authoritarian supervision is based upon practices like 'I told you to do this.' This kills the creative ability and initiative of the teachers and is a hindrance in improving instruction.

Authoritarian supervision forces and prescribes methods. An authoritarian thinks that because a method works well for him, it must be used by the teacher and that it will succeed in the same way and to the same extent. Authoritarian supervision fails to take account of the fact that what produces results for one teacher in his particular situation with his individual personality may not produce same results in the case of the other.

Authoritarian supervision implies that the supervisor is a master, or super teacher, who can walk in, take over the class and get the desired results. The teacher works in such a situation not by actually doing and experiencing but by being 'told.'

2. Corrective: This is also known as 'fault-finding' expedition. In this case the Inspector visits a school to pick holes here and there and is always in the look out of bringing out inconsistencies and gaps to the notice of the head of the institution. Such an inspection does not serve any useful purpose. It simply makes the teachers unhappy. An Inspector must remember that progress depends upon a judicious combination of encouragement to good work and removal of defects.

3. Creative: According to Fred C. Ayer, "Creative supervision should encourage the discovery of all kinds of better ways of learning, teaching and community improvement, not merely those who relate to self-expression and problem-solving."

Barr, Burton and Bruecknor think, "Creative Leadership in the long run is vitally necessary to the success of democratic life."

Creativeness has been linked closely with such words as *self-expression, inventiveness, initiative, originality, experimentation and improvement*.

Supervision seeks for latent talents. It provides opportunity for the exercise and originality and for the development of unique contributions.

William T. Melchoir stresses the following points as being characteristic of creative supervision:

(a) Creative supervision encourages teachers to feel free to think for themselves in matters pertaining to objectives, curriculum, organisation and content, methods of teaching and methods of evaluation.

(b) It encourages teachers to share voluntarily with the supervisor, and co-workers that which they think.

(c) It never stifles the inclination of a teacher to experiment with his own ideas, though the dangers of experimentation are kept in mind.

(d) It does more than encouragement; it inspires teachers to be themselves and to do for themselves; it imbues them with self-confidence and the power of self-evaluation.

4. Democratic: Democratic supervision eliminates the feeling that the supervisor is a superior being and the teacher an inferior worker. Democratic supervision tends to cooperative endeavour for the common goods. Democratic supervision does not allow the supervisor to impose his will upon the teachers. It builds upon the power of the teacher to exercise self-direction through his participation in the formulation of methods and procedures for improving instruction. Democratic supervision seeks for the development of the highest potentialities in all. Democratic supervision recognises the dignity and worth of the individual.

Democratic leadership generates more leadership by providing opportunities to more and more persons to exercise leadership. It must be adapted to the levels of professional ability and to the differences in teachers—whether they be novices or veterans, weak or strong, poorly trained or professionally prepared.

Democratic supervision provides for group planning. It connotes a better organisation among both groups—teachers and children.

Democratic supervision is also concerned with coordinating the work of groups in different schools and on various levels.

Democratic supervision encourages freedom while furnishing direction, advice and suggestion.

5. Humanistic: This type of supervision aims at developing healthy human relationships among all the partners of the educational enterprise, i.e., the pupils, the teachers, the parents, staff personnel, the managers and the supervisors.

6. Inspirational: It inspires teachers, lifts them above themselves, and reinvigorates their flogging spirits. True inspirational supervision must strive to broaden the base of leadership by utilising the full potential of teachers. It will nurture qualities like initiative, originality, creativity, sincerity and honesty. It will discourage rigidity and sameness in teaching. It will meet the needs of teachers sufficiently to serve as the foundation for a good programme of supervision.

Inspirational supervision allows the freedom so necessary for real growth.

7. *Leissez Faire* Type: Like economic *laissez faire*, this type of supervision means letting each teacher as he pleases. He may teach the way he wants to teach. Supervisors are unable to make any impact.

8. Preventive: This type of supervision helps the teachers to anticipate new situations and to find ways and means to remove them. It is obvious that this type of inspection is helpful to teachers.

Types of Inspection According to Supervisory Procedures

1. *Annual Inspection.* This is a detailed and comprehensive inspection of all aspects of the school; its staff, all subjects in all classes; its equipment and organisation.

2. *The Follow-up Inspection.* Follow-up inspection is conducted to ensure that the previous recommendations have been carried out.

3. *Partial Inspection.* This may constitute the inspection of the teaching of one subject only or some special aspect of the school life.

4. *Surprise or Unannounced Visits.* Supervisors visit schools without giving any prior notice. The idea behind such visits is to observe the working of the school under normal situations.

13.5 EPITHETS GIVEN TO SCHOOL INSPECTION

1. School inspection is ad-hoc and unplanned.
2. School inspection is autocratic.

3. School inspection is bureaucratic.
4. School inspection is a 'clog' in the wheel of progress of education.
5. School inspection is detective.
6. School inspection is dreadful.
7. School inspection is hasty.
8. School inspection is lop-sided.
9. School inspection is perfunctory.
10. School inspection is picking holes.
11. School inspection is policing.
12. School inspection is report-oriented.

13.6 SCOPE OF SUPERVISION: CONTENTS OF SUPERVISION AND INSPECTION

1. Supervision of Instructional Work. The Supervisor or the Inspector supervises the effectiveness of the methods of teaching used in a particular institution, the audio-visual aids employed to make teaching interesting and effective, the time-table enforced to carry out the instructional work, distribution of work among the members of the staff; distribution of the prescribed curriculum in suitable terms in the school year, written work done by the students and experiments conducted etc. In fact, he is concerned with the entire planning of the institutional work. He inspects the teachers' diaries also.

2. Supervision of Co-curricular Activities. As the present education is not concerned with the mere teaching of three Rs, the supervisors also supervise the work carried on in the co-curricular field. They are concerned with scouting, games and sports, clubs, school government, school magazine, library service, hobbies, school museum, school exhibition and the like.

3. Supervision of School Environment. The supervisors are concerned with the discipline of the students, their personal habits, their general behaviour, etc. They look up into the cleanliness of students, cleanliness of the school surroundings, beautification of the school, hygienic conditions of the school canteen, proper drinking water arrangements, cleanliness of urinals and latrines. They evaluate the steps taken by the school authorities for the welfare and the safety of the students.

4. Supervision of School Registers. The inspecting staff examines all sorts of school records and registers. They scrutinise all accounts and boys funds. They see whether or not proper use of school funds is being made. They examine the school apparatus and equipment also.

5. Supervision of Developmental Aspects. The supervisors try to assess whether the school is justifying its existence or not. They examine the various steps taken by the school to serve the locality in which it is situated. They report about the school's participation in the social, cultural and recreational programmes of the community.

Supervision of Pupil's Growth. The supervisors are also concerned with the many sided development of the children.

13.7 SCOPE OF SUPERVISORY ACTIVITIES

- Administrative Duties
  - (a) Transfers of teachers within the District
  - (b) Office routine
  - (c) Investigating complaints etc.
- Planning
- Instructional Supervision
  - Guidance to Teachers and Principals
  - Regular and surprise Inspections
- Supervision of co-curricular activities
- Checking of School Accounts
- Collection of statistics
- Dealing with Aided and Unaided Schools and the Managing Committee

13.8 CHANGING CONCEPTS OF SUPERVISION AND INSPECTION

Today supervision is greatly influenced by the increasing insight into the aims of education, the relation of school to the society in which it exists, by the scientific method, and by the democratic philosophy. Supervision is becoming participatory and cooperative, that is, democratic; is increasingly oriented towards the fundamental aims of education and of society.

Beginning slowly in the twenties, developing rapidly in the thirties and forties, was the concept of cooperative supervision and democratic leadership, the supervisor being regarded as an individual who served to assist the staff, as consultant and friend, rather than as inspector and critic. Democratic supervision demands respect for personality. It makes ample provision for self-direction on the part of teachers, and participation to a great extent in their in-service growth.

13.9 AIMS AND OBJECTIVES OF SUPERVISION

1. Improving class-room teaching.
2. Evaluating the scholastic performance of the students.
3. Assessing the teachers with a view to sustaining excellence, helping and encouraging.
4. Knowing the genuine difficulties of the teachers in teaching and organising various activities and suggesting ways and means for overcoming them.
5. Promoting the professional growth of the teachers by providing them in-service education.
6. Discovering whether school is related to the community and if not suggesting ways and means to do so.

7. Ensuring that there is a reasonable balance of intellectual physical, social and moral activities.
8. Acquainting the department with the progress of the scheme of education and giving a factual account of the working of schools.
9. Demonstrating instructional, administrative and supervisory techniques which are found effective.
10. Disseminating effective teaching methods and techniques in various schools.
11. Preventing misdirecting of resources and energies.
12. Helping administrators and teachers to deal successfully with the increasing complexity of the responsibilities of the profession.

The Kothari Commission (1964–66) realised the importance of a dynamic inspectorate and stated, "A sympathetic and imaginative system of supervision and administration is essential for initiating and accelerating educational reforms."

13.10 DEFECTS IN THE PRESENT SYSTEM OF SUPERVISION AND INSPECTION

Though a period of more than a hundred and fifty years has passed since the system came into vogue, yet it is considered as a 'clog' and not as a 'spoke' in the wheel of progress of education in our country. The dawn of independence was expected to make material changes in the system of inspection and supervision but by and large, it has failed to make any substantial contributions to the developmental aspects of schools.

The Sadler Commission of 1919 remarked, "Inspection in most cases is hurried and lacking the friendly suggestions as to the methods of teaching and organisation which are most valuable functions of school inspection."

Hartog Committee (1928) reported, "We have referred many times to the absence of an adequate number of well-qualified and experienced inspectors and inspectresses and to the waste and ineffectiveness in the system of education which we believe to be due in large part to that inadequacy."

The Secondary Education Commission (1952–53) remarked, "It was pointed out by several witnesses that inspections were perfunctory, that the time spent by the inspector at any particular place was insufficient, that the greater part of this time was taken up with routine administration."

The Education Commission (1964–66) outlined the following seven reasons for the weakness of the programme.

- the large expansion in the number of institutions which has not been accompanied by a corresponding increase in the number of inspecting officers;
- the combination of administrative and supervisory functions in the same officer which affects supervision adversely because administrative work, which has increased greatly in recent years, always has priority;
- the use of supervisory officers, when they are members of the block development team, for non-educational world leaving them very little time for their own responsibilities;

— continuance of old techniques of supervision oriented to control rather than to development; and
— lack of adequate competence in the inspecting staff.

13.11 AN INTERESTING ACCOUNT OF AN INSPECTOR'S TRADITIONAL VISIT: SHORTCOMINGS IN THE INSPECTION

Michael West gave the following interesting picture of an inspector's visit in his book — *Education, Selective, Specific, Compensatory* (1967): "The quality of the work is tested by a weary sub-inspector who has trudged some four or five miles through the heat. He hears a boy read and another class meanwhile does a sum which he has written on a stale or a much-pitted black-board. The boys stumble occasionally in the reading. The sum is done wrong by the head boy in the class: all the rest copy him and so are all wrong." The sub-inspector writes, "Reading fair, Arithmetic bad."

Supervision in Schools of Himachal Pradesh

The Himachal Code does not use the term 'Supervision'. Instead it uses the term 'Inspection'.

13.12 SUPERVISORY OR INSPECTION STAFF

1. The Director of Education shall be responsible for the supervision and inspection of all schools in the State.
2. For the purpose of sub-rule (1), the Director may assign all or any of the functions relating to the supervision and inspection to such officer subordinate to him, and as may be authorised by him in this behalf.
3. Every officer, authorised by the Director of Education under sub-rule (2), shall discharge his duties of supervision and inspection under the direction, control and supervision of the Director of Education.
4. The Director of Education may also form a team/panel of persons with special knowledge and experience of different subjects taught in school, to carry out inspections of the schools.
5. The Director of Education may also carry out surprise inspections through any officer authorised by him in this behalf.
6. Every inspecting officer, other than the Director of Education, inspecting a school shall within 15 days from the completion of the inspection, submit a report to the next higher authority with a copy to the concerned school and Director of Education for such further necessary action and compliance, as might be deemed fit in the matter.
7. When the Director of Education himself makes the inspection, he shall send a copy of the inspection note to the head of the concerned school with a copy to the District Education Officer and the Deputy Director of Education of the concerned zone for necessary action and compliance. He may also send a copy to Secretary (Education) for information.

13.13 INSPECTION REPORT: NORMS OF INSPECTION

The report of every inspection shall be made on the proforma.

The different inspecting officers must adhere to the following norms of inspections in an academic year:

(i) The District Education Officer should inspect all the middle and high schools of his district. He shall also pay surprise visits to senior secondary schools in his district.

(ii) The Zonal Deputy Director of Education should inspect all senior secondary and 60 middle and high schools in the respective zone.

(iii) The Additional Director and Joint Director of Education (Schools) shall inspect schools as may be assigned by the Director of Education.

(iv) The Additional Director and Joint Director of Education (Colleges) should inspect all such institutions as may be assigned by the Director of Education.

(v) The Additional Director (Admn.) shall inspect such institutions as may be assigned by the Director of Education.

(vi) The Director of Education may assign the inspection of district and zonal offices to any other officer as he may deem proper and report is to be submitted on prescribed proforma as given in office manual.

Advance Notice of Inspection to be Given to Schools

Except in the case of surprise visits, intimation of the proposal to carry out the inspection of a school shall be given preferably, one month in advance to the head of the school.

Every inspection shall be as objective as possible and shall be aimed at bringing about an improvement in the standards of teaching in the school.

13.14 SUPERVISION REPORT

While making the inspection, the following items should be critically examined and inspection report based on these points:

(a) academic work, i.e., actual teaching and its different aspects including teacher diary.

(b) Libraries and its service to students and teachers.

(c) Games and sports and their organisations.

(d) Co-curricular activities.

(e) The overall environment and interpersonal relations of the teachers among themselves with the parents of the students and the community in general.

(f) Administration and organisation of the school.

(g) Accounts of the school and their maintenance.

(h) The school plan and physical needs of the school.

(i) Discipline and punctuality in the school.

(j) Adherence to the rules and instructions by the school.

(k) National integration/emotional education/value education and other items as incorporated in the inspection programme.

(l) Calendar of activities.

(m) Celebration of annual function.

13.15 STEPS IN SUPERVISION

The inspecting officer shall go to each class and watch the teaching in at least two classes of each teacher and shall specifically note the good and bad points observed.

All the inspecting officers shall ensure that follow up action on report is taken promptly

Guidelines for Inspecting Officers

The supervision or inspection shall;

(i) aim at providing academic guidance to the teacher and help the institution in the promotion of a higher standard of education;

(ii) not aim at fault finding of the teachers and their work, but for providing concrete suggestions for the improvement of teaching, class work, home work and its correction;

(iii) help the institution in organisation of co-curricular programmes in a manner conducive to the all-round development of the students and help in the co-curricular development of the school.

(iv) The supervising and inspecting officers shall:

  (a) formulate a definite plan for supervising the subject and classes of each teacher;

  (b) focus his attention on the teaching-learning situation and not on the teacher as a person;

  (c) emphasise the professional growth of the teacher by developing his/her powers of self direction;

  (d) give the teachers requisite freedom to try out new experiments, methods and innovations in the process of teaching;

  (e) help the teachers to understand the role of the school, and the objectives to be achieved through the teaching-learning process in the school.

13.16 INSPECTION OF MIDDLE SCHOOLS, BY HEADS OF COMPOSITE SCHOOLS

Heads of composite schools will also be responsible for efficient and proper functioning of middle schools under their control. They will ensure proper maintenance of accounts of funds and other relevant records of the schools, punctuality and discipline among the staff and students. He will make surprise visits and two half-yearly inspections of the school(s) and will report to the District Education Officer. He will also do detailed annual inspection and will report on prescribed proforma (Annexure-I), under relevant items, to the District Education Officer.

Specific Guidance: Role of the Supervisor/Inspector

1. *To provide professional leadership* to educational institutions so as to improve their work and put them on right direction and path.

2. *To set suitable goals* for the educational institutions.

3. *To appraise the work of the educational* institutions and to give suitable

suggestions of work being carried on.

4. To *guide and offer technical service to teachers* in the form of instructional aids, specific suggestions for the improvement of instruction and assistance in pupils diagnosis and measurement.

5. To develop in teachers a *growing recognition* of the factors that affect learning.

6. To help teachers to *define and use the purposes of education* as dynamic force in their work with pupils.

7. To promote the *professional growth of all teachers* by providing them in-service training.

The motto of the Inspectors should not be "check your teachers, frighten your teachers, weaken your teachers and examine them", but its variant, "train your teachers, inspire your teachers and trust them," writes an educationist.

(*Source* : *Education Code* : Himachal Pradesh)

13.17 GUIDELINES FOR SUPERVISORS

Supervisors should follow the procedures as shown in the Figure below.

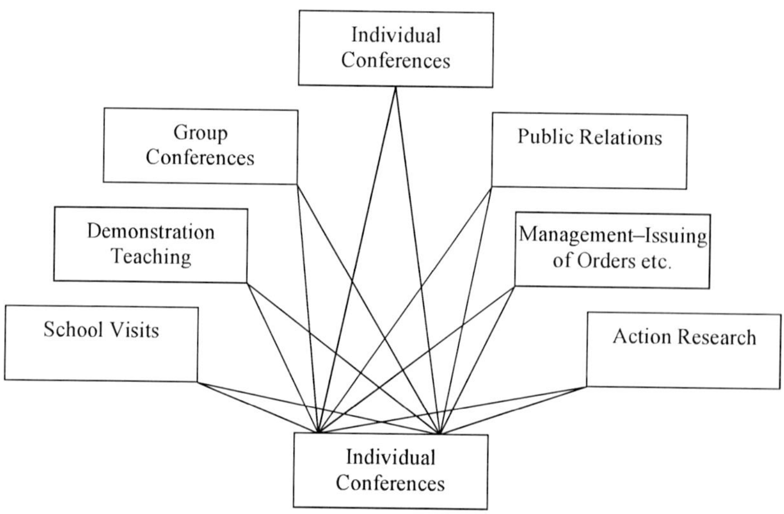

Fig. 13.1: Supervisory Procedures Including Guidance Role of Supervisors/Inspectors

13.18 PURPOSES OF OBSERVATION OR CLASS-ROOM VISITATION

1. Acquainting with teaching-learning situations with reference to:

(a) Physical environment.

(b) Social environment.

(c) Children's behaviour and their responses.

(d) Teacher's behaviour and teaching acts with special reference to the following:

   (i) Introduction of the lesson.

   (ii) Development of the lesson.

   (iii) Suitability of the subject-matter.
   (iv) Methods and techniques.
   (v) Illustrative aids.
   (vi) Interaction with pupils.
   (vii) Recapitulation.
   (viii) Assignments.
   (ix) Evaluation.
2. Solving teacher's problems.
3. Providing instructional leadership.
4. Promoting of research.
5. Identification of talented teachers.

13.19 PRINCIPLES AND PROCEDURES OF OBSERVATION

The following points may be kept in view:

1. The supervisor should plan observation scientifically and wisely.
2. The supervisor should enter the class-room as quietly as possible.
3. The behaviour of the supervisor should be natural and friendly.
4. The supervisor should take special care not to say anything or act in a manner that will impair the status and prestige of the teacher before the students.
5. The supervisor as far as possible should make a mental note of the important points and as soon as he leaves the class-room, he should commit to writing special points that he would like to discuss with the teacher.
6. The supervisor should spend adequate time in the class-room.
7. The supervisor should leave the class-room as quietly as possible.
8. The supervisor should plan follow-up action.

Demonstration

Purposes of Demonstration:

1. Providing in-service education to teachers.
2. Stimulating teacher's professional growth.
3. Solving teacher's problems.
4. Integrating educational theory with practice.

Principles of Demonstration

1. Principle of planning with special reference to the following:
   (i) Careful selection of situations.
   (ii) Preparation of a detailed lesson plan illustrating the procedure of tackling the particular problem.
   (iii) Preparation of the materials needed in demonstration.
2. Principle of natural setting.
3. Principle of correlation.
4. Principle of evaluation.

Workshop

Purposes of the Workshop:

1. Solving professional problems through group process.

2. Encouraging cooperation.
3. Stimulating creative activity.
4. Better utilisation of resources.
5. Providing contact with experts.

Principles and Procedures of Conducting Workshops

1. Planning with reference to:
   - (i) Favourable time.
   - (ii) Suitable place.
   - (iii) Duration.
   - (iv) Frequency.
2. Locating and defining the problem with reference to:
   - (i) Practical utility, and
   - (ii) Jurisdiction of the supervisor.
3. Assigning work to different groups.
4. Drafting and reporting.
5. Evaluating.

13.20 SUPERVISORY PROCEDURES AND GUIDANCE: ROLE OF THE SUPERVISOR

A capable supervisor will not limit his supervisory procedures to the traditional class-room visits and the teachers' meeting. He will render assistance to teachers through such procedures as the following:

(A) **Guidance.** The supervisor or the inspector is expected to help the individual teacher or group of teachers to plan and carry forward out-of-class projects which have a direct bearing on the improvement of learning conditions. These projects are:

(i) Planning, testing programmes and constructing tests.
(ii) Analysing test results and planning remedial procedures.
(iii) Collecting supplementary materials.
(iv) Undertaking special projects in the use of audio-visual aids.
(v) Planning and initiating instructional devices suiting individual students.
(vi) Conducting workshops for the study of special problems.
(vii) Utilising community resources for enriching class-room teaching.

(B) **School and Class-room Visits.** The procedures and techniques of visits are:

(i) Observation of the work of teachers with a view to discovering opportunities for improvement.
(ii) Rating the teacher with some special device for diagnostic purposes.
(iii) Taking up demonstration lessons.
(iv) Making suggestions to teachers regarding new devices and methods, supplementary aids, economy of time, pupil control, adapting methods to pupil differences, and so on.

(C) **Teachers' Meeting and Conferences.** This point may be illustrated under two headings:

(i) *Holding Conferences with the Individual Teacher.* Such conferences will be held as a result of the class-room visits and observations and will involve consideration of teacher's weak and strong points and opportunities for improvement.

(ii) *Holding Teachers' Meeting for Consideration of Major Instructional Problems.* Points of common interests, some difficulties and certain policies are discussed and suggestions made to improve school work.

13.21 CHECK LIST FOR EVALUATION AND SUPERVISION OF INSTRUCTION

Teacher .... Date..

Subject .... Class ....

Note: Check in one of these three columns A,B,C. If a given feature does not appear, check in the column "No".

Class-room Management	*No.*	*A*	*B*	*C*
1. Was sufficient attention given to lighting and ventilation?				
2. Was the equipment of the rooms (for example, desks, black-boards, etc.) in order?				
3. Were there sufficient, audio-visual aids? (for example, maps and charts)				
4. Were supplementary materials effectively arranged?				
5. Was the teacher's voice pleasing and his enunciation, clear?				
6. Was the teacher's dress suitable?				
7. Were the teacher's manners suitable?				
8. Did the teacher show evidence of possession of the following qualities?				
(a) Self-control				
(b) Tact				
(c) Resourcefulness				
(d) Sympathy				
(e) Fair-mindedness				
(f) Enthusiasm				
(g) Decisiveness				
9. Did the lesson begin and end in time?				
10. Did the teacher handle laboratory material efficiently?				
11. Were the students with defective sight or hearing seated on front desks?				
12. Did students enter, leave and move about the room in an appropriate manner?				
13. Were the postures of the students good?				
14. Were pupils' responses well directed and expressed?				
15. Was the attention of the entire class keen and continuous?				
16. Was the group characterised by an attitude of courtesy and cooperation towards all its members?				

Arrangement of the Subject-matter

Class-room Management	*No.*	*A*	*B*	*C*
1. Was the time effectively divided between (i) testing and drilling upon previous assignment, (ii) Assignment and new material. 2. Did the assignment involve activity of the group?				

Teaching Devices

Class-room Management	*No.*	*A*	*B*	*C*
1. Were all pupils kept busy throughout the entire period? 2. Was the proper balance between teacher activity and pupil activity? 3. Was emphasis placed upon the formation of good habits rather than the acquisition of facts? 4. Was sufficient drill given to secure mastery of necessary skills and facts? 5. Did all the students participate in drill? 6. Were the questions suitable? 7. Were the questions well distributed among the members of the group? 8. Did the pupils ask questions spontaneously? 9. Was there any evidence to show that the pupils had been taught how to attack and solve a problem?				

Aim

Class-room Management	*No.*	*A*	*B*	*C*
1. Did the teacher have a clear and worthy aim of the lesson? 2. Was the aim attained?				

Note: Report on other aspects of school organisation and management may also be given in accordance with the proforma prescribed by the department. Normally following aspects are covered:

1. Preliminary – Name of the school etc.
2. Follow-up action on the previous report.
3. Staff statement with qualifications, classes taught etc.
4. Scales of fees and funds.
5. Furniture.
6. Library facilities.
7. Laboratory facilities.
8. Farm/Craft or vocational equipment
9. Co-curricular activities.
10. School results and performance.

11. Service conditions of staff.
12. Maintenance of registers.
13. School finances.
14. Parent teachers association.
15. Compliance of departmental instructions.
16. Community participation.
17. Managing committee.
18. General maintenance of school.
19. School discipline.
20. Supervision diary of the head.

14

Revamping Supervision and Inspection

14.1 DEFECTS IN THE PRESENT SUPERVISION AND INSPECTION

It is generally observed that the present type of supervision and inspection hardly serves the purpose for which it is designed. From time to time, this system has been examined by experts, measures suggested but without any substantial improvement. By and large, it is still the same as was the case before independence.

Here we give the views of some experts on the state of supervision and inspection in India.

The Secondary Education Commission (1952–53) noticed the following defects:

(i) Inspections are perfunctory.

(ii) Time spent by the Inspector is insufficient and greater part of the same is taken up with routine work pertaining to checking of accounts, time-table, curriculum, etc.

(iii) Enough time is not devoted to the academic side.

(iv) Contacts between the teachers and inspectors are casual.

(v) The number of schools entrusted to the care of an inspector is too large and the range too wide for him to be able to acquaint himself with their work and appreciate their problems; nor is he in a position to advise and guide the teaching staff in improving the work of the school.

(vi) The inspector, instead of being "the friend, philosopher and guide" of the school, behaves in such a critical and unsympathetic way that his visit is looked upon with some degree of apprehension, if not of resentment.

In the words of W.M. Ryburn, "The Inspector holds an extremely autocratic position, where, if his will is not exactly law, it is so near to it that for all practical intents and purposes, the teacher and the headmaster regard it as such."

To quote G.S. Shukla: "Till now responsibility of inspectorate in education was considered synonymous with unquestionable authority and superiority demanding unqualified obedience and respect from the teaching profession." He further calls the Inspector of Schools as an 'educational policeman.'

Prof. A.C. Deve Gowda feels that "There is general feeling in the country that the present inspection and supervision of the secondary schools need improvement. It is also realised that this improvement in inspection and supervision may also be helpful in raising the standard of education at the secondary level."

.According to Prof. S.N. Mukherji thinks, "It is also generally admitted that if the system of public education in India is to improve, the department of education should be strong. It needs an adequate staff, both in number and quality. The members of the State Department of Education... can assume leadership of the educational enterprise."

14.2 SUGGESTIONS FOR IMPROVING SUPERVISORY PRACTICES

1. *Frequency of Inspections and Follow-up Work.* With regard to frequency of inspections, it is suggested that there should be at least two inspections in one year, one of them may be informal visit and the other regular annual visit. More visits are desirable specially in the case of those schools which in the view of the Education Officer require special measures to become educationally sound. Needs of each school should be ascertained and remedial measures adopted.

The remarks and suggestions of the Education Officer should be sent to schools within one week of the visit of the supervisor so that these may be considered by school personnel without delay.

School inspections without any regular follow-up programme do not prove to be effective. Planning of follow-up programme is as essential as regular inspection.

2. *Strengthening of the Supervisory Staff.* A major part of the time of the Education Officer is being spent on administrative activities with the result that adequate time is not left him to discharge his supervisory activities. Keeping in view the present situation it is not advisable to separate the administrative and supervisory work. However, it is extremely important that the supervisory staff should be strengthened.

3. *Clerical Staff*. More clerical staff is needed to cope with the routine type of work of supervision and inspection. In many cases supervisory remarks (Reports) remain untyped for months because of the shortage of typists and other clerical staff with the result that schools fail to derive immediate benefit from the supervisory remarks.

4. *Preparation for Class-room Visitation.* The supervisor should prepare himself adequately for a class-room visit. A wise supervisor will secure as much information as possible concerning the professional background and abilities of the teacher.

Class visitation may be announced or unannounced. Announced visitation offers the teacher an opportunity to prepare the best work of which he is capable.

Unannounced visitation enables the supervisor to observe the normal class-room work. Such visitation is favoured by most of the principals and teachers.

The advantages and disadvantages of the two types of visitation suggest that no one type should be used exclusively. There should be a judicious combination of both.

5. *Changes in the Techniques of Supervision.* Since environmental conditions vary from time to time, teacher to teacher, subject to subject, and group to group, supervisory techniques cannot be wedded to any set theory and practice, and therefore, the Education Officer should have a plan ready in

hand as to 'what,' 'where,' 'when' and 'how' to observe and revise the plans periodically.

6. *Encouraging Professional Growth.* Very little is done by the Education Officer for the professional growth of teachers.

A number of teachers may be asked to demonstrate the techniques in which they are most successful. Discussion should always follow immediately after the demonstration. Observers should be given an opportunity to ask whatever question they wish. All suggestions should be made and accepted like an ideal sportsman.

Motion pictures and film strips may be used wherever possible.

The demonstrator should explain the application of principles in his procedure after the demonstration is over.

Adequate preparation should be made by the supervisor while giving a demonstration lesson as this is likely to serve as a model for teachers. It should be well thought-out and well planned and efficiently executed.

7. *Behaviour of the Supervisor.* The supervisor should greet the teacher in a friendly and courteous manner. Usually he should seat himself at the rear of the room. Generally speaking he should not interrupt the work of the class or take over any part of the instruction. He should record his observations as objectively as possible.

8. *In-service Training for Principals and Teachers.* Refresher courses, seminars, workshops, study circles, etc., should be organised for the benefit of principals and teachers. These will enable them to be in touch with the day-to-day changes in the field of education.

9. *Inter School Visitation.* In many cases, teachers can offer valuable assistance or guidance to one another by mutually visiting their classes. For this it is very essential that a cooperative attitude may be developed among the teachers.

10. *Dissemination of Educational Literature.* Supervisor may issue a bulletin at regular intervals for encouraging professional growth among teachers. Following types of material may be included in the bulletin:

(a) Abstracts or brief quotations from books, articles or speeches.
(b) References to articles appearing in current educational periodicals to which the teachers have access.
(c) News items of what various schools or teachers are doing.
(d) News items of achievements in the Zone or Circle itself.
(e) Results of research, reports, etc., which have come to the attention of the supervisors.
(f) Brief reviews of the latest educational literature.
(g) Articles from teachers and other educationists on different aspects of education.
(h) Bibliographies of good references upon selected topics considered of immediate interest to teachers.

The Inspectorate of Education may take up the publication of an educational journal.

11. *Strengthening of Teachers' Reference Libraries.* Teachers may be

stimulated to read literature on professional and general topics. This is possible only when reading material is easily available.

Professional magazines and books may be placed in the reading room. Central teachers' libraries and reading rooms may be established.

12. *Supervisor's Meetings with Teachers.* There are three chief types of teachers' meetings which should be held:

(i) Meetings for routine administrative purposes.

(ii) Meetings for social purposes.

(iii) Meetings that deal with the improvement of instruction.

These meetings should help in stimulating a desire to learn among school personnel for solving their own problems.

13. *Contact with the Public.* School in a democratic society is the source and centre of all development. Hence it is very necessary that the supervisory staff should maintain contacts with local people. At present such contacts are extremely negligible.

14. *Need for Research and Its Relation to Supervision.* Action research seems to be completely missing in our educational institutions. The present day requires research in the field of education on account of the growing emphasis on the democratic way of living.

J.P. Naik feels that in absenceof research "policies continue to be framed on the basis of subjective opinion of individuals—and very often, the same few individuals— and this generally leads to sectoral prejudices and the riding of hobby-horses rather than to comprehensive studies and radical reorganisation."

The Education Officer must acquire a certain amount of knowledge and the skill in the field of educational research so that he can guide the teachers in conducting experiments with regard to the major and minor problems of the school.

15. *Comprehensive Supervision.* Supervision of the work of the teachers should be fairly comprehensive.

16. *Administrative Wing and Supervisor's Recommendations.* The inspection reports generally do not receive their due attention at the hands of the administrative wing. More importance should be given to the recommendations of the supervisory staff by the administrative wing as regards provisions of school furniture and equipment. Every recommendation must be given its due weight.

17. *Spotting out Talented Teachers — State Awards.* Education Officers should spot out talents among the school personnel. Subject experts in various fields from amongst the teachers may be requested to give demonstration lessons from time to time.

18. *Informal Contacts with School Staff.* The supervisory staff should establish contacts with the principals and teachers and discuss their problems, difficulties and plans. Such meetings should be of an informal nature and be confined to small groups. After the regular class-room inspection it is desirable that the Education Officer convenes a meeting of the staff to discuss the problems and difficulties and give them fruitful suggestions. This helps the teachers to come in contact with the inspecting staff.

Programmes like teachers' get-together may be planned periodically and cultural programmes organised on such occasions. Cultural programmes presented by teachers and for teachers prove to be useful in harnessing their energies in fruitful channels and enriching the development of their personality. Educational conferences and exhibitions may also be organised.

19. *Change in Outlook.* Attempts made in recent years to remove the barriers that exist between the supervisory staff and the school personnel should be accelerated. The supervisory staff should have a genuine desire to help the school staff and should always be prepared to cooperate with them to further the cause of education. This work is likely to be facilitated if the supervisory staff finds time to participate occasionally in some activities of the school like games, camps, social service programmes, etc.

20. *In-service Training to Education Officers.* The importance of in-service training to the Education Officers can hardly be minimised. They must orient themselves with new thoughts and techniques in teaching-learning process.

Like all others in the field of education, the education officers also need constant in-service refresher courses, workshops and seminars.

14.3 CONCLUDING REMARKS

It must be remembered that when the teachers feel that the supervisor is one of them and is there to help them as a true friend, philosopher and guide, they will be able to discuss all their problems with the supervisors. All this requires that supervisors must be endowed both with the qualities of head and heart, i.e., keep themselves abreast with the growing latest pedagogical literature as well as develop in themselves the behaviour pattern that would endear themselves to the teachers. This may appear to be a pious hope but the recent studies reveal that all people in the field of education right from the pupils up to the Department feel that the supervisor is an important link that can help the growth of educational institutions in the proper direction. We may bear in mind that respect for personality is fundamental in democratic supervision for it recognises each individual as a person in his own right and as such entitled to growth along the lines of his own social choices.

14.4 HUMAN RELATIONS AND PRINCIPLES OF SUPERVISION AND INSPECTION

Human Relations

It has been rightly observed by A.I. Polack in *Tolerance—Can it be Taught*: "In a world charged with all the electric cross-currents of power politics, partly propaganda and materialistic philosophies—an even greater concentration of effort should be devoted to the task of ensuring that the next generation grows up with the ability to form sound, independent and enlightened judgement based on scientific knowledge and fundamental moral concepts. It is too dangerous to leave this to change. If we cannot solve the problem of human-relations, we perish."

The present-day supervisor is not merely concerned with the all-round improvement of educational institutions under his charge. The democratic set-up expects much from the supervisor. The work of supervision has become very comprehensive and exhaustive, at the same time very complex. The success or the failure of the supervisor depends largely upon the kind of relationships he is able to develop with school personnel.

14.5 PRINCIPLES OF GOOD INSPECTION/SUPERVISION

Inspection, in order to be effective and fruitful, should be conducted according to certain principles which may be listed as:

1. *Principle of General Growth.* Inspection should contribute to the general efficiency of the school and to the professional growth of the teacher.

2. *Principle of Understanding.* Inspection should be done very sympathetically. An inspector should carry with him abundance of sympathy.

3. *Principle of Scientific Attitude.* Inspection implies the impartial observation of facts. The inspector must maintain a scientific and critical attitude and should be free from prejudices.

4. *Principle of Thoroughness.* Inspection should be very comprehensive and thorough. It should not merely be concerned with the financial aspect of school management and administrative details but should cover all aspects of school work.

5. *Principle of Espirit De Corps.* Inspectors should try to assess the spirit of a school in addition to its instructional work. The spirit of school may be gauged from the records of staff meetings, co-curricular activities and any experimental work done in educational methods. The standard of discipline on the playing field and outside the class is a sure index of the spirit of a school.

6. *Principle of Appreciation.* The novelty of the teacher's method should be appreciated. The inspector should not insist on "dead uniformity." He should try to understand the methods employed by the teachers and appreciate the good points they contain.

7. *Principle of Justice.* The inspectors should be judicious in their criticism of the work of the teachers. They should not be 'misers' in giving praise when it is deserved.

8. *Principle of All-Round Development.* Inspection should not be cursory in character. At least two or three days should be devoted. The work of the teacher should not be judged in a few minutes. More careful and longer supervision is necessary. Doing is always better than telling. Demonstration lessons by an inspector are more useful than pages of suggestions. However, it must be stressed that it is a wrong policy to give a demonstration lesson then and there when an inspector finds a class weak in a subject or finds unsatisfactory methods being used by the teacher. Such a step is likely to lower the prestige of the teacher in the eyes of students.

9. *Principle of Reality.* The inspecting staff should not expect impossibilities. They should understand the local conditions perfectly well and then decide for themselves what progress may reasonably be expected.

10. *Principle of Integration.* The written work of the students should be carefully assessed. In the case of subjects with practical work, such as science, agriculture and drawing, the inspectors should always get practical work done by the students.

11. *Principle of Linkage.* Inspection should not be confined to the four

walls of the school. As the school is to serve the community and is intimately connected with it, the inspector should help the school to develop proper contacts with the community and to improve its relations with people.

12. *Principle of Planning.* Inspections must be planned in advance. They should not be a hit-or-miss affair. A good-planned inspection will have a set of clearly stated objectives and will contain an outline of the devices, means and procedures which are to be used in the attainment of these objectives. It will also include a clear outline of the criteria, checks or tests which are to be used to the results of inspection in order to determine the success or failure of the programmes.

13. *Principle of Cooperation.* The academic work of the school should be thoroughly checked by a panel of experts with the inspectors as chairman. Inspection should be planned in such a way as cooperation of all concerned is readily available.

14.6 QUALITIES OF A SUPERVISOR/INSPECTOR

Brilly suggests that the motto of an Inspector should not be "check your teachers, frighten your teachers, weaken your teachers and examine them," but its variant. "Train your teachers, inspire your teachers, encourage your teachers and trust them." Important qualities of such an Inspector are:

1. *Man of Educational Vision.* He should be aware of new trends in education, latest techniques in education, recent problems in the field and their solutions. He should not merely assess the academic achievements of the schools but also the all-round progress of the school should occupy his attention.

2. *Man of Faith.* There is no use of being impatient, for growth and improvement always take time. The inspector must have a far-reaching programme, but putting through it, he should proceed item by item.

3. *Man of Experiments.* He must be an experimenter. An able inspector will select forward looking schools where the teachers and the headmasters have a progressive outlook on education and are imbued with the spirit of experimentation and will turn these schools nurseries wherein the seeds of educational reform and progress are sown, cared for and their progress carefully watched and the message carried to other schools.

4. *Man of Planning.* The inspector should plan his work thoroughly and should not undertake it at random.

5. *Man of Sympathy.* He should always show respect for the teacher's personality. A good inspector is one who can inspire and enthuse the teachers without dominating over them like a harsh taskmaster. He should place the teachers on a footing of human equality. He should be cooperative, sympathetic and affectionate.

6. *Constructive Mind.* An inspector should possess constructive mind rather than a destructive one. He should never undertake a visit to school with the pure object of fault-finding. An inspector who fails to praise when commendation is deserved, is failing as much in his duties as one who fails to criticise when criticism is deserved. He should have a problem-solving attitude and should help teachers in tackling the problems with which they are faced.

7. *Organising Capacity.* As he is to serve as 'teacher of teachers,' he should have the capacity to organise refresher courses, meetings, seminars and discussions.

8. *Expert in Various Subjects.* An inspector should be a specialist in many languages and subjects. This is particularly important in our schools where different media of instruction are followed.

9. *Liaison Officer.* The inspector should be a friendly liaison officer between the department and the field workers, a mediator linking up scattered educational experiences and experiments. Dr. Hart of the California University, a specialist in school administration had enumerated seven abilities which every administrator and supervisor should possess in ample degree to discharge his duties well. The first is the ability to recognise the especially worthwhile things that are taking place in the school system. The second is to organise the school system so that essentially worthwhile things discovered are spread throughout the system. The third is to overcome the inefficiencies of others without losing their goodwill. The fourth is to set goals that are within the reach of an individual. The fifth ability is that of making everyone in the school system feel worthwhileness of his job. The sixth is that of helping everyone in the system to grow professionally and grow in service to society. And the seventh is to make those who work for or with the administrator or supervisor personally happy.

To sum up the qualities of an inspector, it may be stated that he should be a man of learning, faith, pulsating with life and energy and imbued with a spirit of progress and experimentation and must be above prejudices of all sorts and petty personal affiliation.